Law, Language, and Warfare

Law, Language, and Warfare

Edited by

Russell Buchan, Emily Crawford and Rain Liivoja

BRILL | NIJHOFF

LEIDEN | BOSTON

Originally published, in part, as Volume 14, Issue 2 (2023) of Brill's journal Journal of International Humanitarian Legal Studies.

Cover illustration: Photograph by Joshua Hoehne on Unsplash.

The Library of Congress Cataloging-in-Publication Data is available online at https://catalog.loc.gov

Typeface for the Latin, Greek, and Cyrillic scripts: "Brill". See and download: brill.com/brill-typeface.

ISBN 978-90-04-71246-1 (paperback)
ISBN 978-90-04-71247-8 (e-book)
DOI 10.1163/9789004712478

This book is printed on acid-free paper and produced in a sustainable manner.

Contents

Introduction: On the Nature of Law, Language, and Warfare 1
Emily Crawford

The Terminology of the Law of Warfare: a Linguistic Analysis of State Practice 6
Emily Crawford, Jacqueline Mowbray and Annabelle Lukin

The International Laws of War: Linguistic Analysis from the Perspectives of Register, Corpus and Grammatical Patterning 32
Annabelle Lukin and Alexandra García Marrugo

International Humanitarian Law: Necessity, Distinction and the 'Standard of Civilisation' 59
Matt Killingsworth

Filling the Gaps: The Expansion of International Humanitarian Law and the Juridification of the Free-Fighter 83
Amanda Alexander

Another Look at the Gendered Constitution of the Laws of War
Semantic Fields, Hegemonic Masculinities and the Reproduction of Heteronormativity 113
Frédéric Mégret

The Language of the Protection of Civilians Mandate and the Primary Responsibility of the State: A Legal Norm for Peace and Security 158
Tamer Morris

Index 187

Introduction: On the Nature of Law, Language, and Warfare

Emily Crawford

When Russia commenced its full-scale invasion of Ukraine on 24 February 2022, President Vladimir Putin did not declare that Russia was at war with Ukraine but rather that the Russian Federation had commenced a 'special military operation' in the region.[1] The term was widely lambasted[2] as an attempt by Russia to avoid the term "war" or "armed conflict" and, in doing so, potentially avoid the manifold legal and political implications that come with the term "war", not least of which is the application of the law of war, better known as the law of armed conflict or international humanitarian law (IHL).

Linguistic sophistry, of the kind seen in the Russian-Ukraine war is, however, by no means limited to this recent example. For decades, States – particularly when dealing with matters of armed conflict and national security – have employed euphemisms and obfuscation to attempt to soften or distract from the reality of warfare. Thus, the Korean War was not an armed conflict but a 'police action';[3] the CIA did not torture detainees at Guantanamo Bay but rather subjected them to 'enhanced interrogation';[4] the conflict in Gaza

---

1 '"No other option": Excerpts of Putin's Speech Declaring War', *Al Jazeera*, 24 February 2022, https://www.aljazeera.com/news/2022/2/24/putins-speech-declaring-war-on-ukraine-translated-excerpts.

2 'Do Not Call Ukraine Invasion a 'War', Russia Tells Media, Schools', *Al Jazeera*, 2 March 2022, https://web.archive.org/web/20230731123354/https://www.aljazeera.com/news/2022/3/2/do-not-call-ukraine-invasion-a-war-russia-tells-media-schools; 'Word of the Year 2022: Special Military Operation', *American Dialect Society*, https://americandialect.org/woty/all-of-the-words-of-the-year-1990-to-present/#2022; Michael Schmitt, 'Russia's "Special Military Operation" and the (Claimed) Right of Self-Defense', *Articles of War*, 28 February 2022, https://lieber.westpoint.edu/russia-special-military-operation-claimed-right-self-defense/; Andrei Kolesnikov, 'How Putin's "Special Military Operation" Became a People's War', *Carnegie Politika*, 10 April 2022, https://carnegieendowment.org/russia-eurasia/politika/2023/03/how-putins-special-military-operation-became-a-peoples-war?lang=en.

3 Harry S. Truman, 'The President's News Conference of June 29, 1950', *Teaching American History*, https://teachingamericanhistory.org/document/the-presidents-news-conference-of-june-29-1950/.

4 Report of the Senate Select Committee on Intelligence, *Committee Study of the Central Intelligence Agency's Detention and Interrogation Program*, 9 December 2014, https://www.intelligence.senate.gov/sites/default/files/publications/CRPT-113srpt288.pdf&ved=2ahUKEwijx_rO9feGAxVk4TgGHfFlBYYQFnoECCsQAQ&usg=AOvVaw01WWzZKinJMeiAXJIJpERH, XI.

 | DOI:10.1163/9789004712478_002

required not a "ceasefire" but a 'humanitarian pause'[5]; and it is never a matter of civilian deaths but rather unavoidable 'collateral damage'.[6]

In the study of law, the concept that language influences the perception and execution of the law is not a particularly groundbreaking notion – there is, of course, an entire field of study relating to treaty and statutory interpretation, and how words should be understood in order for laws to be understood. Indeed, the entire field of linguistics is dedicated to the study of language and there are manifold studies on how language shapes an individual's perception of the world.[7] What the authors of the papers contained in this volume wanted to do was channel the notion of the intersection between law and language, and apply it to one particular field of shared interest – that of the documents and language of the law of armed conflict. To that end, in April 2022, a group of scholars gathered at the University of Sydney Law School to workshop papers under the thematic banner of 'law, language, and war'. In our various fields of research - including international law, linguistics, and international relations – we have all been interested in how the language employed in legal discourse and legal documents creates a particular conception of the world and prefigures our engagement with that conceived world.

That workshop led to a symposium, published in the *Journal of International Humanitarian Legal Studies*, and recreated here in this volume. Our collection starts with a chapter by Emily Crawford, Annabelle Lukin, and Jacqueline Mowbray, which looks at the very terms that describe this field of law – the law of war (LoW), the law of armed conflict (LOAC), and international humanitarian law (IHL). Crawford, Lukin and Mowbray note the background to these differences in terminology, asking why and when these changes of terminology occurred, with a particular focus how these changes were received in State practice, and what that might say about what these terms mean – namely, are they value-neutral descriptors of an extant body of law or do they carry deeper,

5 Emanuela-Chiara Gillard, 'Humanitarian Pauses and Ceasefires – What are the Differences?', Chatham House, 6 November 2023, https://www.chathamhouse.org/2023/11/humanitarian-pauses-and-ceasefires-what-are-differences.

6 Stephen Rockel and Rick Halpern (eds), *Inventing Collateral Damage: Civilian Casualties, War, and Empire* (Between the Lines 2009).

7 See for example Scott Bruck, 'Lost in Translation: How Language Affects Perception During Armed Conflict', *Small Wars Journal*, 7 May 2019, https://smallwarsjournal.com/jrnl/art/lost-translation-how-language-affects-perception-during-armed-conflict; Mustafa Altun, 'The Power of Language: Exploring Its Significance in Shaping Perceptions, Beliefs, and Relationships' (2023) 10 *International Journal of Social Sciences & Educational Studies* 362; Bodo Winter, *Sensory Linguistics: Language, Perception and Metaphor* (John Benjamins Publishing Company 2019).

politicised qualities that have impacted their acceptance in State practice. While exploring the origins of the terms is not new to the literature, what the chapter utilizes is novel corpus linguistic tools to analyse Security Council and General Assembly resolutions relating to armed conflict, which reveal some interesting insights into how these varied terms have been used in practice, and what that might mean - namely, as Crawford, Lukin, and Mowbray write, 'that while the terms were largely considered unproblematic at their introduction, practice in relation to the deployment of the terms suggests deep tensions regarding the nature and purpose of the law and how and when it applies.'

From there, the volume turns to the study of linguistics, where Annabelle Lukin uses corpus linguistic analysis to examine the texts of the law of armed conflict. As Lukin writes, 'Like every other text, a legal text depends on the semiotic principles which enable every act of meaning, legal or otherwise. These principles, which derive from linguistic theory, help us to understand the nature of these texts, both what makes them unique, and the ways in which they are part of wider textual practices, including the ideologies of the communities in which they operate.' Lukin's chapter explores how the texts of the law of armed conflict have both a legal as well as an ideological role, replete with both power and contradiction, and the site of an 'impossible synthesis between violence and restraint'. Lukin examines the texts of international humanitarian law as a 'register' which 'denotes language variation based on context, and recognises social and cultural context as the dominant shaping force of language both as a generalised semiotic system and in each specific use of language', arguing that IHL introduced a 'new semiotic ecosystem, providing a semiotically constructed home in which to develop and maintain the meanings that give this textual practice its unique identity'. From this study, Lukin shows us the dominant semantic patterns of the law of armed conflict, applying lexicogrammatical analysis to reveal the 'linguistically seamless contradictions within international war law' between moderation and violence.

The next chapter comes from the field of international relations, where Matt Killingsworth explores the contradictions identified in Lukin's chapter – that the 'modern laws of war exist as an uneasy reconciliation' between moderation and violence, and demonstrate a 'continuity of double standards as they relate to protections afforded by the modern laws of war'. Killingsworth identifies the language of the law of war as central to entrenching and enforcing this double-standard, in which the law has historically de-humanised belligerents via the language of the 'standard of civilisation'. In making this argument, Killingsworth draws 'attention to the historical centrality of the state and the role it has played in establishing conditionality with regards to protections afforded by the modern laws of war through the language of raison d'état and the standard of civilisation.' For Killingsworth, the language of the law of armed conflict, embedded as it is in the notion of standards of civilization and state sovereignty, was wielded as a tool of colonial exclusion, and remains central to notions of who should be afforded protections under international humanitarian law. Killingsworth demonstrates how raison d'état and 'standards of civilisation' continues to be a motivating factor informing constraint during combat, and through case studies of the First Gulf War, and the War on Terror, demonstrates how 'the state, self-anointed as 'civilised', continues to use the language of the standard of civilisation as an informant of who should be afforded protections by IHL, and in turn, a concept by which we can continue to understand the gulf between the (universal) humanitarian underpinnings of IHL, and violations of the laws of war.'

The next chapter in the volume is from Amanda Alexander, who picks up on Killingsworth's engagement with the alienating quality of the language of the law of war and applies it to the classification of combatants under the law. As Alexander notes, the law of armed conflict traditionally limited combatant rights 'to those fighting in a state's army; only those in uniform, disciplined, law-abiding and under effective command would fall within the law's regime. These requirements left many people outside the law - in particular, the 'uncivilised' and the 'savage'.' As the law of armed conflict developed and progressed, more categories of legitimate fighter began to be included in the law. But rather than seeing this as an expansion of the law per se, instead, it revised the idea of the irregular as recognised under the law only so long as they resembled the social and legal strictures of war as a heroic and legitimate endeavours. Thus, the irregular must follow the rules of the regular fighter. While the law, 'for a moment, appeared the tool of a political struggle', instead, the law 'did not change the formal, neutral, non-ideological character of the law. Rather it reasserted and multiplied the same form of legal criteria.' Thus, as Alexander notes, 'the expansion of international law has not overturned the formal law of the state with ethical or political objections; rather the formal law, which is synonymous with the state, is continually reaffirmed'.

Frederic Megret's chapter picks up on Alexander's engagement with language as a tool of exclusion and marginalisation, in his chapter looking at the gendered constitution of the laws of war. In his paper, Megret explores how 'the role of gender is even more constitutive than has typically been thought so far'; that '[r]ather than operating only at the level of the law's internal categories ... it is the very categories of the regulation of war within the broader architecture of international law which, themselves, expresses a peculiar gendered sensitivity'. Megret looks at the concept of gender in IHL as having paid scant attention to the notion of 'military masculinities' – that warfare has been 'a place of intense socialization among men and production of expectations about masculinities' and that the language of the law of war, rather than upholding some neutral universality, instead involves 'recurring and even psychologically obsessive conversations about the place of manhood (with men as an evident proxy) in society and the subtle and not-so-subtle crafting of masculine domination', and that 'rhetorical structures in the law that can be understood to be gendercoded even when they are not gender explicit. In the process, it will show the fluid construction of masculinity-through-war and war-through-masculinity as part of an ongoing gendered "performance."'

Finally, Tamer Morris explores the role of language in limiting and delimiting the permissible acts of peacekeepers in UN mandated peacekeeping operations, specifically with regards to the protection of civilians mandate. Morris looks at how the protection of civilians mandate is more than just a guide for UN action, but rather the language of the mandate essentially places an obligation on the State to halt all violence, obliging the State to end to the conflict (rather than the UN to keep the peace). As Morris notes, '[u]nlike the obligations in IHL that allows the existence of conflict, the primary responsibility of the State through the lens of the protection of civilians mandate, is that the existence of conflict by its nature is in violation of the obligation of the State. Therefore, it is suggested in the mandate that the State's obligation to protect their civilians can only be achieved by halting the conflict.' The language used in protection of civilians mandates is thus acting to create a new norm for States in NIAC – essentially one that suggests that it is not enough for States to follow the rules of IHL in on-going NIAC. Rather States can *only* fulfil their IHL obligations by taking all reasonable steps to conclude the conflict.

Collectively, these chapters present a novel insight into the complex intersections between the law of armed conflict and the language of armed conflict. They demonstrate the strengths and fissures in the law, showing how the choice to employ certain terms – even when such choice was unquestioned, perhaps even unconsciously made – can have lasting ramifications. In the realm of armed conflict, which is so beset by rapid technological and political changes but for which the law governing that realm often changes slowly, it is incumbent on us all to pay heed to the generational impacts of the words employed to govern human behaviour at times when all humanity is lost.

The Terminology of the Law of Warfare: a Linguistic Analysis of State Practice

Emily Crawford, Jacqueline Mowbray and Annabelle Lukin

Abstract

The body of international law that regulates the conduct of armed conflicts has been known, at various points in time, as the law of war, the law of armed conflict, and international humanitarian law. While 'the law of war' was a term widely used in State practice throughout the 18th and 19th centuries, both 'the law of armed conflict' and 'international humanitarian law' were terms introduced in the 20th century by one organisation: the International Committee of the Red Cross. In this paper, we use international law and corpus linguistic tools in a pilot study, examining how the terms were first introduced into international law and how quickly they were incorporated (if at all) into the practice of States. Using the ongoing conflict involving Israel and its neighbours, this pilot study charts the appearance and recurrence of these terms in the practice of States in the United Nations to examine how the terms were received and used. We conclude by offering some initial assessments, noting that, while the terms were largely considered unproblematic at their introduction, practice in relation to their deployment suggests deep tensions regarding the nature and purpose of the law and how and when it applies.

Keywords

law of armed conflict – international humanitarian law – linguistics – State practice – law of war

 | DOI:10.1163/9789004712478_003

1 Introduction

It is almost standard practice in the literature of the law of armed conflict to include reference, sometimes even protracted reference, to the different terms used to describe the field of law. The literature on the topic will note that US texts prefer the terminology of 'the law of war' (LOW) or 'the law of armed conflict' (LOAC);[1] that 'international humanitarian law' (IHL) is merely the latest term to define an increasingly expansive field of law;[2] and/or that the terms LOAC and IHL are[3] (or are not[4]) fundamentally interchangeable. Frequently, the texts in question will then go on to state that, for the most part, little turns on the different terminology.[5]

A closer linguistic analysis, however, raises interesting questions regarding the differences in terminology that we explore in this paper. In particular, we consider the background to these differences in terminology, asking *why* these changes of terminology occurred, *how* the changes were received in State practice, and what the *why* and *how* that might say about *what* the terms mean – namely, whether they are value-neutral descriptors of an extant body of law or have become imbued with politicised qualities that have impacted their acceptance in State practice.

Historical records show that the move from LOW to LOAC to IHL was first manifested in the language of the relevant treaties: the term 'armed conflict'

---

1 Pål Wrange, 'Historicising International Humanitarian Law' in Mats Deland, Mark Klamberg and Pål Wrange (eds), *International Humanitarian Law and Justice: Historical and Sociological Perspectives* (Routledge 2019) 9.

2 Dieter Fleck, 'Introduction' in Dieter Fleck (ed), *The Handbook of International Humanitarian Law* (4th edn, OUP 2021) 4.

3 Gary Solis, *The Law of Armed Conflict: International Humanitarian Law in War* (3rd edn, CUP 2022) 18; Robert Kolb and Richard Hyde, *An Introduction to the International Law of Armed Conflicts* (Hart 2008) 16–17; Emily Crawford and Alison Pert, *International Humanitarian Law* (2nd edn, CUP 2020) 33.

4 For example, Mary Ellen O'Connell, while for the most part considering IHL to be synonymous with LOAC, notes that there are parts of the law of armed conflict that might not be considered part of IHL (such as the law of neutrality) because they lack sufficient humanitarian aims: Mary Ellen O'Connell, 'Historical Development and Legal Basis' in Dieter Fleck (ed), *The Handbook of International Humanitarian Law* (4th edn, OUP 2021) 21.

5 M Cherif Bassiouni, 'The Normative Framework of International Humanitarian Law: Overlaps, Gaps and Ambiguities' (1998) 8 Transnational Law & Contemporary Problems 199, 200; Hilaire McCoubrey, *International Humanitarian Law: Modern Developments in the Limitation of Warfare* (Ashgate 1998) 2.

replaced the term 'war' with the adoption of the Geneva Conventions in 1949, and the term 'international humanitarian law' emerged in the 1960s and was used in negotiating and drafting documents that led to the adoption of the 1977 Additional Protocols.[6] Critically, and most important to note for this analysis, the shifts in treaty terminology did not emanate from States (through State practice or from State sponsorship at treaty conferences), but instead from advocacy by the International Committee of the Red Cross (ICRC). Given that the changes came from civil society, what was the reaction of States? Was there resistance to such changes in terminology or were they generally accepted without question? And, connected to this, how quickly – and how – did States accept the new terminology in their own practice, if at all? Did they do so in a uniform manner, or was adoption of the new terms patchy?

Exploration of the origins and development of the terms LOW, LOAC and IHL is not new; as noted above, there are notable examples in the literature that address the changes.[7] However, what is new to the analysis is our approach. We draw on the tools of corpus linguistics, which allows for the linguistic analysis of large bodies of text. This enables us to map, in general terms, when and how particular terminology starts to be used within legal discourse. Of course, the analysis of all State practice since the adoption of the Geneva Conventions in 1949 would be a mammoth task. For this initial case study, we have therefore chosen to focus on a much smaller corpus of texts, namely UN Security Council and General Assembly resolutions relating to the ongoing conflict between Israel, Palestine and other States in the Middle East region. Security Council and General Assembly resolutions provide important evidence of State practice, while the Israel conflict provides a useful case study for our purposes because it has been ongoing since before the adoption of the Geneva Conventions of 1949.

Part Two of this paper traces the historical development of the terminology of LOW, LOAC and IHL. We then turn in Part Three to explain the corpus linguistics techniques we have used to analyse Security Council and General

---

6 For an excellent history of this change and its theoretical underpinnings, see further Amanda Alexander, 'A Short History of International Humanitarian Law' (2015) 26 European Journal of International Law 109.

7 In addition to the works cited above, see Page Wilson, 'The Myth of International Humanitarian Law' (2017) 93 International Affairs 563; Françoise J Hampson, 'Law of War/ Law of Armed Conflict/International Humanitarian Law' in Michael J Bowman and Dino Kritsiotis (eds), *Conceptual and Contextual Perspectives on the Modern Law of Treaties* (CUP 2018).

Assembly resolutions relating to the conflict in the Middle East. Following this, we set out the results of the linguistic analysis. In the final part of the paper – Part Four – we explore what these linguistic results reveal about how States have used different terminology to refer to the law of warfare, and what this means – namely, that while the terms were largely considered unproblematic at their introduction, practice in relation to the deployment of the terms suggests deep tensions regarding the nature and purpose of the law and how and when it applies. We conclude by discussing what these results suggest for future research on this issue.

2 The History of the Terminology of the Law Relating to Wars and Armed Conflicts

From the earliest writings in the field of international law, authors called the rules that had emerged in practice relating to protracted armed engagements between States 'the law of war'.[8] Indeed, many of the earliest, and most significant, writings in international law were primarily about this field. Hugo Grotius's seminal international law text was titled *De jure belli ac pacis* (*On the Law of War and Peace*, 1625); Italian jurist Alberico Gentili published *De jure belli libri tres* (*Three Books on the Law of* War, 1598); and Francisco de Vitoria wrote *De Indis et de jure belli* (*The Indians and the Law of War*, 1532). These works were followed in later years by Emer de Vattel's *Le droit des gens, ou Principes de la loi naturelle, appliqués à la conduite et aux affaires des nations et des souverains* (*The Law of Nations: Or, Principles of the Law of Nature Applied to the Conduct and Affairs of Nations and Sovereigns*, 1758) and Christian Wolff's *Jus naturae methodo scientifica pertractatum* (*The Law of Nations Treated According to the Scientific Method*, 1729). Common to these books was the examination of the laws of war as they had developed in State practice over the centuries, and the rules that should rightly apply to such conflicts. Also common to the texts was that they all referred to a state of 'war' (*belli* – the Latin of which translates to 'of war'; or *guerre*, which translates from the French to 'war') rather than 'armed conflict' (*conflit armé* in French or *arma* in Latin). For example, Book 3, Chapter 1 of *On the Law of War and Peace* began by noting that, having

8 This part of the paper will not include a detailed history of the development of the law of armed conflict generally, but rather a history of the use of the terms in treaty law.

considered those who wage war and why such war may be waged, 'we should determine what is permissible in war, also to what extent, and in what ways, it is permissible.'[9]

By the 18th century, States had begun the process of codifying these rules into documents, continuing the practice of referring to armed clashes as 'war'. The first of these documents was the so-called Lieber Code, drafted to codify the contemporary laws of war for use by the Union Army during the US Civil War. Adopted in 1863, the Instructions for the Government of Armies of the United States in the Field were issued by the Union government as General Orders No 100.[10] Within the 157 articles of the Lieber Code, repeated mention was made to 'war' and 'the laws of war'. For instance, in Article 11, it was stated:

> The law of war does not only disclaim all cruelty and bad faith concerning engagements concluded with the enemy during the war, but also the breaking of stipulations solemnly contracted by the belligerents in time of peace, and avowedly intended to remain in force in case of war between the contracting powers.[11]

Reference to 'the law of war' continued throughout the written rules of armed conflict in the late 18th and early 19th centuries. The 1864 Geneva Convention[12] provided, in Article 4, that '[t]he material of military hospitals being subject to the laws of war, the persons attached to such hospitals may take with them, on withdrawing, only the articles which are their own personal property'; the 1868 St Petersburg Declaration noted that 'the only legitimate object which States should endeavour to accomplish during war is to weaken the military

9 Hugo Grotius, *On the Law of War and Peace* (1609) Book 3, ch 1, § 1 (from Stephen Neff (ed), *Hugo Grotius on the Law of War and Peace* (CUP 2012, with English translation by Francis Kelsey) 325). In the original Latin: "Cui quibusq ex causus bellum gerere liceat dictum est Videamus nunc quantum liceat".

10 See generally Richard Shelly Hartigan, *Lieber's Code and the Law of War* (Precedent 1983) 2–14.

11 US Department of War, Instructions for the Government of Armies of the United States in the Field, General Orders No 100, 24 April 1863 (Lieber Code) art 11.

12 Convention for the Amelioration of the Condition of the Wounded in Armies in the Field (adopted 22 August 1864, entered into force 22 June 1865) 129 CTS 361.

13 Declaration Renouncing the Use, in Time of War, of Explosive Projectiles Under 400 Grammes Weight (adopted and entered into force 11 December 1868) 138 CTS 297, preamble.

14 Convention (II) with Respect to the Laws and Customs of War on Land (adopted 29 July 1899, entered into force 4 September 1900) 187 CTS 429.

forces of the enemy';[13] the 1899[14] and 1907[15] Hague Conventions contained numerous provisions that referenced the law of war, such as Article 1 of the 1899 Convention II, which provided that 'the High Contracting Parties shall issue instructions to their armed land forces, which shall be in conformity with the "Regulations respecting the laws and customs of war on land" annexed to the present Convention'; and Article 1 of the Regulations annexed to the 1907 Convention IV stated that '[t]he laws, rights, and duties of war apply not only to armies, but also to militia and volunteer corps'.[16]

Both the 1899 and 1907 Hague Regulations applied only in situations of 'declared war'; there was, at the time, a customary and conventional requirement that, before a State initiated armed hostilities against another State, a formal declaration of war was necessary.[17] For example, under Article 1 of the 1907 Hague Convention (III) Relative to the Opening of Hostilities,[18] it is stated that '[t]he Contracting Powers recognize that hostilities between themselves must not commence without previous and explicit warning, in the form either of a reasoned declaration of war or of an ultimatum with conditional declaration of war'. Declarations of war were legally necessary to trigger the application of the law of war between belligerents, and to clearly delineate to other States that the law of neutrality would apply to any States not engaged in the conflict. Serious international legal ramifications would follow for a State that breached the laws of neutrality by aiding a State engaged in armed conflict.[19]

---

15 Convention (IV) Respecting the Laws and Customs of War on Land (adopted 18 October 1907, entered into force 26 January 1910) 187 CTS 227.

16 Regulations Respecting the Laws and Customs of War on Land, annexed to Convention (IV) Respecting the Laws and Customs of War on Land (adopted 18 October 1907, entered into force 26 January 1910) 187 CTS 227.

17 See generally Clyde Eagleton, 'The Form and Function of the Declaration of War' (1938) 32 American Journal of International Law 19.

18 Convention (III) Relative to the Opening of Hostilities (adopted 18 October 1907, entered into force 26 January 1910) 205 CTS 264.

19 See, for example, the *Alabama Claims Arbitration* (1872) 1 Moore Intl Arbitrations 495, a case brought by the US against Great Britain claiming that Great Britain had violated the law of neutrality by allowing the fit-out of a Confederate vessel, the CSS *Alabama*, despite Great Britain's declaration of neutrality. See further Tom Bingham, 'The Alabama Claims Arbitration' (2005) 54 International and Comparative Law Quarterly 1.

However, practice in the 19th and early 20th centuries had shown that some States avoided formally declaring war,[20] even at times outright denying that they were engaged in a war, in order to, among other reasons, avoid the political and legal ramifications that would eventually follow.[21] For example, Japan did not declare war against China in 1937, instead calling the conflict an 'incident' rather than a war. In doing so, historians have noted that Japan was hoping to achieve two aims: first, Japan could claim that the rules on the obligations of occupiers during armed conflict,[22] and the treatment of Chinese prisoners of war,[23] did not apply, as it was not at war; second, Japan could avoid the activation of the US Neutrality Act, which would have limited Japan's ability to trade with the US.[24]

Prior to the commencement of the Second World War, the ICRC advocated for the reaffirmation and expansion of the rules relating to armed conflict.[25] In particular, the ICRC believed that the Conventions should apply to all kinds

---

20 In 1883, Sir John Frederick Maurice undertook a study to examine how many wars between 1700 and 1870 commenced only *after* a formal declaration: he could find fewer than 10 instances where formal declarations of war were made before the commencement of hostilities: John Frederick Maurice, *Hostilities without Declaration of War: An Historical Abstract of the Cases in Which Hostilities Have Occurred between Civilized Powers prior to Declaration or Warning from 1720 to 1870* (HM Stationery Office 1883) 4.

21 See Tanisha M Fazal, 'Why States No Longer Declare War' (2012) 21 Security Studies 557; ICRC, *Commentary on the First Geneva Convention: Convention (I) for the Amelioration of the Condition of the Wounded and Sick in Armed Forces in the Field* (2016) para 204 <https://ihl-databases.icrc.org/en/ihl-treaties/gci-1949/article-2/commentary/2016>, which notes: 'Under the traditional theory of declared war, the mere fact that States are engaged in armed violence is insufficient to displace the law of peace and trigger the applicability of humanitarian law. Therefore, declared war in its legal meaning starts with a declaration of war, which is interpreted as the only expression of the States' belligerent intent' (footnote omitted).

22 As outlined in the 1907 Hague Regulations.

23 Under the Convention Relative to the Treatment of Prisoners of War (adopted 27 July 1929, entered into force 19 June 1931) 118 LNTS 343. See also Yuki Tanaka, *Hidden Horrors: Japanese War Crimes in World War II* (Westview Press 1996) 73.

24 See further Haruo Iguchi, 'The Secrets behind Japan's Ability to Cope with U.S. Economic Sanctions, 1940–1941' (2010) 34 Diplomatic History 177; Edward S Miller, *Bankrupting the Enemy: The U.S. Financial Siege of Japan before Pearl Harbor* (United States Naval Institute Press 2007); Haruo Iguchi, *Unfinished Business: Ayukawa Yoshisuke and U.S.-Japan Relations, 1937–1953* (Harvard University Press 2003).

25 ICRC, 'Report on the Interpretation, Revision and Extension of the Geneva Convention of July 27, 1929' (report prepared for the 16th International Conference of the Red Cross, London, 1938) <https://library.icrc.org/library/docs/CI/CI_1938_DOC11_ENG.pdf>; 'Mémorandum adressé par le Comité international de la Croix-Rouge aux Gouvernements des États parties à la Convention de Genève et aux Sociétés nationales de la Croix-Rouge' (1945) 314 Revue Internationale de la Croix-Rouge 85.

of hostilities. The special commission that was enlisted to study the question of updating the Conventions posited, in particular, 'whether it would not be proper to replace the word "war", which occurs frequently in the Convention, particularly in the Preamble and in Articles 24, 25, 29 and 37, by the expressions "armed conflict between States", "hostilities", or "recourse to force"'.[26] Further work on updating the Conventions was delayed by the outbreak of the Second World War. At the cessation of hostilities, the ICRC recommenced its work on updating the 1929 Geneva Conventions, putting forward, in 1946, draft Conventions that would be applicable 'from the moment hostilities have actually broken out, even if no declaration of war has been made and whatever the form that such armed intervention may take'.[27] This was revised in 1947: 'The present Convention is applicable between the Contracting Parties, from the outbreak of any armed conflict, whether the latter is or is not recognised as a state of war by the parties concerned.'[28]

What these draft Conventions effectively did was replace the terminology of 'war' with that of 'armed conflict'. The ICRC did this intentionally. As noted in the Commentaries to the Conventions:

> The substitution of this much more general expression for the word 'war' was deliberate. One may argue almost endlessly about the legal definition of 'war'. A State can always pretend, when it commits a hostile act against another State, that it is not making war, but merely engaging in a police action, or acting in legitimate self-defence. The expression 'armed conflict' makes such arguments less easy. Any difference arising between two States and leading to the intervention of armed forces is an armed conflict within the meaning of Article 2, even if one of the Parties denies the existence of a state of war. It makes no difference how long the conflict lasts, or how much slaughter takes place. The respect due to human personality is not measured by the number of victims.[29]

---

26 ICRC, 'Report on the Interpretation' (n 25) 7–8.

27 ICRC, *Report on the Work of the Preliminary Conference of National Red Cross Societies for the Study of the Conventions and of Various Problems Relative to the Red Cross, Geneva, July 26–August 3, 1946* (1947) 14.

28 ICRC, *Report on the Work of the Conference of Government Experts for the Study of the Conventions for the Protection of War Victims, Geneva, April 14–26, 1947* (1947) 8. See also ICRC, *Draft Revised or New Conventions for the Protection of War Victims Established by the International Committee of the Red Cross with the Assistance of Government Experts, National Red Cross Societies and Other Humanitarian Associations* (1948).

29 Jean Pictet (ed), *Commentary to Geneva Convention I for the Amelioration of the Condition of the Wounded and Sick in Armed Forces in the Field* (ICRC 1952) 32.

When States convened in Geneva to debate the draft Conventions, there was little debate about the use of the term 'armed conflict';[30] from the travaux préparatoires, it seems that States considered 'armed conflict' an uncontroversial substitution for the term 'war', such that the conference eventually adopted the Conventions as applying to 'all cases of declared war or of any other armed conflict which may arise between two or more of the High Contracting Parties, even if the state of war is not recognized by one of them'.[31]

In the years following the adoption of the Geneva Conventions, the terminology of 'armed conflict' essentially replaced that of 'war' in the treaty discourse. Although 'war' was still used in some instances (for example, in reference to 'prisoners of war'), 'armed conflict' remained the dominant terminology in the treaty discourse – for example, in 1954, States drafted and adopted the Hague Convention for the Protection of Cultural Property in the Event of Armed Conflict.[32]

However, at the same time, a new term for the law of armed conflict began to emerge: 'international humanitarian law'. That phrase was not used in the Geneva Conventions, but seemingly first appeared in the ICRC Commentaries to the Conventions, published in four volumes over an eight-year period between 1952 and 1960.[33] The word 'humanitarian' (rather than 'international humanitarian law') was first seen in the Commentary to Convention I, published in 1952, where reference was made, inter alia, to the 'humanitarian principles'[34] of the Geneva Conventions, which were described as 'humanitarian Conventions'.[35] Indeed, the term 'humanitarian' appears nearly 100 times in the Commentary to Convention I, but was not, at that stage, part of the larger term 'international humanitarian law'. That would come with the publication in 1960 of the Commentary to Convention II on the wounded,

30 *Final Record of the Diplomatic Conference for the Establishment of International Conventions for the Protection of War Victims and Held at Geneva, 21 April – 12 August 1949* (1949) vol IIB, 9–15.

31 ibid vol IIB, 128.

32 Convention for the Protection of Cultural Property in the Event of Armed Conflict (adopted 14 May 1954, entered into force 7 August 1956) 249 UNTS 215.

33 Dietrich Schindler attributes the introduction of the term 'international humanitarian law' to the ICRC as early as the beginning of the 1950s; however, he does not cite an 'origin document' in which the term first appeared or was used. See further Dietrich Schindler, 'International Humanitarian Law: Its Remarkable Development and Its Persistent Violation' (2003) 5 Journal of the History of International Law 165, 171.

34 Pictet, *Commentary to Geneva Convention I* (n 29) 26.

35 ibid 28.

sick, and shipwrecked,[36] where the authors noted that 'humanitarian law affects nearly everyone'.[37]

As the 1960s progressed, the term 'humanitarian law' began to appear more frequently in the legal discourse – for example, one of the chief advocates for the law of armed conflict, Jean Pictet, wrote in 1966 on 'The Principles of International Humanitarian Law'.[38] However, it was the 1968 UN Conference on Human Rights in Tehran that arguably contributed the most to cementing the notion that the law of armed conflict and humanitarian law were synonymous.[39] At that Conference, a resolution was adopted calling for the Secretary-General to study '[s]teps which could be taken to secure the better application of existing humanitarian international conventions and rules in all armed conflicts' and '[t]he need for additional humanitarian international conventions or for possible revision of existing Conventions'.[40] Partly in response to that resolution, the ICRC began a program of work that would eventually result in the adoption of the 1977 Additional Protocols.

In 1969, the ICRC took a major step towards 'installing' 'international humanitarian law' as the preferred terminology. In a report submitted to the 21st International Conference of the Red Cross in 1969, the ICRC noted that its focus should be on:

> developing and reaffirming the laws and customs 'of a humanitarian nature'. It may rightly have been said that the law of war, properly interpreted, generally presents that character. Nevertheless, the ICRC considers that efforts should be directed essentially towards the rules of a distinctly

36 Convention (II) for the Amelioration of the Condition of the Wounded, Sick, and Shipwrecked Members of Armed Forces at Sea (adopted 12 August 1949, entered into force 21 October 1950) 75 UNTS 85.

37 Jean Pictet (ed), *Commentary to Geneva Convention II for the Amelioration of the Condition of the Wounded, Sick and Shipwrecked Members of Armed Forces at Sea* (ICRC 1960) 21.

38 J Picket, 'The Principles of International Humanitarian Law' (1966) 6 International Review of the Red Cross 455. Interestingly, Pictet would himself be reticent about using the terms 'international humanitarian law' and 'the law of armed conflict' interchangeably. Writing in 1975, he felt that the term 'international humanitarian law' 'could be thought to exclude some parts of the laws of war ... whose primary purpose is not humanitarian. Indeed, the term "international humanitarian law" could be seen as implying that the laws of war have an exclusively humanitarian purpose, when their evolution has in fact reflected various practical concerns of states and their armed forces on grounds other than those which may be considered humanitarian': Jean Pictet, *Humanitarian Law and the Protection of War Victims* (AW Sijthoff 1975) 11.

39 See generally O'Connell (n 4) 11–13; Solis (n 3) 21–25.

40 Human Rights in Armed Conflicts, Resolution XXIII adopted by the International Conference on Human Rights, Tehran (12 May 1968).

> humanitarian nature; those concerning the protection of the human being or the essential assets of humanity.[41]

In particular, the ICRC expressly eschewed the use of the phrase 'law of war' in favour of 'international humanitarian law', explaining its reasoning as follows:

> The words 'revision' or 'restoration', of the law of war, which are convenient expressions for the sake of brevity, are often uttered and will sometimes be employed hereafter. But the ICRC deliberately refrained from using them in the title of this Report – they can create confusion, controversy, and are associated with the idea of war in the formal sense. In this way the ICRC desires to show that it is deeply aware of the changes which have occurred in the international community since the time when the 1899 and 1907 Hague Conferences codified the 'law of war' and resort to war was considered as a legitimate means of State policy … By avoiding the words 'law of war', the ICRC is also desirous to take account of the deep aspiration of the peoples to see peace installed and the disputes between human communities settled by pacific means. For some years past the ICRC, together with the whole Red Cross, has therefore decided to strengthen its contribution to a peaceful spirit in the world.[42]

The ICRC continued to position 'humanitarian law' as the replacement term for the large bulk of rules relating to armed conflict, arguing in its 1971 report to the Conference of Government Experts (who were tasked with the process of drafting new treaties on the law of armed conflict) that 'international humanitarian law' was now the 'more usual expression'[43] to refer to the law of armed conflict, even though it had not appeared in treaty law to that date. The ICRC justified this by stating that 'international humanitarian law' was the best term to encompass all:

> those rules of the law of armed conflict which are clearly humanitarian in nature, namely those which protect human beings and the property essential to them. Consequently, the term covers not only the Geneva Conventions but also treaty or customary law rules which, for humanitarian

41 ICRC, *Reaffirmation and Development of the Laws and Customs Applicable in Armed Conflicts* (XXIst International Conference of the Red Cross, Istanbul, September 1969) 10.

42 ibid 10–11.

43 ICRC, 'Introduction' (Doc CE/1), submitted by the ICRC to the Conference of Government Experts on the Reaffirmation and Development of International Humanitarian Law Applicable in Armed Conflicts (Geneva, 24 May – 12 June 1971) (1971) 25.

> reasons, lay down limits to be observed in the conduct of hostilities, the use of weapons, the behaviour of combatants and recourse to reprisals, as well as norms intended to ensure the proper application of those rules.[44]

As in 1949, if States objected to the term 'international humanitarian law' in the lead-up to the 1974–1977 Diplomatic Conferences, there is little record of it. No mention of possible resistance to the new terminology appears in the Reports of the Conferences of Government Experts in either 1971[45] or 1972,[46] though there was debate as to what was included within the definition,[47] with one expert calling for a definition 'as this term was now for the first time used in an international instrument'.[48] However, the debate seems to stop there, and when the community of States met to debate and eventually adopt what would become the Additional Protocols over a period of three years (1974–1977), it did so at a drafting conference entitled the Diplomatic Conference on the Reaffirmation and Development of International Humanitarian Law Applicable in Armed Conflicts.[49] The term 'international humanitarian law' was now officially part of the law.

But what exactly was the term 'international humanitarian law' understood to cover? The dominant or orthodox account of this development suggests that 'international humanitarian law' is simply the new terminology for 'the law of armed conflict': following adoption of the Additional Protocols in 1977, the 'laws of war had, for all useful purposes, been replaced by international humanitarian law'.[50] On the other hand, critical accounts suggest that this claim is problematic from both legal and political perspectives: that conflating the laws of war with the principles of humanitarian law applicable in armed

44 ibid.

45 ICRC, Conference of Government Experts on the Reaffirmation and Development of International Humanitarian Law Applicable in Armed Conflicts (Geneva, 24 May – 12 June 1971), *Report on the Work of the Conference* (1971).

46 ICRC, Conference of Government Experts on the Reaffirmation and Development of International Humanitarian Law Applicable in Armed Conflicts (Geneva, 3 May – 3 June 1972), *Report on the Work of the Conference* (1972).

47 ICRC, Conference of Government Experts 1971 (n 45) 35.

48 ICRC, Conference of Government Experts 1972 (n 46) 174, para 4.18.

49 See *Official Records of the Diplomatic Conference on the Reaffirmation and Development of International Humanitarian Law Applicable in Armed Conflicts*, 16 vols (Swiss Federal Political Department 1978).

50 Alexander (n 6) 124.

conflicts is legally incorrect, and that this conflation does political and ideological work, including making the conduct of warfare primarily subject to humanitarian considerations rather than the principle of military necessity.[51] From a purely practical perspective, as indicated in part 1 above, it is noteworthy that the terms 'law(s) of war' and 'law of armed conflict' continue to be used in particular contexts. Against this background, we turn now to consider whether, and how, the new terms 'law of armed conflict' and 'international humanitarian law' are picked up in State practice, through corpus linguistics analysis of the language used by States.

3 Putting Words into Practice – Using Corpus Linguistic Tools to Chart the Reception of the Terms 'the Law of Armed Conflict' and 'International Humanitarian Law' in State Practice: a Case Study of Conflict in the Middle East from 1948 to 2020

Corpus linguistics involves the study of large bodies of texts: a 'corpus' is a defined body of searchable text data deemed appropriate for the study of some particular research questions and of a scale not amenable to manual analysis.[52] While corpus linguistics allows for the analysis of large bodies of text, assembly and preparation of the relevant corpus or dataset is a time-consuming matter. In order to make the scope of our inquiry manageable, we needed to set specific parameters – time and space limitations did not permit us, at this first instance, to study all State practice following 1949 (when States adopted the term 'armed conflict' in the 1949 Geneva Conventions) and 1977 (when States adopted the term 'international humanitarian law' in the Additional Protocols) in relation to armed conflicts. We therefore needed to narrow the case study, either to the practice of a particular State or States, or to the practice in relation to a particular conflict or conflicts.

We made the admittedly not-unproblematic choice to look at resolutions in the General Assembly and the Security Council, as these are the major public forums where States engage with international law. State participation in General Assembly and Security Council resolutions is generally accepted as an example of State practice[53] and can be important in determining how particular legal questions or issues are viewed by the international law

51 See, for example, Alexander (n 6); Wilson (n 7).

52 Anthony McEnery and Andrew Hardie, *Corpus Linguistics: Method, Theory, Practice* (CUP 2012).

53 International Law Commission, 'Ways and Means for Making the Evidence of Customary International Law More Readily Available' (July 1950) UN Doc A/CN.4/34, 368–72.

community.[54] However, we are aware that mere acceptance of the term 'international humanitarian law' or 'the law of armed conflict' in a resolution does not necessarily mean that States have unequivocally accepted the terms as their own preferred descriptor for the body of law applicable in armed conflicts.

We came to the decision to select, as a 'pilot study', one umbrella conflict – that of Israel and the Arab world. This was done for the primary reason that the time period for both the Israel conflict and the changing terminology aligned: the Conventions were introduced in 1949 and, since its creation in 1948, Israel has engaged in, or been engaged in, numerous conflicts with its neighbours, including the Six Day War and the Yom Kippur War, as well as continuing to occupy specific regions in the area. This provided a context in which to chart the changing terminology to see whether it changed with the conflict.

With these parameters in mind, we then looked to all General Assembly and Security Council resolutions adopted between 1947 and 2020 (for the General Assembly) and between 1948 and 2016 (for the Security Council) to see how many times the 'target' terms of 'the law of armed conflict' and 'international humanitarian law' appeared. We assembled a corpus of UN resolutions referring to the Israel-Palestine conflict over this time period, in both the Security Council and the General Assembly. With the age of this data, the texts came in various pdf formats, and so some manual editing was required to clean the data of extraneous text (such as other resolutions not relevant to the data set, or summaries of decisions made at a plenary session). Some resolutions were in both English and French: we resolved to study only the English versions of these resolutions; the French text was removed. Once the data was assembled, we loaded it into a corpus linguistics software program called #LancsBox,[55] which, among other techniques, allows researchers to check on word frequencies[56] and normalised frequencies (typically measured per 10K or per million words, allowing the comparison of frequency across data sets of

54 *Texaco Overseas Petroleum Company and California Asiatic Oil Company v Government of the Libyan Arab Republic* (1978) 17 ILM 1 at 27. See also Stephen Schwebel, 'The Effect of Resolutions of the UN General Assembly on Customary International Law' (1979) 73 ASIL Proceedings 301.

55 Vaclav Brezina, Pierre Weill-Tessier and Anthony McEnery, #LancsBox v. 5.x. [software] (2020) <http://corpora.lancs.ac.uk/lancsbox>.

56 The word count of these two corpora is approximate: the data includes tokens (eg numbers indicating footnotes), which ideally should be excluded. In addition, different tools use different definitions of the unit of word. Thus, the word count here is based on the concept of 'word' applied in #Lancsbox.

different sizes) and to view 'concordance lines' (that is, to see a keyword in the context of the words immediately to either side of it).[57]

Table 1 describes the set of texts that constitute this corpus. A total of 75 resolutions have been passed by the Security Council between the years 1948 and 2016, compared with 666 resolutions passed by the General Assembly[58] between the years 1947 and 2020. General Assembly resolutions are not only more numerous (by a factor of nearly 9 to 1) but, on average, more than three and a half times the length of Security Council resolutions.

Table 2 sets out the terms searched across these two corpora. The common terms to refer to this body of law, including 'law(s) of war', 'law of armed conflict' and 'international humanitarian law', were searched across the two data sets. Of these, 'law(s) of war' and 'law of armed conflict' did not appear in any of the total of 741 texts. 'International humanitarian law' appeared in 7% and 18% of the Security Council and General Assembly texts respectively. The first usage is in 1974, in a General Assembly resolution (A/RES/3237 (XXIX) – 'Observer Status for the Palestinian Liberation Organization'), and then the term does not reappear until 1993. In the Security Council resolutions, the term appears a total of seven times, in five resolutions, with the first appearing in 2002. Given that two of these key terms have abbreviations – LOAC and IHL – these were searched but no instances were found.

The term 'international law' appears in both data sets, including in 5% of Security Council resolutions[59] and 40% of General Assembly resolutions, making it the highest term of our set within the General Assembly resolutions. The term 'international instruments' makes a marginal appearance in the General Assembly resolutions (appearing in 3% of the texts) from 1971 to 1992.

TABLE 1 Texts constituting the corpus

	Security council	General assembly
Years	1948–2016	1947–2020
Number of texts	75	666
Word count	24,649	803,823
Average words per text	327	1,207

57 McEnery and Hardie (n 52).

58 Some early resolution texts contain more than one resolution. If the text has only one identifying number, we have treated it as one resolution.

59 For example, in Resolutions 271, 478, 1544 and 2334.

In the Security Council resolutions, there is also reference to the 'General Armistice Agreement' in the years from 1950 to 1966. General Assembly

TABLE 2 Use of terms to reference the law of international war in resolutions pertaining to the Israel-Palestine conflict

	Security council resolutions				General assembly resolutions			
Term	**Raw freq**	**Normalised freq: per 10K words**	**Text dispersion**	**Time frame**	**Raw freq**	**Normalised freq: per 10K words**	**Text dispersion**	**Time frame**
law of war	0	–	–	–	0	–	–	–
laws of war	0	–	–	–	0	–	–	–
law of armed conflict	0	–	–	–	0	–	–	–
General Armistice Agreement	34	13.79	11/75	1950–1966	0			
Geneva Conventions	2	0.81	1/75 (1%)	1969	70	1.02	32/666 (5%)	1968–1972; 1993–2018
Geneva Convention	44	17.85	25/75 (33%)	1979–2016	856	12.41	245/666 (37%)	1968–2020
international humanitarian law	7	2.84	5/75 (7%)	2002–2016	225	3.26	121/666 (18%)	1974 … 1993–2020
international law	6	2.43	4/75 (5%)	1969–2016	755	10.95	265/666 (40%)	1948 … 1970–2020
international instruments	0	0	0	0	22	0.32	22/666 (3%)	1971–1992

resolutions also frequently refer to *specific* instruments: 14 General Assembly resolutions reference 'Convention IV of the Hague 1907' and 65 reference the Geneva Convention Relative to the Protection of Civilian Persons in Time of War (Geneva Convention IV)[60] – this is mainly in reference to occupied territory. 'International humanitarian law' tends to be referenced in more recent resolutions. For example, in a 2020 resolution, the General Assembly '[c]alls upon Israel, the occupying Power, to comply strictly with its obligations under international law, including international humanitarian law'. However, within the same resolution, there is also specific reference to Geneva Convention IV. Likewise, Security Council resolutions tend to refer to 'international humanitarian law' only after 2002.[61]

By reading a selection of these texts, it became clear that, particularly before the 1990s, other terminology (rather than 'the law of armed conflict' or 'international humanitarian law') was used to reference this body of law. For instance, there is frequent reference to 'the' Geneva Convention. In fact, the term 'the Geneva Convention' is referenced in one-third of the Security Council resolutions[62] and just over one-third of the General Assembly resolutions. By using the concordance function, it is apparent that this term is referencing Geneva Convention IV. Figures 1 and 2 are screenshots of

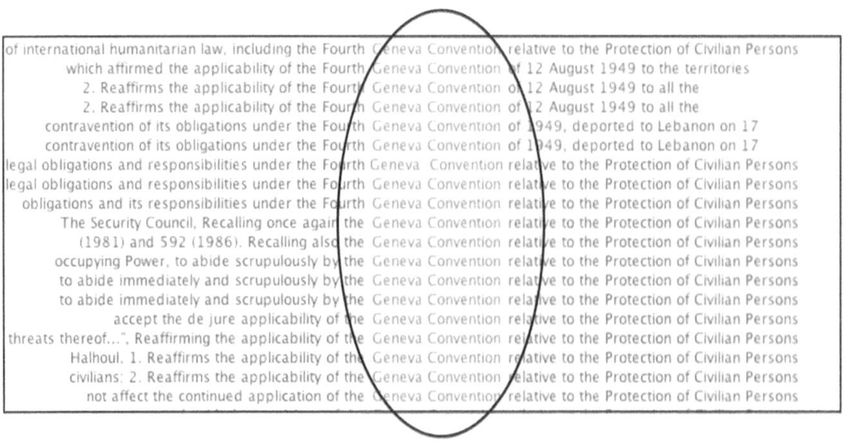

FIGURE 1 Concordance lines illustrating the use of 'Geneva Convention' in UN Security Council resolutions

60 Convention (IV) Relative to the Protection of Civilian Persons in Time of War (adopted 12 August 1949, entered into force 21 October 1950) 75 UNTS 287 (Geneva Convention IV).

61 For example, in Resolutions 1397, 1405, 1435, 1544 and 2334.

62 For example, in Resolutions 271, 446, 465, 469, 471, 476, 592, 605, 607, 636, 641, 468, 469, 672, 681, 694, 726, 799 and 904.

concordance lines, which confirm that it is this convention being referred to in these resolutions. The time period for referencing Geneva Convention IV is 1979–2016 for the Security Council resolutions, and 1968–2020 for the General Assembly resolutions. Reference to the Geneva Conventions in plural terms is made, but much less frequently than to the specific Geneva Convention IV: the plural form appears in only 1% of the Security Council resolutions, and 5% of the General Assembly resolutions.

4 Analysing the Results: Tensions in the State Practice of the Language of LOAC

Perhaps the most interesting finding from this small case study is that the terms 'law of war' and 'law of armed conflict' do not appear in the General Assembly or Security Council resolutions at all, while the term 'international humanitarian law' does. This suggests that, at least for these UN bodies, and in the context of resolutions relating to this particular conflict, 'international humanitarian law' is the preferred global term to describe this body of law.[63]

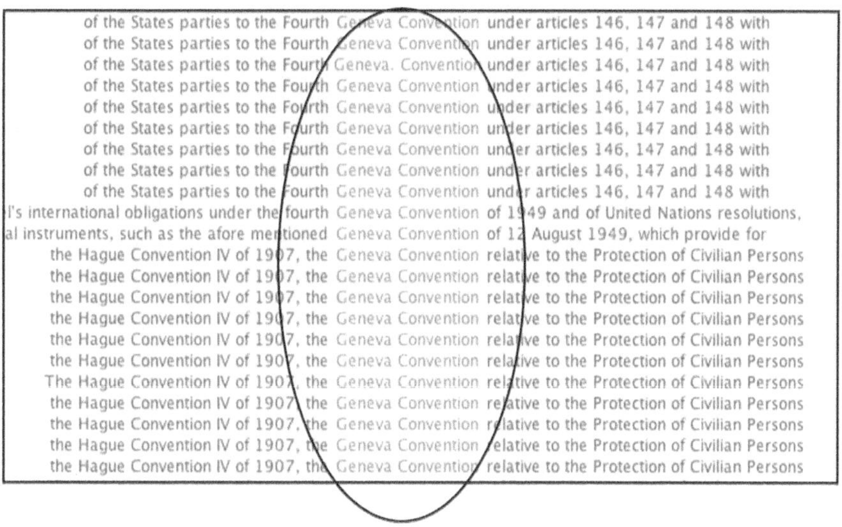

of the States parties to the Fourth Geneva Convention under articles 146, 147 and 148 with
of the States parties to the Fourth Geneva Convention under articles 146, 147 and 148 with
of the States parties to the Fourth Geneva. Convention under articles 146, 147 and 148 with
of the States parties to the Fourth Geneva Convention under articles 146, 147 and 148 with
of the States parties to the Fourth Geneva Convention under articles 146, 147 and 148 with
of the States parties to the Fourth Geneva Convention under articles 146, 147 and 148 with
of the States parties to the Fourth Geneva Convention under articles 146, 147 and 148 with
of the States parties to the Fourth Geneva Convention under articles 146, 147 and 148 with
of the States parties to the Fourth Geneva Convention under articles 146, 147 and 148 with
l's international obligations under the fourth Geneva Convention of 1949 and of United Nations resolutions,
al instruments, such as the afore mentioned Geneva Convention of 12 August 1949, which provide for
the Hague Convention IV of 1907, the Geneva Convention relative to the Protection of Civilian Persons
the Hague Convention IV of 1907, the Geneva Convention relative to the Protection of Civilian Persons
the Hague Convention IV of 1907, the Geneva Convention relative to the Protection of Civilian Persons
the Hague Convention IV of 1907, the Geneva Convention relative to the Protection of Civilian Persons
the Hague Convention IV of 1907, the Geneva Convention relative to the Protection of Civilian Persons
the Hague Convention IV of 1907, the Geneva Convention relative to the Protection of Civilian Persons
The Hague Convention IV of 1907, the Geneva Convention relative to the Protection of Civilian Persons
the Hague Convention IV of 1907, the Geneva Convention relative to the Protection of Civilian Persons
the Hague Convention IV of 1907, the Geneva Convention relative to the Protection of Civilian Persons
the Hague Convention IV of 1907, the Geneva Convention relative to the Protection of Civilian Persons
the Hague Convention IV of 1907, the Geneva Convention relative to the Protection of Civilian Persons

FIGURE 2 Concordance lines illustrating the use of 'Geneva Convention' in UN General Assembly resolutions

63 Although, as noted above and discussed further below, these bodies seem to prefer either using more general terms ('international law' or 'international instruments') or making more specific reference to particular treaties (Geneva Convention IV, for example).

This confirms the orthodox account regarding the use of these terms, namely that 'international humanitarian law' is the contemporary terminology used to refer to what was previously known as the 'law of war' and the 'law of armed conflict'.[64] As Hampson has written, since 1977, '[t]he use of the term [international humanitarian law] became more and more widespread, until now it is the term used by the United Nations Security Council and General Assembly, the International Court of Justice (ICJ), the International Committee of the Red Cross (ICRC) and the human rights machinery of the United Nations'.[65]

As foreshadowed above, however, critical accounts of the history of these terms challenge the assumption that international humanitarian law is simply the new term used to describe the laws of armed conflict and raise questions about the political and ideological implications of this terminology. Many of these accounts emphasise the distinction between traditional rules of the law of war relating to the conduct of hostilities (as embodied, for example, in the Hague Regulations) and those relating to the treatment of 'victims of war'[66] (as embodied, for example, in the Geneva Conventions) and argue that 'international humanitarian law' properly so-called should refer only to the latter. These scholars argue that the use of the term 'international humanitarian law' to describe both of these bodies of law is at best 'something of a misnomer'[67] and at worst a 'myth',[68] a 'political project by and for international humanitarian and human rights organizations in support of their own political objectives'.[69] Thus, Page Wilson describes 'a concerted effort to rebrand' the law of armed conflict as international humanitarian law 'first led by the International Committee of the Red Cross (ICRC), and then taken up by human rights groups from the 1980s onwards'.[70] For Wilson, the use of the term 'humanitarian' to describe this body of law was pursued by these organisations for political and ideological reasons, to shape the law and its application to their humanitarian agenda. On this account, unifying Hague and Geneva law under the umbrella of 'international humanitarian law' serves to subsume the idea of 'military necessity' in Hague law under the overriding imperative of humanitarianism, as well as making the interpretation of the law

64 Wilson (n 7) 563; Hampson (n 7) 538–39; Alexander (n 6).
65 Hampson (n 7) 539.
66 ibid 538.
67 ibid 539.
68 Wilson (n 7).
69 ibid 579.
70 ibid 565.

open to 'anyone claiming a stake in humanitarian issues'.[71] In other words, the law of armed conflict is no longer the domain of military lawyers alone, but also that of humanitarian and human rights NGOs.

Alexander, similarly, has shown how the field of 'international humanitarian law' has a relatively 'short' history: rather than being the natural successor of the law of war, it was created relatively quickly through a 'contested and contingent process'[72] driven in particular by the work of the ICRC to expand the scope of its remit, but also by other actors seeking to expand the application of human rights principles to the regulation of armed conflict. These actors include not only human rights NGOs such as Human Rights Watch, as emphasised by Wilson, but also international legal scholars and key figures such as Seán MacBride, Secretary-General of the International Commission of Jurists and co-founder of Amnesty International, who advocated for the expansion of the human rights regime to the regulation of armed conflict.

On Alexander's account, and as described in part 2 above, the term 'international humanitarian law' first came to prominence in 1971 with the ICRC Conference of Government Experts on the Reaffirmation and Development of International Humanitarian Law Applicable in Armed Conflicts.[73] As Alexander demonstrates, the term was used throughout the negotiations at the Diplomatic Conference, although there was some 'inconsistency in the commentary', with some speaking of, for example, 'the international humanitarian law of armed conflict'.[74] Following the Conference and the adoption of the Additional Protocols in 1977, however, Alexander notes that 'commentators and states began to express concerns about Additional Protocol I', fearing that 'the new international humanitarian law was too humanitarian to be adopted'.[75] Many States refused to sign or did not ratify, including the US, the UK, France and Australia.[76] And it was generally accepted that Additional Protocol I did not represent customary international law, so the obligations contained in it were not applicable to States that had not ratified. Thus, legal commentary on the First Gulf War in the early 1990s, for example, generally argued that the obligations in Additional Protocol I were not applicable, as neither the US nor Iraq was a party. This, Alexander notes, was 'connected with a widespread perception that the legal regime governing the Gulf War was not really a humanitarian law', as the 'central principle of the *ius in bello* was not

71 ibid 577.
72 Alexander (n 6) 110.
73 ibid 122.
74 ibid 123.
75 ibid 126.
76 Though eventually France ratified in 2001, Australia in 1991, and the UK in 1998.

humanity but, rather, the principle of military necessity'.[77] As a result, at this point in time, there was significant uncertainty about the appropriateness of the term 'international humanitarian law' to denote 'a *ius in bello* that was dominated by military imperatives'.[78]

According to Alexander, this all changed, relatively quickly, with the outbreaks of ethnic conflict in Yugoslavia and Rwanda and international attempts to respond to these events, including through international criminal tribunals. 'Suddenly, there was an institutional environment established to enforce international humanitarian law.'[79] With a rush of enthusiasm for the humanitarian potential of law in responding to these conflicts, lawyers 'almost without exception' would argue that the provisions of Protocol I were accepted as customary international law.[80] Thus, 'the correct understanding of the *ius in bello* by the end of the 20th century was that it was a truly international humanitarian law … in which considerations of humanity trumped military necessity'.[81]

Our findings support Alexander's claim that while the term 'international humanitarian law' came to the fore in the early-mid 1970s, with the Diplomatic Conference, it was not until the 1990s, and the outbreak of the conflict in the Balkans in particular, that it was confidently embraced as an appropriate description of the laws of war. The term 'international humanitarian law' first appears in General Assembly resolutions relating to Israel-Palestine in 1974, with a reference to the Conference itself.[82] It then disappears from use until 1993, from which time it is used fairly consistently. Also of interest is the fact that the term 'international instruments' ceases to be used around the same time that 'international humanitarian law' starts to be used more consistently. The last reference in the Israel-Palestine General Assembly resolutions to 'international instruments' is in 1992, and it is in 1993 that the term 'international humanitarian law' begins to be used consistently. This seems to confirm Alexander's thesis that it is only with the Balkan conflict in the early 1990s that the international consensus shifts to consider provisions of Additional Protocol I to be customary international law, thus justifying the reference to 'international humanitarian law' in Israel-Palestine resolutions

77 Alexander (n 6) 129.
78 ibid 130.
79 ibid.
80 ibid 132.
81 ibid 135.
82 UNGA Res 3237 (22 November 1974) UN Doc A/RES/3237, entitled 'Observer status for the Palestine Liberation Organization'.

rather than specific reference to the 'international instruments' by which the parties to the conflict are bound.

This conclusion, following from analysis of the General Assembly resolutions relating to Israel-Palestine, is supported by analysis of a larger, pre-existing corpus, the United Nations General Debate Corpus, which consists of the General Debate statements in the General Assembly from 1970 to 2020. Analysis of this corpus confirms the linguistic pattern noted in the General Assembly resolutions on Israel-Palestine. It shows that the term 'international humanitarian law' is first used in 1972 and then only sporadically used until 1992, at which point it becomes consistently used every year.

In relation to the Security Council, our results indicate that the term 'international humanitarian law' is not used in Security Council resolutions concerning Israel-Palestine until 2002. Manual analysis of Security Council debates, however, indicates that the relevant body of law starts to be labelled 'humanitarian' in the early 1980s. However, as Alexander notes with respect to the Diplomatic Conference itself, the language used is inconsistent with references to, for example, 'humanitarian principles of international law' or 'humanitarian rules'. By the time of the Balkan conflict, however, 'international humanitarian law' is used consistently.

5 Looking Forward – Possible Future Analyses on the Terminology of LOAC

In general terms, then, our results support Alexander's account of the contingent and contested rise of the term 'international humanitarian law'. In particular, our results support her claim that while the term comes to prominence with the Diplomatic Conference and the adoption of the Additional Protocols in the 1970s, it is not consistently embraced by the international community until the early 1990s and the outbreak of the conflict in the Balkans, in particular. To the extent that our findings support such critical accounts of the history of the term 'international humanitarian law', suggesting that the story of its rise to prominence is more complex than traditionally assumed, a number of questions about the implications of this 'new' terminology follow. Wilson and Alexander note the political implications that may be associated with the change in terminology from 'law of armed conflict' to 'international humanitarian law'. Other scholars note more technical, legal difficulties that may be associated with conflating Hague and Geneva law.[83] From a linguistic

83 Hampson (n 7).

perspective, the change raises interesting questions, in that while 'international humanitarian law' may have an autonomous legal meaning, it nonetheless retains traces of its ordinary meaning, so that the natural connotations of the term 'humanitarian' are likely to influence, in some way, the content of the legal concept itself.[84] As Mégret has noted, the choice of whether to call the relevant body of law the 'law of war' or 'international humanitarian law' is not neutral: 'It is not for nothing that the laws of war are typically referred to in polite company as international *humanitarian* law.'[85] From this perspective, the fact that the General Assembly and the Security Council exclusively use this term in their resolutions relating to Israel-Palestine (and do not refer to the law of armed conflict or the law of war) has important implications, which deserve further study.

Also deserving of further study is the fact that, in spite of UN bodies using the language of 'international humanitarian law', other actors continue to use the terms 'law of war' and 'law of armed conflict'. Hampson notes that 'international humanitarian law' 'is not the term used by a significant number of armed forces. They still prefer either the "law of war" or the "law of armed conflict"'.[86] Wilson similarly notes the dominance of these latter terms in military publications.[87] This suggests that while States use the language of 'international humanitarian law' in some contexts, namely when participating in UN processes, they also use 'law of war' or 'law of armed conflict', particularly when engaging with their militaries. This raises interesting questions of when and why States deploy different terminology, as well as the implications this has for State practice and international law. Future research could fruitfully map the different terminology used by States in contexts beyond General Assembly and Security Council resolutions.

At the same time, our current findings do hint that States may be aware of the political and other difficulties associated with the use of the terms 'international humanitarian law', 'law of armed conflict' and 'law of war'. The results discussed in part 3 indicate that, while the term 'international humanitarian law' is used in the resolutions relating to Israel-Palestine, it is much more common for the General Assembly and the Security Council to use broader terms (such as 'international law' or 'international instruments') or

84 Wilson (n 7).
85 Frédéric Mégret, 'The Laws of War and the Structure of Masculine Power' (2018) 19 Melbourne Journal of International Law 200, 204. Demonstrating the complexity at work here, in this article Mégret demonstrates how the very project of 'humanising' war effects a particular form of masculine domination.
86 Hampson (n 7) 539.
87 Wilson (n 7) 566.

more specific terms, specifying the applicable law as the Geneva Conventions or, much more commonly, the Fourth Geneva Convention. This practice of specifying the law more generally or more particularly may be a response to the legal and political complications associated with the term 'international humanitarian law', not least the fact that, as Wilson has noted, 'there is no international agreement which defines IHL on its own terms, let alone sets down its provisions in a comprehensive way'.[88] The limited nature of our case study raises the question of whether this is a general practice of the General Assembly and the Security Council, or a practice adopted in relation to the particular political situation of conflict with Israel. Future research will consider the language used in relation to other conflicts to draw more general conclusions regarding this phenomenon.

Preliminary research on this issue suggests that there may indeed be particular political considerations that influence the choice of language in relation to the Israel-Palestine conflict. Manual analysis of Security Council resolutions relating to other conflicts suggests that the first reference to 'international humanitarian law' is in 1982 in relation to the Iran-Iraq war, where the Security Council '[c]ondemns all violations of international humanitarian law, in particular, the provisions of the Geneva Conventions of 1949 in all their aspects'.[89] However, the use of this term is not universal, as resolutions passed that year regarding the ongoing Israel-Lebanon war contain no references to 'international humanitarian law'. By 2000, the Security Council is regularly referring to 'international humanitarian law', for example in its resolutions relating to the conflict between Ethiopia and Eritrea. But it is not until 2002 that the Security Council starts to use that language in its resolutions relating to Israel-Palestine. This may suggest that different politics are at work in different contexts, and it raises interesting questions of how the language of this body of law can be manipulated for political ends. Again, further research is needed to confirm whether this is indeed the case, and to explore the political, legal and linguistic dynamics at work here.

6 Conclusion

Over the course of the 20th century, the language used in treaties regulating the conduct of warfare shifted from referring to the 'law(s) of war' to the 'law of armed conflict' and ultimately 'international humanitarian law'. But these

88 ibid 578.

89 UNSC Res 540 (31 October 1982) UN Doc S/RES/540.

changes in terminology were largely driven by civil society, particularly the ICRC, rather than by States. This raises interesting questions of whether the changes in terminology are picked up in State practice – and, if so, how and when. Our larger research project seeks to answer this question using tools of corpus linguistics to help us map language patterns across large bodies of text. For this pilot study, we have focused on a particular type of text that manifests State practice, namely General Assembly and Security Council resolutions, with respect to a particular conflict, namely Israel-Palestine.

The results of this pilot study demonstrated that the terms 'law(s) of war' and 'law of armed conflict' were not used in General Assembly and Security Council resolutions relating to the Israel-Palestine conflict at all. The term 'international humanitarian law', however, was. This would seem to confirm orthodox accounts of the shift in terminology, which view it as linear and neutral, such that 'international humanitarian law' is simply the 'new' name for the 'law(s) of war'. On closer analysis, however, our results suggest that the picture is more complex. Contrary to what orthodox accounts might predict, the term 'international humanitarian law' does not appear in the resolutions in any consistent way until 1993 in the General Assembly and 2002 in the Security Council. Prior to that time, both bodies demonstrate a marked preference for refraining from using a global term to describe this body of law, instead using more general terms ('international law' or 'international instruments') or referring more specifically to particular instruments, notably Geneva Convention IV.

This suggests that the shift to using the terminology of 'international humanitarian law' to cover the field of the *ius in bello* does not result, at least not directly, from adoption of the Additional Protocols in 1977. In this sense, our findings support the argument of scholars such as Alexander, who argue that the rise of 'international humanitarian law' was rather the result of a contingent and contested process, 'the intersection of the work of a diverse group of actors, each focused on their own particular aims, strategies or tasks'.[90] Alexander points, in particular, to changes in legal scholarship and practice following the outbreaks of ethnic conflict in the Balkans and Rwanda in the early 1990s. Our finding that the General Assembly resolutions on the Israel-Palestine conflict start referring to international humanitarian law in a consistent way from 1993 would seem to support this argument. If this is indeed the case, and the shift towards the terminology of 'international humanitarian law' was not linear and neutral, but contingent and contested, then this raises legal, linguistic, political and ideological issues which require further study.

---

90 Alexander (n 6) 136.

Of course, it is important not to overstate the significance of our findings based on this small sample of State practice. It is possible that the way in which language is used in these resolutions does not reflect State practice more broadly. It is also possible that State practice varies in different contexts. Perhaps the particular politics of the Israel-Palestine conflict affect the choice of language used in these resolutions. In this sense, part of the significance of this pilot study is to identify avenues for further research. Most obviously, this includes expanding our study of General Assembly and Security Council resolutions to other conflicts. It could also include expanding our study to consider the way in which States use language outside the context of UN resolutions, such as in General Assembly and Security Council debates. Future research could also combine the use of corpus linguistics analysis with close legal and discourse analysis of particular texts to explore the legal and political implications of choice of language more fully.

In spite of these limitations, two things emerge clearly from our analysis. The first is that States do not automatically embrace the changing terminology in the treaties regulating warfare. The second is that corpus linguistics provides useful tools for mapping the use of legal language across large bodies of text and over time. Combined with traditional tools of legal and linguistic analysis, it has the potential to offer new insights into the language of law and war, as well as its legal, linguistic and political implications.

The International Laws of War: Linguistic Analysis from the Perspectives of Register, Corpus and Grammatical Patterning

Annabelle Lukin and Alexandra García Marrugo

Abstract

All texts, including all legal texts, are constructed in language. All legal constructs and discriminations are an effect of language. As such, linguistics and text analysis should be considered a necessary adjunct to legal studies and, in particular, to critical legal studies. While the disciplines of linguistics and law are increasingly interacting, there is a paucity of linguistic analysis in the field of the international laws of war. This paper seeks to open doors to collaboration, by viewing the texts of the international laws of war from three linguistic perspectives: as a 'register', as a 'corpus', and in terms of their lexicogrammatical patterning. In terms of register, the international laws of war herald a new form of textual practice, the function and effects of which are subject to debate. As a corpus, some dominant lexical habits of these texts are explored and interpreted for their ideological implications and reactances. Finally, an examination of covert lexicogrammatical meanings in this register, via a small extract from Article 8 of the Rome Statute, illuminates the contradictory meanings that these texts navigate. These three perspectives offer a preliminary glimpse into the value of linguistic analysis for critical perspectives on the international laws of war.

Keywords

International laws of war – linguistics – register – corpus linguistics – grammar

 | DOI:10.1163/9789004712478_004

1 Introduction

Legal texts are, by design, complex texts that require specialised training to interpret. They promulgate crucial legal concepts that are dressed in legal regalia. On the surface, these texts appear able to rise above the hurly burly of ordinary, nonlegal uses of language. As such, claims have been made for the special nature of legal discourse. Goodrich in his 1987 book *Legal Discourse* describes it as a 'closed code' and argues that 'the rules of the legal grammatical code' 'transform' or 'translate' ordinary language and meanings into this closed system. A decade earlier, the French linguist Greimas had described legal discourse as a 'secondary metasemiotic', with its own lexicon and syntax and a capacity to create 'autonomous semiotic objects endowed with personality and quasi-organic functions'.

However, while legal texts have unique features, they are in most respects like any other use of language. Like any other text, a legal text depends on the semiotic principles that enable every act of meaning. They are structured and coherent acts of meaning, responsive to and constrained by the nature of their social and cultural context. Those who create, interpret, and study legal texts stand to benefit from linguistic insights into the internal semiotic machinery of language, upon which all texts depend.

This paper brings a linguistic focus to texts variously referred to as the 'laws of war', the 'laws of armed conflict' or 'international humanitarian law'.[1] Until recently, histories of this body of international law were 'characterized by the grand narrative of international law as the purveyor of peace and civilisation to the whole world',[2] as a 'broadly humanist and civilizing force, standing back from war, judging it to be just or unjust, while offering itself as a code of conduct to limit violence on the battlefield'.[3] More recently, this 'standard Western-European-centred view' has been challenged, so that 'virtually no one today thinks that he or she could produce a new grand narrative of international law which would be objective, entirely neutral, absolute and universal'. Alternatives to the 'grand narrative' of international law as a purveyor of peace

1 See A Alexander, 'A Short History of International Humanitarian Law' (2015) 26 European Journal of International Law 109.

2 ET Jouannet and A Peters, 'The Journal of the History of International Law: A Forum for New Research' (2014) 16 Journal of the History of International Law 1, 4.

3 D Kennedy, *Of War and Law* (Princeton University Press 2006) 6.

include claims that the international laws of war, rather than constraining violence and being a force for 'civilisation', are a potent source for the legitimation of violence.

For example, Jochnick and Norman 'challenge [...] the notion that the laws of war serve to restrain or "humanize" war', arguing instead that 'through law, violence has been legitimated',[4] while Mégret argues that treaties, statutes and sources of customary laws of war 'enable, constitute and perpetuate' war and have produced 'the basic building blocks of the international grammar of violence'.[5] Law, he proposes, is 'just another name for fossilized theory that no longer sees itself as theory'. The theorising of the laws of war, Mégret argues, is necessary to 'displace [...] the field's confidence that it is "only law" and can shape our understanding of the laws of war as less immutable, progressive and benign than is typically accepted'.[6] Elsewhere, he has also claimed that the laws of war are intimately tied up with the projection of masculine power, serving to provide a plausible, virulent masculinity that navigates 'an impossible synthesis between violence and restraint'.[7]

Underlying these critiques is an intimation of the constructive power of language. These texts are not merely passive vehicles for a singular and authoritative voice of law, but are, rather, active players in the construction of principles and categories, at least some of which serve to legitimate rather than constrain geopolitical violence. They echo and bolster ideological forces outside the domain of law, not only available as a strategic asset by militaries[8], but as a foundational ideological source for the maintenance of gendered power relations. Given the reliance of the laws of war on language, there is much to be gained by adding theoretical and methodological resources from linguistics to these critical accounts.

While linguistic engagement with legal discourse has a reasonably long history,[9] the intersections are more recent in the field of the international laws of

---

4 CA Jochnick and R Normand, 'The Legitimation of Violence: A Critical History of the Laws of War' (1994) 35 Harvard International Law Journal 49, 50.

5 F Mégret, 'Theorizing the Laws of War' in A Orford and F Hoffman (eds.), *Oxford Handbook on the Theory of International Law* (Oxford University Press 2016).

6 ibid 778.

7 F Mégret, 'The Laws of War and the Structure of Masculine Power' (2018) 19 Melbourne Journal of International Law 200.

8 D Kennedy, *Of War and Law* (Princeton University Press 2006) 8.

9 See JM Broekman and L Catà Backer, 'Jacob Israel de Haan, the First Legal Semiotician' in JM Broekman and L Catà Backer (eds.) *Signs in Law – A Source Book. The Semiotics of Law in Legal Education III* (Springer 2015).

war.[10] The texts of the international laws of war are a natural site of collaboration between linguistics and law: they are made out of language, which gives a natural role for linguistics in their understanding, and they offer to linguistics the challenge of understanding and explaining their power to set the terms of legal geopolitical violence. No doubt part of the power of these texts of the international laws of war derives from the fact that they are interwoven with the threat of violence on which state sovereignty is based;[11] but it would be misguided to think that what Althusser calls the 'Repressive State Apparatus' could function in a semiotic vacuum.[12]

The organised violence that has proliferated in modernity has, as Malešević argues, been enabled by its ideological underpinnings.[13] As such, these texts have not just a legal but an ideological role, shaping collective human thought and individual and institutional behaviour. While part of their own kind of text practice, the meanings of these texts are not confined to the legal field.[14] To understand both their power and their contradictions, we need to understand the specific nature of these texts as a kind of text form, or 'register', and inquire into their semantic patterning via various linguistic approaches.

The paper is divided into three sections. The first examines the international laws of war as a 'register'. The term 'register' denotes language variation based on context and recognises social and cultural context as the dominant shaping force of language both as a generalised semiotic system and in each specific use of language.[15] As we discuss below, modern international laws of

---

10 See for example: A Potts and AL Kjær, 'Constructing Achievement in the International Criminal Tribunal for the Former Yugoslavia (ICTY): A Corpus-Based Critical Discourse Analysis' (2016) 29 International Journal for the Semiotics of Law 525; A Lukin, 'How International Law Makes Violence Legal: a Case Study of the Rome Statute' (2020) 2 Language, Context and Text: The Social Semiotics Forum 91; A Lukin and R Araujo e Castro, 'The Macquarie Laws of War Corpus (MQLWC): Design, Construction and Use' (2022) 35 International Journal for the Semiotics of Law – Revue Internationale de Sémiotique Juridique 2167.

11 M Weber, *Economy and Society* (University of California Press 1978) 54.

12 L Althusser, 'Ideology and Ideological State Apparatuses' in *Lenin and Philosophy* (New Left Books 1971).

13 S Malešević, *The Sociology of War and Violence* (Cambridge University Press 2010).

14 A gaming satirical news site, Hard Drive, published an article in 2021 stating the the 'New Geneva Conventions' was now outlawing the killing of a player away from their keyboard. While these texts are developed by the international legal community, their meanings are open to recontextualisation.

15 MAK Halliday and R Hasan, *Language, Context and Text: Aspects of Language in a Social Semiotic Perspective*, (Deakin University Press 1985); R Hasan, 'Towards a Paradigmatic Description of Context: Systems, Metafunctions, and Semantics' (2014) 1 Journal of Functional Linguistics <https://doi.org/10.1186/s40554-014-0009-y>.

war are based on a new kind of register, i.e., a new way of using language beginning, more or less, with the Paris Declaration of 1856.[16] A new register is a new semiotic ecosystem, providing a semiotically constructed home in which to develop and maintain the meanings that give this textual practice its unique identity. These texts provide the conditions for the creation of the key principles of the international laws of war. Such principles are no more and no less than patterns of wording and meaning that such texts have created and which they sustain.

Section two of the paper treats the international laws of war texts as a 'corpus',[17] a coherent body of searchable texts. It draws on corpus linguistic methods to inquire into their dominant semantic patterns. Using our expertise in linguistics, we constituted this corpus by incorporating all the texts included by the International Committee of the Red Cross in their International Humanitarian Law (IHL) treaties database,[18] a set of 110 texts at the time of writing. It includes all current international treaties pertaining to the governance of war or 'armed conflict', treaties no longer in force, and documents, such as the Lieber Code, considered to have been formative in the development of this field. We demonstrate how key techniques in corpus linguistics, such as word frequency, concordance (viewing a particular word in the context of the words on either side of it), and collocations (a summary of the typical words that co-occur with a word under examination), can be used to explore significant lexical patterns in this body of text.

Finally, while corpus techniques enable certain reading practices over a large data set, texts are not simply bags of words: they are intricately structured, and subject to the grammatical systems of the language in which they are expressed. Section three of the paper provides a third linguistic angle on the international laws of war. It explores two extracts from the Rome Statute,[19] the treaty that established the International Criminal Court, described by former UN Secretary-General Kofi Annan as 'one of the finest moments in the history of the United Nations' and 'a giant step forward in the march towards universal human rights and the rule of law'.[20] In this third section, we employ

---

16 Paris Declaration Respecting Maritime Law (adopted 16 April 1856, entered into force 18 April 1858) 115 CTS 1.

17 A McEnery and A Hardie, *Corpus Linguistics: Method, Theory, Practice* (Cambridge University Press 2012).

18 See <https://ihl-databases.icrc.org/ihl>.

19 Rome Statute of the International Criminal Court (adopted 17 July 1998, entered into force 1 July 2002) 2187 UNTS 90 ('Rome Statute').

20 K Annan, 'Preface' in RS Lee (ed.) *The International Criminal Court: The Making of the Rome Statute* (Kluwer Law International 1999) ix.

a lexicogrammatical analysis, based on Halliday and Matthiessen's work, to explore the meanings that grammatical patterns construe and how a short piece of grammatical structure can interweave deeply contradictory meanings. These three sections are intended to provide avenues for further interdisciplinary collaborations between law and linguistics.

2 The International Laws of War as 'Register'

Open multilateral treaties, treaties to which any state can become a party, are a relatively new text form which appeared in the mid-19th century. It has been argued that the first open multilateral treaty was the 1856 Paris Declaration on Maritime Law, which was the first to attempt to regulate the behaviour of states at war. According to Roberts, it is not simply that the Paris Declaration is the first multilateral laws of war treaty: it is the first multilateral treaty.[21] At a mere 336 words, the Paris Declaration introduces the idea of presenting, in written form, a set of four points, or 'maxims' – the only use of this word across the subsequent nearly 170 years of making of international laws of war – which are agreed upon by those states who declare themselves signatories.

Although this little text foreshadowed the emergence of what in linguistics is called a new 'register' – i.e., a functional variety of language – the idea of 'laws of war' well precedes it. Texts published from as early as 1535, available via the Early English Books Online (EEBO)[22] corpus, show the expression 'laws of war' to be already part of public discourse, perhaps as a function of ordinances on the conduct of war promulgated by medieval kings, or tracts of medieval jurists[23]. Thus, the Paris Declaration enters a stage already prepared by an existing notion of the 'laws of war', but begins a process of textual and legal innovation, by creating a space for international negotiations on the behaviour of states 'in time of war', to quote the preamble. The Paris Declaration was the first step of many towards the creation of a body of international laws of war. Two produced soon afterwards – the 1863 Lieber Code[24] and the 1864 Geneva

21 Ironically, as he argues, the 'basic legal art form of the past 160 years or more' actually emerged in the field of the laws of war, despite the fact that it is 'undoubtedly a particularly difficult legal subject area': AS Roberts, 'Foundational Myths in the Laws of War: The 1863 Lieber Code and the 1864 Geneva Convention' (2019) 20 Melbourne Journal of International Law 158, 164.

22 See <https://ota.bodleian.ox.ac.uk/repository/xmlui/handle/20.500.12024/A00381>.

23 T Meron, 'Shakespeare's Henry the Fifth and the Law of War' (2012) 86 American Journal of International Law 1.

24 *General Orders No 100: Adjutant-General's Office, Instructions for the Government of Armies of the United States, in the Field.* Prepared by Francis Lieber, promulgated as General

Convention[25] – would provide 'foundational stories' about the emergence and function of the international laws of war.[26]

To understand the cultural and linguistic shift entailed in the emergence of the language of the 'laws of war', 'register' enables us to identify the features of the new text forms and appreciate those that may have been taken for granted. Registers have three key defining parameters, described as, (1) the nature of the social activity the text is engaged in (referred to as its 'field'); (2) the nature of the relationships that bring the interactants together (referred to as 'tenor') and (3) the nature of the language contact (referred to as 'mode').[27] Every text is some kind of register, configured by these three principles, because language itself evolved through these same principles of human interaction. These parameters are inescapable features of every act of meaning, with all uses of language being responsive to these three dimensions of context.

By using these linguistic concepts, some significant features of the international laws of war as a register can be identified. For example, the concept of tenor (the nature of the interactant relations) reveals that the international laws of war provided the conditions for the emergence of a new kind of discursive speaker role. These texts, starting with the Paris Declaration, acted as a vehicle for the 'voice' of an open collection of (emerging) nation state entities. Within two years of the Declaration's promulgation, the text had attracted 41 signatories.[28] Language was being used to perform a new kind of interaction, and in the process, the voice of a globalising, institutionalised speaker was constructed.

In the Paris Declaration, this speaker position was known as a collection of 'plenipotentiaries', a Latin term attested at least as early as the mid-17th century in English.[29] It appears in international war law until the 1986 Convention on the Rights of the Child,[30] although its use past 1929 is very minimal. The

Orders No. 100 by President Lincoln, 24 April 1863. The Lieber Code is not a multilateral treaty, so it lacks a key feature of the majority of texts considered to constitute the laws of war. But like the others, it is constituted by a set of principles around declaring legal means of violence, while purporting to provide limits to this violence.

25 Convention for the Amelioration of the Condition of the Wounded in Armies in the Field (adopted 22 August 1864, entered into force 22 June 1865) 129 CTS 361.

26 Roberts (n 21).

27 Halliday and Hasan; Hasan (n 15).

28 Roberts (n 22) 164.

29 "plenipotentiary, adj. and n." (*OED Online*, March 2022) <www.oed.com/view/Entry/145680>.

30 Convention on the Rights of the Child (adopted 20 November 1989, entered into force 2 September 1990) UNTS 1577 3.

1863 Lieber Code introduces the terms 'Contracting Powers' and 'Contracting Parties', the former falling out of use by 1934, and the latter last used in the 2006 International Convention for the Protection of All Persons from Enforced Disappearance. From 1968, the authority of a 'Contracting Power' would share the field with the term 'States Parties', which remains the current term to refer to document signatories.

This changing terminology – from the concept of an individual person invested with the authority to speak on behalf of a ruler, to an abstract, bureaucratic, contractual authority eventually based in statehood – reflects the long-term sociological process of bureaucratic rationalisation where 'personal ties and nepotistic relationships become slowly but steadily replaced with impersonal rules and bureaucratic regulations'[31] – see Figure 1.

While Roberts suggests that the emergence of international cooperation should have been quite unlikely in such a contentious field as that of war, Malešević, argues that, in fact, it the origins of modern bureaucratisation, with its newfound force and reach, is with the military, quoting Weber's point that 'military discipline gives birth to all discipline'.[32] The Paris Declaration can be seen as heralding a process by which an international bureaucratic authority emerges to set the 'rules' of war. It marks a milestone in a sociohistorical process Malešević calls 'the bureaucratisation of coercion', which he argues develops in parallel with war becoming 'a total event involving millions of mobilised and ideologised citizens bent on the destruction of entire societies deemed to be enemies'.[33]

The 'voice' of States Parties (and their predecessors) could only have been enabled and constructed via writing, a point which brings in the concept of 'mode' – the means by which language enables a speaker and addressee to come into contact. The texts of international war law are densely written texts created in the standard languages of the nation state.[34] Their grammatical structures and patterns stand in stark contrast to the grammar of the spoken discourse of everyday life and echo the semantic style of other registers typical of modernity, such as the discourses of science and government administration. These registers – described as 'inherently displaced',[35] that is, registers

31 Malešević (n 13) 5.
32 ibid 6.
33 Malešević (n 13) 7.
34 See B Anderson, *Imagined Communities: Reflections on the Origin and Spread of Nationalism* (Verso 1983); RD Grillo, *Dominant Languages: Language and Hierarchy in Britain and France* (Cambridge University Press 1989).
35 R Hasan, 'Tenor: Rethinking Interactant Relations' (2020) 2 Language, Context and Text: The Social Semiotics Forum 213.

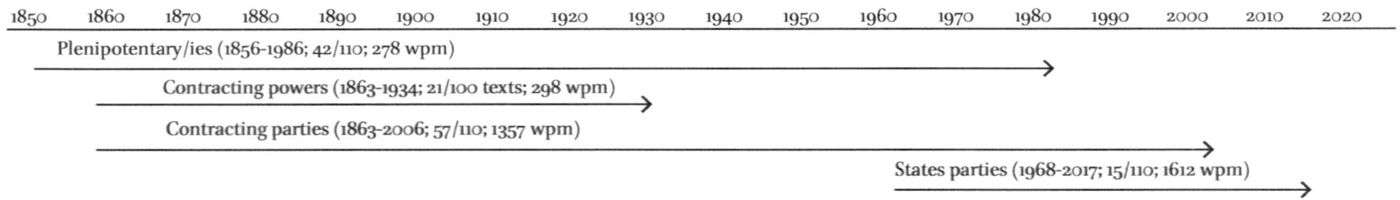

FIGURE 1 Terms describing interactants in texts of the international laws of war 1856–2017, including timeframe of usage and normalised frequency (number of tokens per million words, or wpm, discussed below) across the data

where the reception of meaning is displaced in time and space from its production – have a grammatical complexity known as 'grammatical metaphor'.[36]

Grammatical metaphor describes the grammatical tendencies in registers, such as in law, to favour nominal modes of representation: process being represented as a noun. One example is the concept 'military necessity', where the verb 'to need' has become a noun expressing an abstract thing. This results in reification and abstraction away from material, concrete, everyday experience. As Halliday argues, 'grammatical metaphor allows users of standard languages to 'hold[…] the world still, making it noun-like (stable in time) while it is observed, experimented with, measured and reasoned about'.[37] These linguistic patterns and habits allow communities to create 'a parallel semiotic universe of virtual things, especially virtual entities and virtual processes'.[38]

The 'virtual phenomena' created through grammatical metaphor exist only on a semiotic plane: they have no direct material analogue, and are entirely dependent on their definitions. For example, the key principles of the international laws of war, summarised in Crawford and Pert, are 'distinction', 'military necessity', 'proportionality', 'the prohibition on causing unnecessary suffering and superfluous injury', 'neutrality', and 'humanity',[39] all instances of grammatical metaphor, all relying on the grammatical shift into abstract nouns, a grammatical shift from meanings more directly or concretely expressed through other grammatical structures.

This feature can be seen as soon as we attempt to 'translate' these concepts into everyday language: the principle of 'distinction' can be translated to 'you have to distinguish between ordinary people and the people who belong to the army of a country'; 'the prohibition on causing unnecessary suffering and superfluous injury' could be 'you are not allowed to make people suffer too much and you cannot injure them too much either'. Translated, these concepts lack the mystique and prestige of the abstract form, the capacity to have the status of a legal principle. These concepts depend on the grammar of densely

36 MAK Halliday, 'Written language, standard language, global language' in JJ Webster (ed.) *Linguistic Studies of Text and Discourse. Volume 11 in the Collected Works of M.A.K. Halliday* (Bloomsbury 2013).

37 MAK Halliday, 'Language and the reshaping of human experience' in JJ Webster (ed.) *The Language of Science: Volume 5 in the Collected Works of M.A.K. Halliday* (Continuum 2004) 21.

38 MAK Halliday, 'Language evolving: Some systemic functional reflections on the history of meaning' in JJ Webster (ed.) *Halliday in the 21st Century. Volume 11 in the Collected Works of M.A.K. Halliday* (Bloomsbury 2013).

39 E Crawford and A Pert, *International Humanitarian Law* (Cambridge University Press 2015) 41–49.

written text for their existence and identity. This is the meaning of 'semiotic constructs with no material analogue', and these constructs came into being through the emergence of the international laws of war register.

In summary, the texts of the international laws of war herald a new register, in which a newly forming speaker position (i.e., tenor) – an abstract, international, bureaucratic voice, with the force of nation state militaries – projects itself through the densely crafted and highly elaborated written form, dependent on grammatical metaphor (i.e., mode). The function of this discourse (i.e., field, or nature of the social activity) as these texts accumulate over time, is, as we have already seen, subject to debate and interpretation. While these texts have an overtly stated purpose, often articulated in a preamble, the complex combination of tenor and mode ensures that these texts can be home to discordant meanings and internal contradictions. More detailed analysis of the language of the texts of the international laws of war is one means to bring out such contradictions.

3 The International Laws of War as Corpus

Despite the contest over precisely what semiotic work they perform, the texts of the international laws of war are functionally similar enough to be treated as a 'corpus', that is, as a searchable body of linguistic data. For our purposes, we have assembled all the texts hosted by the International Committee of the Red Cross in its IHL database.[40] While the International Committee of the Red Cross website, which hosts these documents, has improved its search functionality,[41] these texts are now available in a search interface with the full functionality of linguistic corpus technology via the Sydney Corpus Lab[42] under the title of 'Macquarie Laws of War Corpus' (MQLWC), reflecting the institution (Macquarie University) where this corpus development work took place.

40 See <https://ihl-databases.icrc.org/ihl>.

41 See https://www.icrc.org/en/document/searching-ihl-databases-icrc. The site covers treaties, customary law, and documents associated with national implementation, and includes documents in seven languages. The site currently only allows a user to determine if a word or phrase appears in the available documents.

42 The Sydney Corpus Lab is a corpus website directed by Professor Monika Bednerak at the University of Sydney. By requesting a free account, any user can access available corpora at this site: https://sydneycorpuslab.com. For details on the MQLWC, see Lukin and Araujo e Castro (n 10).

The corpus is based on the 110 texts (English only; the corpus excludes Annex II to Protocol Additional to the Geneva Conventions 1949, as it consists of a template only) hosted in the International Committee of the Red Cross IHL database, a corpus totaling c. 392K words,[43] beginning with the Paris Declaration in 1856 and extending up to 2019 when a further amendment to the Rome Statute was made. In this format, this body of international law can now be easily searched with basic corpus linguistic techniques such as word frequencies, concordances (where a word of interest is viewed in relation to words both to the left and right of this word in a corpus) and collocations (i.e., the typical words that co-occur with a specific word),[44] providing the opportunity to study these texts in new ways. In addition, the whole corpus can be downloaded from the Sydney Corpus Lab for offline processing via other popular corpus software tools. This new access to these texts opens them up for a range of inquiries. Here we illustrate this potential with a brief discussion of the data using some corpus linguistic techniques.

Starting with word frequencies,[45] Table 1 provides an example of the kind of information that can be extracted from this body of law. It lists, in order of frequency, the top 20 'open system' lexical items across the MQLWC; that is, the list of top frequency words when grammatical words (articles, such as 'the'; prepositions, such as 'in' or 'of'; and conjunctions, such as 'and', among others) are excluded. The table specifies both 'raw' and 'normalised' frequencies, the first being actual number of occurrences in the data, and the second being a measure of frequency per quantum or words, using a standard measure of 'words per million', or 'wpm'. Normalised frequency allows us to compare patterns in one data set with another. In addition, the metric of text dispersion shows how many texts in the corpus include these words.

This list includes some high frequency items that reflect the bureaucratic process itself of 'states' 'parties' signing up to 'international' 'conventions', which are constituted by 'articles' (and where 'art' is an abbreviation for this term), reflecting that these texts are part Malešević's 'bureaucratization of

43 Different corpus systems have different ways of defining words or 'tokens'. This count, based on the CQWEB system, includes punctuation items.

44 A McEnery and A Hardie, *Corpus Linguistics: Method, Theory, Practice* (Cambridge University Press 2012).

45 Analysing word frequencies provides a measure of dominant word forms and, to some degree, dominant concepts in a corpus.

TABLE 1 Twenty most frequent lexical (content) items in the MQLWC[46]

Rank	Lexical item	Raw frequency	Normalised frequency (wpm)	Text dispersion (n/total n)
1	article	2722	7667	86/100 (78%)
2	convention	1719	4842	77/110 (70%)
3	parties	1645	4638	85/110 (76%)
4	state	1544	4349	68/110 (68%)
5	art	1407	3963	80/110 (73%)
6	war	1401	3946	79/110 (72%)
7	party	1344	3785	63/110 (57%)
8	international	1154	3250	90/110 (81%)
9	states	1047	2949	65/100 (59%)
10	power	970	2732	52/110 (47%)
11	present	846	2383	78/110 (71%)
12	prisoners	832	2344	34/110 (31%)
13	military	827	2329	66/110 (60%)
14	conflict	791	2228	42/110 (38%)
15	court	752	2118	37/110 (34%)
16	persons	712	2005	67/110 (61%)
17	paragraph	675	1901	68/110 (62%)
18	provisions	675	1901	78/110 (71%)
19	powers	665	1873	57/110 (52%)
20	contracting	664	1870	60/110 (54%)

coercion'.[47] Setting these words aside for now, then 'war', 'power', and 'military' can been seen as very dominant concepts across this body of text, empirical findings which can provide evidence for debates about the preoccupations within this register.

46 These frequencies were derived using Lancsbox: V Brezina, P Weill-Tessier, and A McEnery, #LancsBox v. 5.x. [software] (2020). Available at: <http://corpora.lancs.ac.uk/lancsbox>.

47 Malešević (n 13).

While each of these terms merit further investigation, for our purposes we consider in more detail the use of the word 'military' in this corpus. The mirror image of 'military', the word 'civilian', does not appear in the top 20 most frequent terms in this data. While 'military' ranks 13th, 'civilian' ranks at 61st, and appears at less than half the frequency of 'military' (359 for 'civilian'; 827 for 'military'), and is found in approximately 50% fewer texts than 'military' (34% text dispersion for 'civilian'; 60% for 'military'). A further measure of its frequency can be sought by comparing the frequency of the word 'military' in this corpus to a variety of other corpora to consider whether 'military' is particularly frequent in the international laws of war. This is likely to be the case, but a comparison with other data not only provides the evidence for this hypothesis, but can also provide a calibration of the greater frequency of 'military' in the laws of war.

To do this, we selected relevant comparative corpora, such as the British National Corpus (BNC: 100 million word cross-register corpus of British English from early 1990s); AmE06 (1 million word cross-register corpus from American English between 2005–2007); BE06 (1 million word cross-register corpus from British English between 2005–2007); News on the Web corpus (>15 billion words of news data in English across 20 countries from 2010 to current).[48] Figure 2 plots the normalised frequency for 'military' across these five corpora, with the MQLWC clearly showing a strong bias towards the word. The average normalised frequency across the comparator corpora for the word 'military' is 157 wpm. With the normalised frequency of 'military' in the laws of war corpus being 2329 wpm, the comparison shows 'military' to be nearly 15 times more frequent in the laws of war.

Again, these findings are not surprising: but if claims are being made that this discourse form is not restraining but instead enabling violence, then the high frequency of 'military' may be indicative of a legitimising labour that these texts are engaged in. A further step methodologically is to consider the 'collocates' of a lexical item – that is, the words which typically go with (on either side of) a word of interest, for instance, taking five words either side of the lexical item. Collocates can be determined simply on the basis of frequency, but other measures allow collocates to be determined by a combination of frequency and mutual expectancy (the probability that two lexical items will

48 BNC Consortium, The British National Corpus, XML Edition, 2007, Oxford Text Archive, <http://hdl.handle.net/20.500.12024/2554>; P Baker, 'The BE06 Corpus of British English and recent language change' (2009) 14 International Journal of Corpus Linguistics 312; M Davies, 'Corpus of News on the Web (NOW)' 2006, *<https://www.english-corpora.org/now/>*.

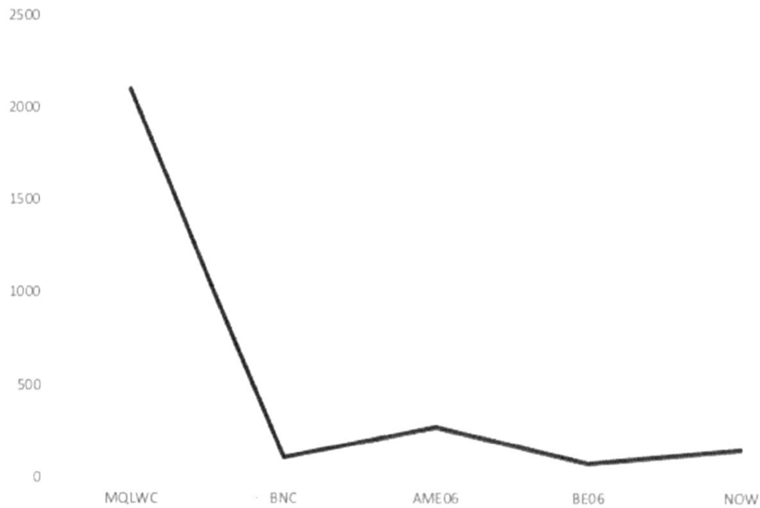

FIGURE 2 Comparing the frequency (wpm) of 'military' in MQLWC with comparator corpora: BNC, AmE06, BE06, NOW

typically co-occur). Table 2 shows the top 20 collocates for the word 'military' in the corpus of the international laws of war (leaving out function words).[49]

These collocates give 'military' a rational underpinning, by associating it with lexical items that imply organisation and planning, such as 'objective/s', 'operations', 'objects' and 'purposes'. Military power is authorised by its association with the words 'authority/ies'. The conjunction of 'military' and 'action' creates a large category of behaviour without any specificity, thereby standing back from the embodied violence of the specific 'actions' that militaries engage in, which include invading, bombing, killing, injuring, destroying, etc. 'Action' is instead a neutral, catch-all phrase that avoids the negativity of other likely word selections.

The conjunction of 'military' with 'necessity' can also be observed in this list, in addition to various synonyms such as: 'advantage', 'imperative' and 'considerations'. As Lukin and Araújo e Castro note, the international laws of war are *the* semiotic ecosystem in which the concept of 'military necessity' was

49 See V Brezina, T McEnery, and S Wattam, 'Collocations in Context: A New Perspective on Collocation Networks' (2015) 20 International Journal of Corpus Linguistics 139. The collocates in Table 3 are based on the following collocation parameters: MI3 (9); L5-R5;C5; NC5, that is, a minimum threshold of MI3 of 9; a collocate window of 5 left and 5 right; a minimum collocate frequency of 5 and a minimum frequency of collocation of 5.

TABLE 2 Top 20 collocates of 'military' in MQLWC

	Lexical item	MI3	Freq (collocation)	Freq (corpus)
1	objectives	21.40	89	109
2	operations	20.21	83	202
3	objective	18.88	40	57
4	necessity	18.80	46	91
5	aircraft	18.49	72	433
6	advantage	18.25	32	45
7	authorities	17.62	48	235
8	military	17.05	64	827
9	action	16.78	30	103
10	imperative	16.25	17	27
11	direct	16.16	26	103
12	authority	16.15	31	176
13	permit	16.07	24	86
14	objects	15.94	27	134
15	art	15.86	58	1407
16	purposes	15.85	31	216
17	anticipated	15.84	13	16
18	considerations	15.70	14	22
19	concrete	15.54	11	12
20	establishments	15.53	19	62

created, and has been maintained.[50] It is inside of this body of law that 'military necessity' is, albeit very briefly, and in a fundamentally circular fashion, defined for legal purposes. The concept almost does not exist outside of this paradigm context (i.e., it appears as a marginal concept in data sets such as the BNC, the Google Books Corpus, and the News on the Web corpus). The international laws of war provide the 'parallel universe' in which 'military necessity' can operate and have plausibility.

50 Lukin and Araujo e Castro (n 10).

Linguistically, 'military necessity' is only the conjunction of a classifier/ adjective ('military') and a noun ('necessity'). While all words are linguistic entities, 'military necessity', like anything we refer to as a 'principle', exists only within a discursive framework. This is not the case for all entities inside the documents of the international laws of war. One strand in these texts has been around attempts to limit war's lethal technology, such as exploding bullets under 400 grams, landmines, and chemical and nuclear weapons. All of these have a very real and material existence outside the discourse of international law. This does not mean that language is simply a mirror to them – language is always exercising its organising and categorising power. But, 'military necessity' is, as noted above, a 'virtual entity': it has no existence outside of language because it relies, as all such principles do, on grammatical metaphor.

Let's recall its original, and notably circular, definition in Article 14 of the Lieber Code where 'military necessity' is defined as consisting 'in the necessity of those measures which are indispensable for securing the ends of the war, and which are lawful according to the modern law and usages of war'. The definition has no special technical terms: 'necessity' is simply a nominalised form from the verb 'to need', with the conjunction of the term 'military' acting to grant the illusion of a specialised sub-category of 'necessity'. If we attempt to 'de-metaphorise' the concept, that is, to translate the nominalised form into the grammar of our everyday interactions, we end up with an explanation in these terms: 'militaries need to do things'. In these terms, the concept loses the prestige bestowed on it through its nominal form. It becomes vague and starts to resemble an ambit claim. But the concept is validated by its constant repetition in these texts, and by the many validating collocates that come with the term 'military'.

In this section, we have sought to exemplify the potential of corpus linguistics techniques, with a small investigation of the dominant words in this corpus, followed by some more detail on the word 'military'. While there is much to be elaborated on here, we turn now to complement the two approaches previously explored with a final angle from linguistics, namely the study of lexicogrammatical patterns in this data. Given the intricacy of grammar, we take one small section from the 1998 Rome Statute, to consider the meanings made through lexicogrammatical selections and patterning.

4 Grammatical Patterning in the Texts of the International Laws of War

The texts of the international laws of war, like all others, are subject to the semiotic forces which are involved in creating a text, in which grammatical systems are the foundation. For any act of meaning to perform its necessary work, it must have three interwoven strands of meaning, which derive from what Halliday calls the 'metafunctional' organisation of language.[51] All languages, he argues, have three modes of meaning which texts organise through grammatical structures. These three strands of meanings are: experiential meanings, which enable speakers to construe our experience of the world; interpersonal meanings, through which we enact our interpersonal relationships in all their complex variability; and textual meanings, the mode of meaning which brings experiential and interpersonal meanings into a coherent flow of discourse. These modes of meaning reflect the three principles of interaction (field, tenor and mode) outlined earlier.

All texts, legal or otherwise, traverse the grammatical systems of a language. In the creation of a text, speakers and writers make selections from these grammatical systems, and in the process a text's potential meanings are configured. For the purposes of illustrating the ideological potential of grammatical patterns in the laws of war, some examples from a small but significant extract of the Rome Statute are examined below.

As previously mentioned, this treaty established the International Criminal Court and was heralded by Kofi Annan as a very significant step in the history of the UN.[52] The Rome Statute proscribes and criminalises the actions labelled 'war crimes', 'crimes of aggression', 'crimes against humanity' and 'genocide'. As much as it might seem that such crimes are self-evident, within a legal context they require definition to indicate their scope. Only language can provide such definitions: what makes an action a 'war crime' is the meaning that can be attributed, via language, to some forms of action and not others. The act of defining 'war crimes' involves construing through wording the behaviours that will be attached to this crime, and such a definition cannot be achieved without choosing grammatical options from these grammatical systems. Language is not reflecting, but constructing these categories.

Tables 3 and 4 provide two example clauses from Article 8 of the Rome Statute, which carries the burden of defining the meaning of the legal concept 'war crimes'. These examples are analysed with respect to two grammatical systems of Halliday's 'experiential' function of language: the systems of THING TYPE and PROCESS TYPE.[53] All English language text construction is

---

51 MAK Halliday, 'How do you mean?' in JJ Webster (ed.) *On Grammar. Volume 1 in the Collected Works of M.A.K. Halliday* (Continuum 2002).

52 Annan (n 20).

53 The grammatical analysis in this paper is based on MAK Halliday and CMIM Matthiessen, *An Introduction to Halliday's Functional Grammar: Fourth Edition* (Arnold 2014). The small caps formatting is a standard for the name of a grammatical system.

TABLE 3 Example 1 – Article 8 (b) (xx)[54]

Employing	weapons, projectiles and material and methods of warfare [[[55]which are of a nature [[to cause superfluous injury or unnecessary suffering]] || or which are inherently indiscriminate in violation of the international law of armed conflict, || provided that such weapons, projectiles and material and methods of warfare are the subject of a comprehensive prohibition || and are included in an annex to this Statute, by an amendment in accordance with the relevant provisions set forth in articles 121 and 123;]]
Verbal group	Nominal group
Process: material	Goal

TABLE 4 Example 2 – Article 8 (b)(iv)[56]

Intentionally	launching	an attack	in the knowledge [[that such attack will cause incidental loss of life or injury to civilians or damage to civilian objects or widespread, long-term and severe damage to the natural environment [[which would be clearly excessive in relation to the concrete and direct overall military advantage [[anticipated]]]];
Adverbial group	Verbal group	Nominal group	Prepositional Phrase
Circumstance: manner	Process: material	Scope	Circ: location

54 Rome Statute (n 19).

55 Double square brackets '[[...]]' denote an embedded clause, i.e. a clause which functions as a constituent element, or part of a constituent element, within a clause; two vertical lines '||' denote a clause boundary. See MAK Halliday and CMIM Matthiessen, *An Introduction to Halliday's Functional Grammar: Fourth Edition* (Arnold 2014).

56 Rome Statute (n 19).

TABLE 5 Example 1 – Article 8(b)(xx) of the Rome Statute (n 19)[57]

		Article 8(b)(xx) of the Rome Statute
Words	Employing	weapons, projectiles and material and methods of warfare [[which are of a nature [[to cause superfluous injury or unnecessary suffering]] || or which are inherently indiscriminate in violation of the international law of armed conflict, || provided that such weapons, projectiles and material and methods of warfare are the subject of a comprehensive prohibition || and are included in an annex to this Statute, by an amendment in accordance with the relevant provisions set forth in articles 121 and 123;]]]]
Grouping	Verbal Group	Nominal Group
Function (?)	Process: Material	Goal

subject to the options of these grammatical systems: all texts have some kinds of entities or 'things' that construct content meanings in a text (THING TYPE) and all texts include lexical verbs or processes (PROCESS TYPE). The analysis of patterns in these grammatical systems will enable us to see a little more deeply into the semiotic mechanics of the ways in which the violence of war is constructed in this body of law.

Example 1 in Table 3 consists of two constituent parts: a 'verbal group' construing the process, and a 'nominal group' construing an entity or 'thing' pertinent to this context.[58] Nominal groups are responsible for creating what humans want, need, or dream up. A 'thing', grammatically, can be short and sweet, such as 'poison or poisoned weapons',[59] a simple and relatively unelaborated flow of words. Presumably the lack of elaboration in the nominal group 'poison or poisoned weapons' is because the harm of such weapons appears to

57 Rome Statute (n 19)

58 While the terminology of 'verb' and 'noun' is likely to be more familiar, these concepts are not robust enough to capture the semiotic work done by the structures Halliday calls verbal and nominal groups, and which have a variety of functional roles in a clause.

59 Rome Statute (n 19) art 8(b)xvii.

TABLE 6 Example 2 – Article 8 (b)(iv) Rome Statute (n 19)[60]

	Article 8(b)(iv) of the Rome Statute			
Words	Intentionally	launching	an attack	in the knowledge [[that such attack will cause incidental loss of life or injury to civilians or damage to civilian objects or widespread, long-term and severe damage to the natural environment [[which would be clearly excessive in relation to the concrete and direct overall military advantage [[anticipated]]]];
Grouping	Adverbial group	Verbal Group	Nominal Group	Prepositional Phrase
Function (?)	Circumstance: Manner	Process: Material	Scope	Circumstance: Location

be uncontested, so no further elaboration, conditions or caveats are required to understand this particular category of thing.

Legal texts are home to both elaborated and abstract things, and the examples in Tables 3 and 4 each show clauses in which one constituent element (the nominal group) is highly elaborated. The length of these structures is one key indicator of this complexity. The presence of long, complex nominal groups in a legal text is not in any way a surprise: but neither are such structures arbitrary or to be taken-for-granted. These 'things' in this text are expressed through nominal groups with extensive elaboration or 'post-qualification' (i.e., wording that follows the noun, and which is required to clearly specify the category of thing being invoked in the text).

Example 1 in Table 3 consists of two parts, a simple verbal group (only one word is required for this constituent to do its job), and a long and complex nominal group which construes a highly specific entity in the text. With so much intricacy in a nominal group structure like this, it is perhaps also unsurprising that we find within this structure contradictory semantic currents,

60 Rome Statute (n 19)

TABLE 7 Nominal group structure of Goal element in Examples 1 and 2

Example 1	null	weapons, projectiles and material and methods [of warfare]	[[which are of a nature [[to cause superfluous injury or unnecessary suffering]] || or which are inherently indiscriminate in violation of the international law of armed conflict, || provided that such weapons, projectiles and material and methods of warfare are the subject of a comprehensive prohibition || and are included in an annex to this Statute, by an amendment in accordance with the relevant provisions set forth in articles 121 and 123;]]
Example 2	The	Knowledge	[[that such attack will cause incidental loss of life or injury to civilians or damage to civilian objects or widespread, long-term and severe damage to the natural environment [[which would be clearly excessive in relation to the concrete and direct overall military advantage [[anticipated]]]];
	Determiner	Thing	Post-qualifier

described by Mégret as the 'impossible synthesis between restraint and violence'.[61] Example 1 starts by heading towards the restraining of some particular war-like behaviour, but before we get too far into this clause, we encounter the placing of limits on these limits. The grammar of this clause gives with one hand, and then takes with the other.

Table 7 shows the internal group structure analysis of the 'thing' or nominal group element of the clause. The lack of determiner (e.g., *the, some, those, these* etc.) or any other premodification means this instance includes all members of the category 'weapons, projectiles and material and methods of warfare',

61 F Mégret, 'The Laws of War and the Structure of Masculine Power' (2018) 19 Melbourne Journal of International Law 200.

creating the appearance of a broad all-encompassing sweep of prohibition. Eight words into this structure, the post-qualifying element (the words following the central noun) begins, adding a further 72 words, and in the process considerably reduces the scope of reference of this nominal group. This post-qualifier begins by reducing the category 'weapons, projectiles and materials and methods of warfare' to those which cause 'superfluous' or 'unnecessary' injuries and suffering.

These adjectives are relative: they can only be analysed from a particular, and potentially variable, benchmark which is unspecified. This clause is joined to the next by the conjunction 'or', providing an alternative means by which this category of 'weapons …etc' is curtailed, i.e., if 1. they are shown to be 'indiscriminate' in a way that violates international law (again, a contestable principle) and 2. if they have been subject to comprehensive prohibition, and 3. if they are listed in the annex to the Statute. In summary, the only weapons, projectiles and means and methods of warfare prohibited are those 'which are *w*, or which are *x*, provided that they are *y* AND that they are *z*'. This is quite a hurdle to have to pass for a weapon or method of war to be prohibited. To date, no form of weapons, projectiles or materials and methods of warfare has been so listed in an Annex to this Statute.[62]

Example 2 (Table 4) is a variation on this theme, although now the complex thing being constructed is the state of mind or 'knowledge' of the belligerent. This clause in Article 8 criminalises only those attacks carried out 'intentionally', and 'in the knowledge that … etc' – a point echoed in Article 30 of the Statute ('Mental Element') which states the requirement of knowledge and intent for criminality – essentially, the long-held common law principle of *mens rea*.[63] As such, two of the four constituents of this clause are devoted to giving weight not to an action or its consequences, but to the consciousness brought by the belligerent to this action. The second of these constituents, as shown in Table 5, is a lengthy discourse spelling out what kind of 'knowledge' results in an attack being criminalised. It is not the fact of, or scale of, the incidental killings, woundings or suffering caused. Instead, such loss, injury or damage must be shown to be 'excessive' relative to the 'military advantage [[anticipated]]'.

62 <https://asp.icc-cpi.int/sites/asp/files/asp_docs/Publications/Compendium/RomeStatute-ENG.pdf>.

63 According to Ausserladscheider Jonas (2021), the Rome Statute is the only international instrument with a definition of *mens rea* (Article 30), although it is also present in customary international law. See L Ausserladscheider Jonas, *Individual Criminal Responsibility for Financing Entities Involved in Core Crimes* (Brill 2021) 40, 40–44.

As we have seen before, a lexical item like 'excessive' is relative to some particular, and potentially variable, threshold – it is not a self-evident quantifier. Furthermore, the thing to which the threshold is relative is a highly abstract concept, namely 'military advantage', also known as 'military necessity' – as discussed above, a legal fiction which exists only within the confines of the international laws of war. Around this concept, we again can see two contradictory currents: the advantage has to be 'concrete' and 'direct', an attempt to try to ground this highly abstract concept in evidence. Yet, at the same time, the measure is not actual 'military advantage', but only that which was 'anticipated'. In other words, the advantage has to be concrete and direct at least in the mind of the author of the attack prior to it taking place. This second example shows us, again, the grammar restraining violence on the one hand and enabling it with the other – all within the confines of one single element in one single clause.

As all the material and methods of warfare are indisputably lethal, Article 8 is attempting to provide some magical space in which this lethal technology can be used by some legal justification. For those who claim that these texts work to constrain violence, the text of the Rome Statute clearly shows itself attempting to regulate actions and place limits of weapons. In addition, the florid elaboration of entities in the text creates the appearance of attention to the detail of what is in and what is outside of this definition, as if international legal minds have striven for, and achieved, a profound degree of specificity. The elaboration seen in these two entities (but of which there are many more in the text) is reiterated at another scale: the list of war crimes in Article 8 is spread over 4 subsections with eight listed in 8(a), 26 in 8(b), 4 in 8(c), and 15 in 8(e), creating the impression of significant semiotic energy being devoted to precisely pinning down the scope of the category 'war crimes'.

Language has indeterminacy as one of its key features, a function of the fact that it is a 'theorizing of the human condition' in which it manages 'a massive reconciliation of conflicting principles of order – this being the only way of 'semioticizing' our complex ecosocial environment in a way that is favourable to our survival'.[64] Some degree of indeterminacy is therefore unavoidable: but language allows its speakers and writers key choices that bring semantic consequences.

For example, the long list of proscribed actions under the umbrella of 'war crimes' have a key characteristic, which is also a consequence of a grammatical choice. An action verb can be transitive or intransitive. A transitive verb or

64 MAK Halliday, 'On the Architecture of Human Language' in JJ Webster (ed.) *On Language and Linguistics. Volume 3 in the Collected Works of M.A.K. Halliday* (Continuum 2003).

process construes an action that extends to another entity and impacts upon it. 'Killing' is transitive; 'injuring' and 'wounding' are transitive', 'torturing' is transitive; 'attacking', 'destroying', 'pillaging', 'raping', 'displacing', 'conscripting' and 'starving' are all transitive verbs.[65] Again, this comes as no surprise – surely the very essence of the methods of war are actions which are construed as highly impactful. It is a key feature of the overall tone of Article 8 that it contains such a long list of transitive processes, whose impact is unequivocally negative.

Violence which is stigmatised requires that it be construed in specific and transitive terms, so that its consequences are made explicit. But the choice of transitive grammar and semantics is not simply reflecting these actions, it also constructs them since language always offers alternative words and wording. An example of such contrasting wording is found in the Article (2)(e), pertaining to torture. While torture is criminalised, it is only torture when defined as 'intentional infliction of severe pain or suffering'. By contrast, if the same pain or suffering simply 'arises' as a consequence of 'lawful sanctions', this does not fit the definition of torture, even if such pain and suffering inheres in (and is therefore caused by) the belligerent action. Here, the line between legal and unlawful is resolved by a grammatical selection, the contrasting of the transitive verb 'to inflict' with the intransitive verb 'to arise'. In the first, pain and suffering is 'inflicted', while in the second it merely 'arises', and in this construction, agency and causation is made invisible.

The use of transitive grammar and semantics generates a set of proscribable and illegitimate actions – and so this language is working to constrain forms of violence. The extensive list of such actions adds weight to this sense of constraint. Mégret has argued that the laws of war enact their semantics of restraint in a theatrical fashion,[66] perhaps as a means to draw attention from the many ways this language is also legitimising violence. Since this theatricality has to be an artefact of language use in these texts, arguably it is produced through the seemingly exhaustive list of crimes, their articulation as transitive processes, the repetition and redundancy across the various sub-sections of Article 8, and the florid qualification of things.

One further feature of this text could be added here: the apparent intent to ensure all alternatives of some category are voiced. One of the textual measures of this final point is the pervasive use of the conjunction 'or'. The frequency

65 For a more detailed discussion of the grammar of Article 8 of the Rome Statute, see A Lukin, 'How International Law Makes Violence Legal: A Case Study of the Rome Statute' (2020) 2 Language, Context and Text: The Social Semiotics Forum 91.

66 Mégret (n 61).

TABLE 8 Ratio of 'and' to 'or' of MQLWC compared with BNC, BE06 and AmE06

	'and'	'or'	Ratio and/or
BNC	26, 615	3, 732	7.64
BE06	24, 330	3, 147	7.73
AmE06	24,487	3,170	7.72
MQLWC	23, 648	16, 158	1.46
1998 Rome Statute	22, 290	25, 322	0.88

of the conjunction 'or' in this text can be calibrated against the corpus as a whole, and this corpus against other corpora: Table 8 sets out the frequency of 'or' compared with the most frequent of all conjunctions, 'and' in the Rome Statute, compared with the MQLWC as a whole, and with the BNC, the BE06 and the AmE06 corpora. In the comparator corpora, the ratio of 'and' to 'or' is more than 7 to 1. In the MQLWC, the figure is around 1.5 to 1, and in the Rome Statute, the frequency of 'or' is actually higher than 'and'.

In this short analysis of a very small extract from the Rome Statute, we begin to see how effortlessly grammatical systems are recruited to both constrain and enable the violence of states. Across a variety of micro-grammatical choices exemplified here, lethal action is proscribed, but perhaps more importantly, is seen to be proscribed, while simultaneously, and within one and the same grammatical structure, such proscriptions are limited, opening the semantic spaces for forms of violence to be given the imprimatur of legality.

5 Conclusion

The aim of this paper has been to show how linguistic theory and method can assist in examining the kind of semiotic work that the international laws of war perform. Each of the three sections of the paper approached this aim in different ways: section 2 introduced the concept of 'register', a necessary linguistic concept to understand the way in which these texts are unique products of deep cultural forces, creating not only the voice of a bureaucratic international community, but a semiotic ecosystem for the development of the defining principles of the international laws of war.

In section 3, the potential of corpus linguistics to study this body of law was examined and illustrated with reference to the word 'military', a very dominant concept in this discourse. Its very high relative frequency shows the international laws of war to be a semiotic environment which gives this concept a very big platform to accrue associations. An examination of collocations of this word showed these associations to be deeply legitimating. Finally, section 4 brought the focus to the intricate work of grammatical structure, and the ways that its patterns covertly generate semantic currents with significant ideological consequences.

These three linguistic angles on these texts show the role language has played in constructing this discourse form, furnishing the environment for the development of legal principles which define this field, and providing the lexicogrammatical patterns that both proscribe and legitimate the violence of war. Each of these demonstrations provides a starting point for further interdisciplinary collaborations to enhance understanding about the power of language in a context where its processes and products have such profound human consequences.

International Humanitarian Law: Necessity, Distinction and the 'Standard of Civilisation'

Matt Killingsworth

Abstract

The modern laws of war are an integral foundation of 19th century efforts to establish and maintain order within the then emerging international society of states. But membership was conditional; only 'civilised' states were permitted entry to international society. Engaging with the concept of 'the standard of civilisation', the aim of this paper is to demonstrate a continuity of double standards as they relate to protections afforded by the modern laws of war. It will argue that these double standards have been, and continue to be, underpinned by attempts to de-humanise belligerents via the language of the 'standard of civilisation'. In making this argument, the paper will draw attention to the historical centrality of the state and the role it has played in establishing conditionality with regards to protections afforded by the modern laws of war through the language of raison d'état and the standard of civilisation.

Keywords

international humanitarian law – standard of civilisation – necessity

1 Introduction

The modern laws of war are the result of a centuries long process, which tacitly acknowledges the inevitably of conflict, while attempting to place limitations on battlefield conduct. They have evolved from customary norms and agreements between warring European actors to a universally accepted body

 | DOI:10.1163/9789004712478_005

of international law, underpinned by the 1949 Geneva Conventions and the three 1977 Additional Protocols. In this respect, the modern laws of war exist as an uneasy reconciliation between principles of distinction, proportionality and humanitarianism, on the one hand, and military necessity on the other.

The modern laws of war are also an integral foundation of 19th century efforts to establish and maintain order within the then emerging international society of states. But membership was conditional; only 'civilised' states were permitted entry into international society. Engaging with the concept of 'the standard of civilisation', the aim of this paper is to demonstrate a continuity of double standards as they relate to protections afforded by the modern laws of war. It will argue that these double standards have been, and continue to be, underpinned by attempts to de-humanise belligerents via the language of the 'standard of civilisation'. In making this argument, the paper will draw attention to the historical centrality of the state and the role it has played in establishing conditionality with regards to protections afforded by the modern laws of war through the language of *raison d'état* and the 'standard of civilisation'.

The paper is presented in five parts. The first introduces the concept of the 'standard of civilisation' demonstrating how the concept was utilised as a tool of exclusion in the 19th century, preparing for the argument that it remains an informant of who is be afforded protections under international humanitarian law (IHL). Part two explores how the laws of war evolved in lockstep with the European state-system, traces the evolution from customary to treaty based 'humanitarian' law, and argues that despite the purported humanitarian underpinnings of modern laws of war, IHL represents a safeguarding of the 'politico-military interests [...] of the Great Powers and, to some degree, those of lesser states'.[1] Part three presents an exploration of the relationship between the four core principles of IHL, and makes the argument that the claimed shift from sovereignty to humanitarianism is not as complete as often argued, and that rather, *raison d'état* continues to be a motivating factor informing constraint during combat. Part four, through examples from the War on Terror, will demonstrate how the state, self-anointed as 'civilised', continues to use the language of the 'standard of civilisation' as an informant of who should be afforded protections by IHL, and in turn, a concept by which we can continue to understand the gulf between the (universal) humanitarian underpinnings of IHL, and violations of the laws of war.

1 Antonio Cassese, 'Current Challenges to International Humanitarian Law' in Andrew Clapham and Paola Gaeta (eds.), *The Oxford Handbook of International Law in Armed Conflict* (Oxford: Oxford University Press, 2014) 6.

2 The Standard of Civilisation

The 'standard of civilisation' concept, while having deep roots in international law, is also a key concept of the English School of International Relations, primarily as a tool (albeit contested) by which to explain inclusion and exclusion in the expansion of European international society in the late 19th and early 20th centuries. Its strong association with colonial attitudes and practices means that while appropriate to use it when looking at pre-1945 international society, its usefulness as an analytical tool for contemporary world politics is generally regarded as limited.

However, the concept has experienced a renaissance of sorts, and in agreeing with Barry Buzan, and taking up his challenge to 'raise the profile of the 'standard of civilisation' not just in its historical work, but also in its analysis of the post-colonial world',[2] it is argued here that the concept remains valuable in better understanding continuities of double standards as they relate to protections afforded by the modern laws of war.

Civilisation, a term coined in the 18th century, came to be associated in its 19th century usage with the idea of progress 'and the theory that nations advance through different stages of development'.[3] Europeans increasingly came to use the term as a comparative 'other', believing they were 'endowed with an advanced level of social complexity, in opposition to 'barbarous' nations, who could possibly acquire civilisation if they conformed to certain values, or 'savages', who were condemned to never access it'.[4] This was most clearly articulated by Scottish lawyer James Lorimer, who divided humanity into three distinct spheres; the civilised, the barbarian (semi-civilised) and the savage (un-civilised); of these three categories, only the first enjoyed full political status, membership of international society, and thus political recognition under international law.[5]

In terms of giving rise to the European 'standard of civilisation', the adjective 'civilised', and its counter concept 'uncivilised' (or 'barbarian') found its way into the writings of publicists, as well as judicial decisions and treaties. The two terms 'described and evaluated peoples, nations or states in their

---

2 Barry Buzan, 'The Standard of Civilisation as an English School Concept' (2014) 42 Millennium: Journal of International Studies 577.

3 Lillian Obregon, 'The Civilised and Uncivilised' in Bardo Fassbender and Anne Peters (eds.), *The Oxford Handbook of the History of International Law* (Oxford: Oxford University Press, 2012) 917.

4 Ibid.

5 See Ntina Tzouvala, *Capitalism as Civilisation: A History of International Law* (Cambridge: Cambridge University Press, 2021) 51.

relation to sovereignty […] the civilised, those endowed with civilisation, were recognised as proper subjects of international law. The uncivilised, those lacking civilisation, were left outside international law'.[6] Thus, the 'standard of civilisation' 'supported a partly racist taxonomy of 'savage, barbarian and civilised' as a way of classifying the non-European world in relation to Europe' and became the means by which people or states were admitted or barred from the international society of states.[7] Indeed, as Linklater suggests, 'The idea of civilisation was regarded as having a transcendent quality that provided an image of a future political condition in which European peoples reached a higher state of civilisation by eradicating unnecessary suffering in warfare'.[8]

Although never codified as such, Gong's criteria for a state to be civilised, and thus be accepted into international society, is the most widely cited; non-western states needed to (1) guarantee basic rights, as understood in the west, for foreign nationals; (2) have an organised an efficient political bureaucracy with capacity for self-defence; (3) have a domestic system of courts and codes, and adhere to international law; (4) have diplomatic institutions in order to engage in international relations; and (5) conformity with western mores, norms and customs.[9]

Not identified by Gong, but nonetheless a further element that underpinned the emergence of a standard of civilisation was 'the increasing dominance of positive over natural law in western thinking and practise during the 19th century'.[10] While natural law assumed the equality of humans under the sight of God, positive international law, emanating from sovereign states, was explicitly the law of civilised European states.[11] In this respect, "civilisation' –

6 Obregon (n 3) 918.

7 Buzan (n 2) 578 and Brett Bowden, 'The Colonial Origins of International Law: European Expansion and the Classical Standard of Civilisation' (2005) 7 Journal of the History of International Law 1. See also Zhang, who argues that the standard of civilisation, as it developed in the 19th century, was developed to practically protect 'European life, liberty and property in a culturally different and potentially hostile non-European world', and philosophically protect 'how to determine which non-European countries deserved legal recognition and legal personality in international law informed exclusively by the European tradition and civilisation'; Yongjin Zhang, 'The Standard of Civilisation Redux: Towards the Expansion on International Society 3.0?' (2014) 42 Millennium: Journal of International Studies 674, 679.

8 Andrew Linklater, *Violence and Civilisation in the Western States-Systems* (Cambridge: Cambridge University Press, 2016) 394.

9 Gerrit Gong, *The Standard of Civilisation in International Society* (Oxford: Clarendon Press, 1984) 14–21.

10 Buzan (n 2) 579.

11 See Martii Koskienniemi, *The Gentler Civiliser of Nations: The Rise and Fall of International Law*, 1870-1960 (Cambridge: Cambridge University Press, 2001) 73–5 and 99–116.

as a condition, came to supersede Christianity and Europe as the principle means of demarcation of the boundaries of international society'.[12]

The degree to which such a standard ever existed is debated, but also unimportant. As Keene identifies, 'we need to appreciate the importance of the idea of civilisation not merely as a standard for regulating the entry of new states in international society, but also for validating an entirely different set of legal rules and political institutions in its own right'.[13] Arguing that the existence of a standard to govern entry into the 'community of international law' didn't exist in the 19th century, Koskenniemi nonetheless acknowledges that the '*language of a standard*' existed, 'which gave the appearance of fair treatment and regular administration to what was simply a conjectural policy'.[14] Thus, as identified by Keene and Koskenniemi, the belief in a standard of civilisation by European and western powers permitted them to exclude those who didn't meet the expectations of the standard from the protections afforded by the newly forming body of international law.

One of these new formations of international law included the laws of war. Existing primarily as customary agreements between belligerents for much of the modern period, 'the 19th century codification of the laws of war distinguished between insiders and outsiders of international society, with the former subject to rules that determined the scope of legitimate violence, not least that it should be discriminate and proportional, and the latter considered to be outside such rules'.[15] The link between the idea of civilisation and humanitarian laws of war as they emerged in the 19th century can be seen, for example, in the St Petersburg Declaration (1868), which contended that in the relations between 'civilised nations', it was essential to identify the moment at which the 'necessities of war ought to yield to the requirements of humanity'.[16] Similarly, the Lieber Code and Martens Clause both famously

12 Jacinta O'Hagan, 'The Role of Civilisation in the Globalisation of International Society' in Tim Dunne and Christian Reus-Smit (eds.), *The Globalisation of International Society* (Oxford: Oxford University Press, 2017) 191.

13 Edward Keene, *Beyond the Anarchical Society: Grotius, Colonialism and Order in World Politics* (Cambridge: Cambridge University Press, 2002) 117.

14 Martii Koskenniemi, 'The Legacy of the Nineteenth Century' in David Armstrong (ed.), *Routledge Handbook of International Law* (New York: Routledge 2009) 134–135 (emphasis in original).

15 Buzan (n 2) 580–581. See also Lacy Pejcinovic, *War in International Society* (Abingdon: Routledge, 2013) and Casper Sylvest, 'International Law in Nineteenth-Century Britain' (2005) 75 British Yearbook of International Law 9.

16 Linklater (n 8) 394.

make reference to 'civilised nations';[17] the Lieber Code, in defining military necessity, suggests that the law is both the product of, and applicable only to, civilised nations; somewhat similarly, although more explicitly, the Martens Clause also assumes protections for non-combatants to have evolved only from interactions between civilised nations.

The darker actualisation of the 'standard of civilisation' as it related to the application of newly codified laws of war was borne out through what Mégret calls 'international humanitarian law's original sin'; European colonial powers that developed multilateral legal constraints on the waging of war in the name of humanity and civilisation only did so on the basis that it applied to war between civilised peoples, excluding non-European 'savages'.[18] In a similar vein, Mazower identifies the effects of a 'standard of civilisation' in action with what he argues is the inherent hypocrisy of the 1899 Hague Conventions, which expressly prohibited signatories from dropping bombs from balloons, yet 'bombing from the air offered colonial powers a low-cost method of supressing native discontent'.[19]

This double standard extended into the 20th century. Writing in 1927, US Army Captain Elbridge Colby proffered advice on dealing with 'savage tribes':

> It is good to be decent. It is good to use proper discretion. It is good to observe the decencies of international law. But it is a fact that against uncivilized people who do not know international law and do not observe it, and would take advantage of one who did, there must be something else. The 'something else' should not be a relaxation of all bonds of restraint. But it should be [a] clear understanding that this is a different kind of war, this which is waged by native tribes, than that which might be waged between advanced nations of western culture. Ferocity and ruthlessness

17 Linklater notes further that the Lieber Code 'was derived not from any existing legal text but from the core beliefs and practices of 'civilisation'; ibid 392.

18 Frédéric Mégret, 'From 'Savages' to 'Unlawful Combatants': A Postcolonial Look at International Law's 'Other'' in Anne Orford (ed.), *International Law and Its Others* (Cambridge: Cambridge University Press, 2006) 269.

19 Mark Mazower, *Governing the World: The History of an Idea* (London: Allen Lane, 2012) 78–79. See also Jennifer Welsh, 'Empire and Fragmentation' in Dunne and Rues-Smit (n 12) 155. Additionally, Mégret argues that 'the benefit of precisely what the Hague Regulations had sought to achieve – the moving of humanitarianism from the province of moral or chivalrous compulsion to positive law – was thus denied to non-European peoples, effectively leaving Europeans' relations with them in a pre-modern realm of fragile natural obligations'; Mégret (n 18) 283.

> are not essential; but it is essential to recognize the different character of the people.[20]

Specific invocations of the 'standard of civilisation' slowly disappeared during the interwar period and in the aftermath of the Second World War, due in no small part to the fact that application of the standard had granted Germany pride of place in international society.[21] Similarly, blatant distinctions between 'civilised' and 'barbarian' or 'savage' have also since disappeared. But as Fidler observes, 'the rejection of the 'standard of civilisation' as a driving force of international law has been more apparent than real'.[22] O'Hagan also notes a resurgence in the language of 'the standard of civilisation' as part of a 'creeping return to the tenets of empirical or conditional sovereignty of imperial international society, where sovereign autonomy was dependent on conformity with standards and practices defined by powerful external actors and international institutions'.[23] Rather than conditional sovereignty, as such, the remainder of this paper will demonstrate how conditionality as it relates to protections provided by the modern laws of war were originally defined by the state and realised through the language of the 'standard of civilisation', and how, after a Cold War hiatus, have returned in an historically informed symbiosis of law, war, civilisation and the state to again undermine the universal aspirations of the modern laws of war.

3 The State, War and IHL

For much of the modern era, the evolution of attempts to limit war via international law have been intrinsically linked with the evolution of the modern nation-state. This is not to deny pre-modern constraints on warfare, informed variously by notions of chivalry and customary rules of war. Nonetheless, contemporary IHL finds its genesis in the post-Enlightenment epoch, when the European state-system started to establish itself as the dominant form of political organisation. Concurrently, this period also bears witness to the increasing crystallisation of contemporary conceptions of the international,

20 Elbridge Colby, 'How to Fight Savage Tribes' (1927) 21 American Journal of International Law 279, 287.

21 Tzouvala (n 5) 84.

22 David Fidler, 'A Kinder, Gentler System of Capitulations? International Law, Structural Adjustment Policies, and the Standard of Liberal, Globalised Civilisation' (2000) 35 Texas International Law Review 387, 388–389.

23 O'Hagan (n 12) 199–200.

and a symbiotic relationship whereby states legitimated themselves via their membership of international legal institutions, and the emergence of an international society of states in which order was increasingly underpinned by the doctrine of sovereignty, whereby states 'increasingly sought to base their legal obligations on clearer, more precise, more formal and, most of all, more consensual foundations'.[24] In this respect, and elaborated on below, the modern laws of war, articulated as either IHL or the law of armed conflict (LOAC), are best understood as an historical balancing process between attempts to regulate the conduct of hostilities between belligerents and the self-perceived rights of states to use force to achieve desired ends.

The state's emergence as the dominant form of political organisation was due in part to its capacity over time, to monopolise the use of violence, which it did in two, interrelated ways. First, as the war making endeavours of European sovereigns expanded, and the cost of waging war dramatically increased, smaller, decentralised administrative units proved incapable of managing this new enterprise. The increasingly centralised state proved itself more adept not only at raising the capital required for this new militarism, but also, as Tilly identifies, the states' increased capacity for raising revenue and streamlining administrative capacities enabled it to 'monitor, control and monopolise the effective means of violence'.[25] Second, through a long historical process, the modern state was able to successfully disarm competitors.[26] The disarming of non-state actors, sometimes through bargains struck with societal groups, but mostly via a long and bloody struggle, was a process which ended through 'Violence being shifted from the non-state, economic and international realms of authority into the state, domestic and political realms of authority … the transformation entailed the states' monopolisation of the authority to deploy violence beyond its borders *and* the state's acceptance of violence emanating from its territory'.[27]

In the pre-modern period, war existed as a form of spectator sport, with a set of rules that existed more as mutual obligations on warring parties than law, as such:

---

24 David Armstrong, Theo Farrell and Helene Lambert, *International Law and International Relations* (Cambridge: Cambridge University Press, 2012) 61.

25 Charles Tilly, *Coercion, Capital and European Sates, AD 990–1992* (Cambridge, Mass.: Blackwell, 1992) 68.

26 Janice Thomson, *Mercenaries, Pirates and Sovereigns* (Princeton: Princeton University Press, 1994) 4.

27 Ibid 4 (emphasis in original). See also Matt Killingsworth, 'The International Criminal Court and Global Justice' in John Adlam, Tilman Kluttig and Bandy Lee (eds.), *Violent States and Creative States: From the Individual to the Global* (London: Jessica Kingsley Publishers, 2018) 237–250.

> The 'rules of the game' that constituted the laws of war at this time, however, were of little relevance to the feudal peasants that constituted the foot soldiery of European armies, nor were they believed to be of any application to wars against *uncivilised enemies* – infidels and primitive peoples.[28]

As noted above, up until the middle of the nineteenth century, attempts to restrain the use of force during conflict existed mainly as customary rules, often agreed to amongst warring (European) parties and, most importantly, generally existing without consistent punishments for violations of said rules and customs. Nonetheless, it would be incorrect to assume that war was fought without any boundaries or restrictions. As Keegan notes:

> War may have got worse with the passage of time, but the ethic of restraint has rarely been wholly absent from its practise [...] Even in the age of total warfare when war was considered a normal condition, and the inherent right of sovereign states presided, there remained taboos, enshrined in law and thankfully widely observed.[29]

Not until the creation and subsequent crystallisation of the European states-system do we start to see what we now recognise as modern international law.[30] Beginning in the middle of the nineteenth century, this is a period that bears witness to a flurry of treaties aimed at restraining behaviour during conflict, the number and significance of which was staggering, especially when one considers the historically sclerotic advances up to then.[31]

This period also bears witness to a shift towards 'humanitarian' laws of war, which for much of the modern period were divided into 'Geneva Law', which is mainly concerned with the protection of victims of armed conflict;

---

28 David Turns, 'The Law of Armed Conflict (International Humanitarian Law)' in Malcolm Evans (ed.), *International Law* (Oxford: Oxford University Press, 2010) 822 (emphasis in original).

29 John Keegan, *War and Our World* (New York: Vintage Books, 2001) 26.

30 Koskenniemi elaborates on this point, arguing that the 'long nineteenth century' bears witness to a complicated amalgam of events that constitute European modernity – 'the formation of the nation-state, the tension between sovereignty and liberal individualism, influence of technology and economic growth on state power, secularism, rationalism and belief in progress as a lingua franca between international elites' – all of which international law is an outgrowth of; Koskenniemi (n 14) 142).

31 Adam Roberts, 'Land Warfare: From Hague to Nuremberg' in Michael Howard, George Andreopoulas and Mark Shulman (eds.), *The Laws of War: Constraints on Warfare in the Western World* (New Haven: Yale University Press, 1994) 119.

and 'Hague Law', named in reference to the 1899 and 1907 Hague Conventions, which is concerned with controlling types of weapons and means and method of warfare. Historically, IHL was used in reference primarily to 'Geneva' Law; however, it has become the norm for IHL to incorporate both the 'Geneva' and 'Hague' dimensions of *jus in bello* law.[32]

It is generally established that Henry Dunant's *Memories of Solferino*, in which Dunant described the horror of witnessing the suffering of 40,000 Austrian, French, and Italian soldiers wounded on the battlefield of Solferino (1859), was the foundational moment in the establishment of humanitarian focused laws of war. Specifically, Dunant's observations served as the catalyst for establishing the landmark Geneva Convention for the Amelioration of the Condition of the Wounded in Armies in the Field (1864), its core provision being the neutrality of the wounded and those who cared for them.[33] Dunant's experience also led him to play a leading role in the establishment of the International Committee of the Red Cross (ICRC), which was to become 'a promoter and custodian of the humanitarian idea and the primary initiation for its transition into international humanitarian law'.[34] 'Geneva Law' evolved through two subsequent Conventions for the Amelioration of the Condition of the Wounded in Armies in the Field in 1906 and 1929 respectively, designed to strengthen protections for *hors d'combat* and complemented further by the 1929 Convention relative to the Treatment of Prisoners of War, all of which were further revised and subsequently redrafted at the end of the Second World War as the 1949 Geneva Conventions.[35]

The first international treaty to prohibit a particular weapon was the 1868 'St. Petersburg Declaration Renouncing the Use, in Time of War, of Explosive Projectiles Under 400 Grammes Weight', and it is notable for articulating two ideas that subsequently underpin the fundamentals of modern IHL; military necessity and proportionality: 'The only legitimate object which States should endeavour to accomplish during war is to weaken the military forces of the

32 Hilarie McCoubrey, *International Humanitarian War: Modern Developments in the Limitation of Warfare* (Aldershot: Ashgate, 1998) 2.

33 See Gary Solis, *The Law of Armed Conflict: International Humanitarian Law in War* (Oxford: Oxford University Press, 2010) 46–49.

34 Cited in Michael A. Meyer and Hilaire McCoubrey (eds.), *Reflections on Law and Armed Conflicts. The Selected Works on the Laws of War by the late Professor Colonel G.I.A.D. Draper, OBE* (Kluwer Law International, The Hague/Boston/London, 1998) 69. For a critical examination of this traditional narrative, see Amanda Alexander, 'A Short History of International Humanitarian Law' (2015) 26 European Journal of International Law 109.

35 See Emily Crawford and Alison Pert, *International Humanitarian Law* (Cambridge: Cambridge University Press, 2015) 13–15.

enemy' and 'for this purpose it is sufficient to disable the greatest possible number of men'.[36]

The relative success of the St. Petersburg conference paved the way for the second set of substantive, pre-World War One treaties – the Hague Conventions of 1899 and 1907. While representatives from the twenty-six states that attended the first Hague Conference failed to reach concrete agreements on arms limitations, they did, in the shape of the Convention on the Laws and Customs on War on Land, conclude the first general codification of laws of land war in the form of a multilateral treaty.[37] The final act of the 1899 Conference was agreement on the need for a further conference, which was subsequently held in 1907. Building on the pattern of the first, there was once again no general agreement on arms limitation. However, with a substantially increased state representation, authors and commentators are in general agreement that the thirteen conventions adopted in 1907, when considered alongside the 1880 Oxford Manual of the Laws and Customs of War and the 1899 Hague Conventions, represented a high-water mark in codified attempts to limit warfare. For Rues-Smit, the Hague Conferences should be regarded as more than merely an instance of emerging multilateralism, but rather, serving as examples of judicial interpretations of the law, a step in the realisation of a civilised polity 'and thus a desirable feature of a society of civilised states'.[38]

Despite being a period in which 'the law of war entered its epoch of highest repute',[39] the turn to positivism did not reconcile the tension between emerging humanitarian concern in warfare, and the historic predilection of military necessity as informed by *raison d'état*. Indeed, Best refers to this period as the 'militarisation of the humanitarians',[40] and Kolb argues that the Hague Conventions, through their marginal concern with civilians and their

36 'St. Petersburg Declaration Renouncing the Use, in Time of War, of Explosive Projectiles Under 400 Grammes Weight' in Adam Roberts and Richard Guelff (eds.), *Documents on the Laws of War* (Oxford: Oxford University Press, 2000) 55. For more on the importance of the St Petersburg Declaration to modern IHL, see Emily Crawford, 'The Enduring Legacy of the St Petersburg Declaration: Distinction, Military Necessity, and the Prohibition of Causing Unnecessary Suffering and Superfluous Injury in IHL' (2018) 20 Journal of the History of International Law 544 and Janina Dill and Henry Shue, 'Limiting the Killing in War: Military Necessity and the St. Petersburg Assumption' (2012) 26 Ethics & International Affairs 311.

37 Roberts (n 31) 121.

38 Christian Rues-Smit, *The Moral Purpose of the State: Culture, Social Identity and Institutional Rationality in International Relations* (Princeton: Princeton University Press, 1999) 142.

39 Geoffrey Best, *Humanity in Warfare* (London: Weidenfeld and Nicholson, 1980) 129.

40 Ibid 143.

protections, remained primarily military law (as opposed to humanitarian law); 'it was a special law for the combating forces rather than a general law protecting persons in general'.[41] While Kolb's criticism is not incorrect, it does underestimate the degree to which the Hague Conventions 'define an extensive and detailed list of persons to be protected in various ways'.[42] Thus, in agreeing with Rues-Smit and Johnson, it is argued here that we see in both the St. Petersburg Declaration and the Hague Conventions not only the emergence of positivist IHL, but also the development of international law premised on humanitarian concerns, albeit law that continued to reflect the prevailing ideals of sovereignty and independence, and as such a continued, if only tacit, understanding that states could continue to conduct their military operations as informed by effective ends.

The onset of the First World War and the subsequent devastation halted the pre-World War enthusiasms for further codification of laws designed to limit warfare.[43] The mood following the end of the Second World War, however, was discernibly different. Policy makers, scarred by two world wars and the Great Depression, set about the construction of a new, liberal world order, underpinned by the idea of 'never again', to be realised through the establishment of multilateral institutions. The United Nations stands as the most obvious representation of this post-war order, but of greater significance with regards to IHL are the four Geneva Conventions of 1949 and the three 1977 Additional Protocols, which form the cornerstone of IHL. Underpinning the humanitarian aims of the Geneva Conventions is Article 3 common to the four Conventions, which 'sets out the minimum humanitarian guarantees in all armed conflicts', comprising of 'humane treatment, non-discrimination and the obligation to collect and care for the wounded and sick'.[44]

Countering the claim made in Common Article 3, it will be argued in the next section, through a focus on the relationship between the core principles of IHL, that the historically evolved underpinnings of the laws of war ensure that the central characteristic of IHL is that it continues to allow states to conduct wars constrained by *raison d'état*, and not humanitarian concerns.

---

41 Robert Kolb, 'The Main Epochs of Modern International Humanitarian Law since 1864 and their Related Dominant Legal Constructions' in Kjetil Mujezinović Larsen, Camilla Guldahl Cooper and Gro Nystuen (eds.), *Searching for a 'Principle of Humanity' in International Humanitarian Law* (Cambridge: Cambridge University Press, 2013) 38–39.

42 James Johnson, 'Maintaining the Protection of Non-Combatants' (2000) 37 Journal of Peace Research 421, 431.

43 In an interesting aside, Roberts points out that 'ghastly as all this carnage of the land battles was, for the most part it was not contrary to the laws of war'; Roberts (n 31) 125.

44 Giulia Pinzauti, 'Common Article 3' in Dražan Djukic and Niccolò Pons (eds.), *The Companion to International Humanitarian Law* (Leiden: Brill, 2018) 256

4 Core Principles of IHL (With a Focus on Military Necessity)

The UK Ministry of Defence's *Manual on the Law of Armed Conflict*, noting that while much customary IHL has been codified into treaty form, identifies four fundamental principles that underly the law of armed conflict: 'military necessity, humanity, distinction, and proportionality'.[45] This section will explore each of these four core principles, explain how they relate to each other, and as identified in the introduction, explore the controversial nature of military necessity.

4.1 *Distinction*

The principle of distinction has been qualified by the International Court of Justice (ICJ) as one of the 'intransgressible principles of international customary law' and is to be seen as one of the 'cardinal principles' of IHL.[46]

The first codification of discrimination, albeit being somewhat vague, occurs in the Lieber Code (1863), which required unarmed citizens to be spared 'as much as the exigencies of war will admit'.[47] Further codified in the 1907 Hague Regulations, distinction was not properly codified until the 1977 Additional Protocols, where it provides that parties to an armed conflict must 'at all times distinguish between the civilian population and combatants and between civilian objects and military objectives and accordingly shall direct their operations only against military objectives'.[48] As Heinsch identifies, the principle recognises only two categories to be distinguished under IHL, civilians and combatants; while combatants can be lawfully targeted to achieve military advantage, civilians must not be targeted or made the object of attack.[49] A further aspect of the principle, relating to objects rather than persons, stipulates 'the parties to the conflict must at all times distinguish between civilian objects and military objects. Attacks may be directed only

45 U.K. Ministry of Defence, *The Manual of the Law of Armed Conflict* (Oxford: Oxford University Press, 2004) 21. The International Committee of the Red Cross identifies the Fundamental Principles of IHL as: 'the principle of humanity; the principle of distinction between civilians and combatants, and between civilian objects and military objectives; the principle of proportionality; and the principle of military necessity', available at https://casebook.icrc.org/glossary/fundamental-principles-ihl (accessed 1.8.2021)

46 Cited in Robert Heinsch, 'Distinction' in Djukic and Pons (n 44) 307.

47 Cited ibid 308.

48 Protocol Additional to the Geneva Conventions of 12 August 1949, and Relating the Protection of Victims of International Armed Conflicts, Geneva, 8 June 1977, in force 7 December 1978, 1125 UNTS 3 ("AP I"), art. 51.

49 Heinsch (n 46) 308.

against military. Attacks must not be directed against civilian objects'.[50] Elaborating on its importance, the ICRC notes of Additional Protocol 1, Article 48:

> It is the foundation on which the codification of the laws and customs of war rests: the civilian population and civilian objects must be respected and protected in armed conflict, and for this purpose, they must be distinguished from combatants and military objectives. The entire system established in the Hague in 1899 and 1907and in Geneva from 1864 to 1977 is founded on this rule of customary law.[51]

While simple at its core, protections afforded by the principle of distinction are not always straightforward. The distinction principle is underpinned by the assumption that civilians do not pose a threat, and are thus not to be targeted, 'unless and for such time they directly participate in hostilities'.[52] This means that during the time that civilians directly take part in hostilities, they can be directly attacked.[53] Thus, as Fleck argues, as 'more and more civilians are engaged in and around hostilities […] the situation on the ground is more blurred and the principle of distinction harder to implement'.[54]

4.2 *Proportionality*

In summary, the principle of proportionality requires 'that any military advantage obtained by a particular operation must outweigh the damage caused to civilians and civilian objects'.[55] It is codified in Additional Protocol I, Article 51, which defines as indiscriminate 'an attack which may be expected to cause incidental loss of civilian life, injury to civilians, damage to civilian objects, or a combination thereof, which would be excessive in relation

50 Jean-Marie Henkaerts and Louise Doswald-Beck, *Customary International Humanitarian Law*, vol.1 (Oxford: Oxford University Press, 2005) 25.

51 International Committee of the Red Cross, 'Commentary of 1987 Protocol Additional to the Geneva Conventions of 12 August 1949, and relating to the Protection of Victims of International Armed Conflicts (Protocol I), 8 June 1977', para 1863, available at https://ihl-databases.icrc.org/applic/ihl/ihl.nsf/Comment.xsp?action=openDocument&documentId=83C5B3FC27BB6F00C12563CD00434537 (accessed 1.8.2021).

52 AP I, art. 53(1).

53 For a discussion on what constitutes direct participation in hostilities, see Nils Melzer, *Interpretive Guidance on the Notion of Direct Participation in Hostilities under International Humanitarian Law* (ICRC, 2009).

54 Dieter Fleck 'Historical Development and Legal Basis' and Dieter Fleck (ed.), *The Handbook of International Humanitarian Law* (Oxford: Oxford University Press, 2021) 87.

55 Crawford and Pert (n 35) 44.

to the concrete and direct military advantage anticipated'.[56] The key term here is 'incidental'; as Gardam notes, IHL accepts 'the incidence of some civilian casualties' as the result of military operations.[57] However, arguments suggesting that Article 51 authorises any sort of attack, so long as it does not cause excessive loss or damage in relation to the military advantage expected, are justifiably refuted by the ICRC:

> In order to comply with the conditions, the attack must be directed against a military objective with means which are not disproportionate in relation to the objective, but are suited to destroying only that objective, and the effects of the attacks must be limited in the way required by the Protocol; moreover, even after those conditions are fulfilled, the incidental civilian losses and damages must not be excessive.[58]

Thus, the principle of proportionality 'rules out measures which are unnecessary or unsuitable to achieve the legitimate aim of forcible action, or which entail excessive or inappropriate sacrifice to other competing values and interests'.[59] It is also closely related to the principles of distinction and necessity, in that the principle of proportionality 'seeks to limit damage, injury and death to civilians and civilian objects', while still allowing for the military objectives to be met.[60]

4.3 *Humanity*

The meaning of the principle of humanity, as Cross notes, 'may at first be thought self-evident; a matter of common sense'.[61] But as Hayashi points out, this is not always the case, noting that 'humanity' has been defined:

> as a notion that 'forbids the infliction of suffering, injury, or destruction not actually necessary for the accomplishment of legitimate military

56 AP I, art. 51.

57 Judith Gardam, 'Necessity and Proportionality in Jus ad Bellum and Jus in Bello' in Laurence Boisson de Chazournes and Philippe Sands (eds.), *International Law, the International Court of Justice and Nuclear Weapons* (Cambridge: Cambridge University Press, 1999) 283.

58 International Committee of the Red Cross, 'Commentary of 1987 – Article 51 – Protection of the Civilian Population', para 5, available at https://ihl-databases.icrc.org/en/ihl-treaties/api-1977/article-51/commentary/1987 (accessed 1.8.2021).

59 Enzo Cannizzaro, 'Proportionality in the Law of Armed Conflict' in Clapham and Gaeta (n 1) 351.

60 Crawford and Pert (n 35) 45.

61 Matthew Cross, 'Humanity' in Djukic and Pons (n 44) 396.

> purposes', as synonymous with the prohibition of superfluous injury and unnecessary suffering; an equivalent to the Martens Clause; and a vehicle through which international human rights law has made its way into the regulation of armed conflicts.[62]

Both Cross and Solis make the compelling argument that humanity is perhaps best understood when considered in its relationship with military necessity: ' ... to some extent, the two concepts are mirror images, each qualifying the other. The principle of humanity does not absolutely forbid the use of force and the infliction of human suffering, but it does, at least, establish that such conduct is exceptional'.[63]

The now famous Martens Clause, appearing for the first time in the Preamble of the 1899 Hague Convention, is generally assumed to provide the legal basis for the principle of humanity, and has subsequently been adopted and reinforced in the 1949 Geneva Conventions and the 1977 Additional Protocols:

> Until a more complete code of the laws of war has been issued, the High Contracting Parties deem it expedient to declare that, in cases not included in the Regulations adopted by them, the inhabitants and the belligerents remain under the protection and the rule of the law of nations, as they result from the usages established among civilized peoples, from the laws of humanity and the dictates of public conscience.[64]

Furthermore, it is possible to identify impacts of the principle of humanity in other aspects of codified IHL, including the prohibition on certain weapons, including dum-dum bullets and poisonous gasses; it is also possible to identify the impact of the principle of humanity in the Rome Statute of the International Criminal Court, which includes amongst its crimes arbitrary punishment, torture, and unlawful deportation or transfer or unlawful confinement.[65]

However, as Cross reinforces, the 'Martens approach' must be treated with caution: 'It does not mean that humanity trumps positivist law. In particular, there seems to be little support in state practice for the view that the principle

62 Nobuo Hayashi, 'Basic Principles' in Tim McCormack and Rain Liivoja (eds.), *Routledge Handbook of the Law of Armed Conflict* (New York: Routledge, 2016) 93.

63 Cross (n 61) 396; Solis (n 33) 270.

64 Cited in Marco Sassòli, Antoine Bouvier and Anne Quintin, *How Does Law Protect in War?* (International Committee of the Red Cross, 2014) available at https://casebook.icrc.org/glossary/distinction (accessed 1.8.2021).

65 See United Nations, *The Rome Statute of the International Criminal Court* (1998) available at https://www.icc-cpi.int/resource-library/documents/rs-eng.pdf (accessed 30.7.2021).

of humanity can be called upon to limit conduct which is permitted by positive rules of IHL.[66] Indeed, as discussed above, and elaborated on below, the application of the humanity principle is not only historically subjective, but also deferential to necessity when it serves the interests of the state.

4.4 *Military Necessity*

According to Schmitt, 'no principle is more central to IHL, nor more misunderstood than military necessity. It has been proffered to both justify horrendous abuses during armed conflicts, and to impose impractical and dangerous restrictions on those who fight'.[67] For Dinstein, 'if military necessity were to prevail completely, belligerent parties would have full freedom of action with a view to winning a war; if humanitarian considerations were the only guide to the conduct of hostilities, the waging of war would become impossible by dint of the death, injury and suffering that unavoidably accompany it'.[68]

Military necessity, as defined by the US, 'is that principle which justifies those measures not forbidden by international law which are indispensable for securing the complete submission of the enemy as soon as possible'.[69] As with all the fundamental or core principles identified here, numerous expressions of the principle of military necessity can be found in treaty and customary international law. Perhaps most famously, the 1863 Lieber Code defined military necessity 'as understood by *modern civilised nations*, consists in the necessity of those measures which are indispensable for securing ends in war, and are lawful according to the modern law and usages of war'.[70] More recently, the preamble of the 1907 Hague Convention identified the aims of the treaty being to 'diminish the evils of war as far military requirements permit',[71] and Article 54 states that underwater power and communications cables between occupied and neutral territories are not to be seized or destroyed 'except in the case of absolute necessity'.[72]

---

66 Cross (n 61) 397.

67 Michael Schmitt, 'Military Necessity and Humanity in International Humanitarian Law: Preserving the Delicate Balance' (2010) 50 Virginia Journal of International Law 795, 796.

68 Yoram Dinstein, 'Military Necessity' in Max Planck Encyclopedia of International Law (2015) available at https://opil.ouplaw.com/view/10.1093/law:epil/9780199231690/law-9780199231690-e333?rskey=xoTuFn&result=1&prd=MPIL (accessed 30.7.2021).

69 Department of The Army, Field Manual 27–10, *The Law of Land Warfare* (Washington: GPO, 1956) para. 3.a., 4.

70 Cited in Solis (n 33) 258 (emphasis added).

71 Convention (IV) respecting the Laws and Customs of War on Land and its annex: Regulations concerning the Laws and Customs of War on Land. The Hague, 18 October 1907 ('Hague IV, 1907'), Preamble.

72 Hague IV, 1907, art. 54.

While not codified as such in the 1949 Geneva Conventions or the 1977 Additional Protocols, part III of the Fourth 1949 Geneva Convention allows parties to 'take such measures of control and security in regard to protected persons as may be necessary as part of the war',[73] and Article 54 of Additional Protocol I provides that civilian crops or livestock may not be removed except by parties in their own territory 'where required by imperative military necessity'.[74]

As discussed in the second section, the modern laws of war, described as either IHL or LOAC, are the product result of a centuries long process. As such, and as elaborated on above, while humanitarian concerns are relatively new, without necessarily describing them as such, there existed forms of distinction and proportionality in pre-modern attempts to restrain battlefield conduct. Similarly, military necessity has always been a consideration during conduct, but at different times in history, the term has meant different things. The degree to which competing understanding of the term military necessity might inform contemporary perceptions of the principle necessitates a discussion on the evolution of the term.

Notions of military necessity appear in the 17th century writings of Dutch jurist Hugo Grotius; writing at the time of the Thirty Years War, Grotius notes 'all engagements which are of no use in obtaining a right, or putting an end to war, but have as their purpose a mere display of strength [...] are incompatible with both the duty of a Christian and with humanity itself'.[75] Even as relatively late as 1814, US Supreme Court Chief Justice John Marshall observed, 'that war gives to the sovereign full rights to take the persons and confiscate the property of the enemy wherever found, is conceded'.[76]

Arguably the most infamous expression of necessity overriding any restraint on conduct during war was the doctrine of *Kriegraison geht vor Kriegsrecht* (necessity in war overrules the manner of warfare), mostly often shortened to *Kriegraison*. In the late 19th and early 20th centuries, a number of German theorists proposed the idea that 'the elevation of necessity over legal norms was justified when the sole means of avoiding severe danger was to violate the law, or when compliance with the law might jeopardise the conflicts ultimate objectives';[77] it was subsequently endorsed by military leaders and politicians

73 Convention Relative to the Protection of Civilian Persons in Time of War. Geneva, 12 August 1949 ('GC IV'), art. 27.

74 AP1, art. 54.

75 Hugo Grotius, *De Jure Belli Ac Pacis*, vol. 2, Francis W. Kelset (trans.) (Buffalo: William Hein, 1995) 743–744.

76 Cited in Solis (n 33) 260.

77 Schmitt (n 67) 797.

between 1871 and 1945.[78] However, as both Schmitt and Solis observe, *Kriegraison* never gained wider traction, and whatever legitimacy the doctrine might have had was extinguished in *The Hostage Case*.[79]

Similarly, Cassese, commenting on the success of the Diplomatic Conferences that completed Additional Protocol I and Additional Protocol II, observed:

> The Protocol places primary emphasis on humanitarian demands and, indeed, in many respects subordinates military exigencies to such demands. On this score, the Protocol markedly departs from the customary law, which in general tends to put military necessity on the same footing as humanitarian demands.[80]

5 Necessity, Raison d'état and the Standard of Civilisation

Of the four principles of IHL discussed here, military necessity is the principle that most clearly reflects the historically developed right of states to determine the conduct of military affairs to suit their own defined ends. While subsequent developments in the laws of war have sought to constrain states' behaviour, and indeed 'the means to achieve military victory are not unlimited',[81] the concept of 'whatever it takes', and the related notion that states still feel relatively comfortable defending the actions of their armed services through references to national interest or *raison d'état*, retain some salience. One of the reasons for this, as argued here, and reinforced by Schmitt, is historical: 'the historical underpinnings of military necessity as a justification for the divergence from the absolute protection of civilians and civilian objects during armed conflict are carried through and reflected in the entire body of IHL'.[82]

---

78 Solis (n 33) 266.

79 See *United States v List* (The Hostage Case), Case No.7 (19th of Feb., 1948), reprinted in *Trials of War Criminals Before the Nuremburg Military Tribunals Under Control Council Law No.10*, 1230, available at https://www.loc.gov/rr/frd/Military_Law/pdf/NT_war-criminals_Vol-II.pdf (accessed 30.7.2021).

80 Antonio Cassese, 'A Tentative Appraisal of the Old and the New Humanitarian Law of Armed Conflict' in Antonio Cassese (ed.), *The New Humanitarian Law of Armed Conflict* (Naples: Editoriale Scientifica, 1979) 481.

81 U.K. Ministry of Defence (n 45) 23.

82 Schmitt (n 67) 798.

The priority given to the state's capacity to use force in the name of the 'national interest' was also evident in the ICJ's advisory opinion regarding the use of nuclear weapons:

> ... the threat or use of nuclear weapons would generally be contrary to the rules of international law applicable in armed conflict [...] however, in view of the current state of international law [...] the Court cannot conclude definitively whether the threat or use of nuclear weapons would be lawful or unlawful in an extreme circumstance of self-defence, in which the very survival of the state would be at stake'.[83]

Dinstein notes that 'the last sentence is most troublesome. The linkage between nuclear weapons and 'extreme circumstances' [...] is hard to digest; it appears to be utterly inconsistent with the basic tenet that [IHL] applies equally to all belligerent states, irrespective of the merits of their cause'.[84]

In a similar vein, Alexander, writing about the 1991 Gulf War, argues that there was:

> a widespread perception that the legal regime governing the Gulf War was not really a humanitarian law. The central principle of the *jus in bello* was not humanity but, rather, the principle of military necessity [...] What was clear [...] was that it was a permissive principle that allowed almost any action if it could be justified by military necessity. It amounted to nothing more than a prohibition on the direct or negligent targeting of civilians'.[85]

Commentating on the destruction of an electricity facility that killed hundreds of civilians during the same conflict, Gardam and Jarvis also argue that:

> The conduct of hostilities in the Gulf conflict indicates that the concept of 'excessive casualties' was restricted to that context. In other words, the military advantage always outweighed the civilian casualties as long as civilians were not directly targeted and care was taken in assessing the nature of the target and during the attack itself. The impact of the practice of states such as the United States and its coalition partners on the

83 International Court of Justice, *Advisory Opinion on the Legality of the Threat or Use of Nuclear Weapons* [1996] ICJ Rep., 263.

84 Yoram Dinstein, *The Conduct of Hostilities under the Law of International Armed Conflict* (Cambridge: Cambridge University Press, 2004) 78.

85 Alexander (n 34) 129.

> formation of custom is considerable and cannot be overlooked. It seems inevitable that the concept of proportionality as a customary norm is limited to the situations outlined above.[86]

But it is also important to acknowledge that the relationship between the core principles of IHL change over time; as Alexander argues with regards to NATO's 1999 intervention in Kosovo, the equilibrium shifted back to the humanitarian principle of IHL:

> When civilians were killed, their deaths were not blamed on the inadequacy of the law but, rather, on the failure of NATO to apply the law properly. When lawyers sought better protection for civilians, they called for better adherence to the law – they did not suggest that better laws were required. In this way, international humanitarian law was cemented not only as the governing regime of *jus in bello* but also as a respected and prestigious regime.[87]

With this in mind, it is argued here that the War on Terror, primarily fought in Afghanistan and Iraq, has again shifted the equilibrium towards the principle of military necessity. Furthermore, the universal underpinnings of IHL are being undermined, and simultaneously justified, through the language of *raison d'état* and the 'standard of civilisation'. Several examples can be highlighted to this end.

The first example concerns the language that the G.W. Bush Administration used when denying IHL protections for 'enemy combatants', which Mégret articulately argues bears notable similarities to the language that was typical of the earlier exclusion of non-Western peoples from the laws of war.[88] Some of the tropes identified by Mégret include the Bush Administration arguing that the adversary, as was the case with savage tribes, was not a party to the relevant treaties; and arguing that Afghanistan was a failed state, and thus 'US obligations towards it could be suspended, echoing the old idea that non-Western lands, being non-sovereign, are lands where no laws apply'.[89] The Bush Administration also argued that 'even if al Qaeda were a nation-state and a party to the Geneva Conventions, its members would still qualify as

86 Judith Gardam and Michelle Jarvis, *Women, Armed Conflict and International Law* (The Hague: Brill, 2001) 834.

87 Alexander (n 34) 135.

88 Mégret (n 18) 299.

89 Ibid 299.

illegal belligerents *due to their very conduct*',[90] which echoes the 'standard of civilisation' criteria discussed above for denying entry in international society, and thus excluding 'barbarians' from the protections of international law.

The second example is via the writings of Marcus Luttrell, a U.S. Navy SEAL veteran of Afghanistan combat, who wrote in 2007:

> These terrorist/insurgents know the rules […] they're not their rules, they're *our* rules, the rules of Western countries, *the civilised side of the world*. And every terrorist knows how to manipulate them in their own favour […] they know we are probably scared to shoot them, because we get charged with murder […] The truth is, in this kind of terrorist/insurgent warfare, no one can tell who's a civilian and who's not. So what's the point of framing rules that cannot be comprehensively carried out by anyone? Rules that are unworkable, because half the time no one knows who the goddamned enemy is, and by the time you find out, it might be too late to save your own life […] Nothing's fair in war, and occasionally the wrong people do get killed. It's been happening for about a million years. Faced with the murderous cutthroats of the Taliban, we are not fighting under the rules of Geneva IV Article 4. We are fighting under the rules of Article 223.556 mm – that's the calibre and bullet gauge of our M4 rifle.[91]

Luttrell's musings, in that they posit a different set of protections between civilised and barbarian belligerents, mimic the instructions offered by Captain Eldridge for fighting 'savages'. Luttrell's comments about IHL being the law of civilised peoples is enlightening. By dehumanising the opposition, and tacitly identifying them as barbarian, Luttrell is subsequently denying terrorist groups the protections that IHL, more so in its customary form, provides all belligerents during combat. Another example of battlefield perceptions of IHL as they relate to fighting 'terrorists', comes from an enlisted veteran from Iraq:

> That I should observe the Geneva Conventions/ Which doesn't apply to a terrorist scum/ So evil and cruel their own people run/ From cold-blooded killers who love to behead/ Shove that mother' Geneva, I'm leaving him dead […] So it's Muj' checkin' out, 'cos I'm going to last.[92]

---

90 John C. Yoo and James C. Ho, *The Status of Terrorists* (UC Berkeley Boalt Working Papers in Public Law, 2003) 10 (emphasis added).

91 Marcus Luttrell with Patrick Robinson, *Lone Survivor: The Eyewitness Account of Operation Redwing and the Lost Heroes of SEAL Team 10* (New York: Little Brown, 2007) 168–170.

92 Cited in Solis (n 33) 338.

The 'terrorist' is the 'savage' or 'barbarian', dehumanised and uncivilised, and thus excluded from the protections afforded 'civilised' belligerents. As with the arguments made by the Bush Administration identified above, the tacit application of a 'standard of civilisation' is also wrapped up in the language of *raison d'état*. Furthermore, the language and actions of Luttrell and the enlisted soldier offer evidence of the degree to which the equilibrium in IHL has shifted towards military necessity.

The third example concerns revelations from the *Inspector-General of the Australian Defence Force Afghanistan Inquiry Report*, more commonly known as the Brereton Report. Although heavily redacted, part of report identifies that 'SOTG (Special Operations Task Group) were prepared to kill in contravention of the Law of Armed Conflict (LOAC)', and that 'none of the witnesses appeared to recognise […] skewed morality, and a disregard for human life (at least, for Afghan human life)'.[93] Australian journalist Mark Willacy's book *Rogue Forces* is replete with examples of Australian SAS soldiers denying protections to Taliban 'terrorists' based on the idea of them being 'uncivilised' or 'barbarian'.[94] Here, the tacit application of a 'standard of civilisation' serves to undermine the universalist aspirations of IHL by validating 'an entirely different set of legal rules'. This is further reinforced by Saul, who notes that the dehumanising of the enemy is 'a moral distancing that treats them as undeserving of the respect of the law',[95] and Fowler, who suggests that there is a certain inevitability to the alleged violations of IHL committed by the SAS in Afghanistan, as 'the Taliban has long been condemned and dehumanised at the highest political and military leadership levels, in Australia and by international allies. A hefty dose of anti-Islamic bias, and a desire to punish for previous attacks, has been part of this narrative'.[96] The application of the 'standard of civilisation', albeit it tacitly, denies the non-state Taliban (and other 'terrorist' groups) entry into international society; the dehumanising of the enemy, based on their conduct,

---

93 *Inspector-General of the Australian Defence Force Afghanistan Inquiry Report* (2020) 331, available at: https://afghanistaninquiry.defence.gov.au/sites/default/files/2020-11/IGADF-Afghanistan-Inquiry-Public-Release-Version.pdf (accessed 8.8.2022).

94 See Mark Willacy, *Rogue Forces: An Explosive Insiders' Account of Australian SAS War Crimes in Afghanistan* (Sydney: Simon and Shuster, 2021).

95 Cited in Ben Doherty, 'How the 'good war' went bad: elite soldiers from Australia, UK and US face a reckoning', *The Guardian*, 2 June 2021, available at https://www.theguardian.com/australia-news/2021/jun/02/how-the-good-war-went-bad-elite-soldiers-from-australia-uk-and-us-face-a-reckoning (accessed 8.8.2022).

96 Alexander Fowler, 'Australian war crimes in Afghanistan: Prosecutions face an uncertain road ahead', *ILA Reporter*, 4 July 2021, available at https://ilareporter.org.au/2021/06/Australian-war-crimes-in-afghanistan-prosecutions-face-an-uncertain-road-ahead-alexandra-fowler/ (accessed 20 December 2022).

reinforces their status as 'barbarian' or 'savage', thus further justifies the denial of protections afforded by IHL.

None of this is to suggest that the laws of war have been rendered useless. Nor is it to suggest that alleged violators of IHL will not be prosecuted. Rather, through the either tacit or explicit invocation of a 'standard of civilisation', the universalist aspirations of modern IHL are being undermined, and relatedly, the historically state-centric foundations of modern IHL are increasingly informing a military necessity bias, underpinned by *raison d'état*, with regards to the relationship between the four core principles of IHL.

6 Conclusion

Through an exploration of the relationship between the state and war, and a study of the way in which the modern laws of war are a culmination of a centuries long process, this paper has identified the modern laws of war as a compromise between the state's historically informed and self-anointed right to use force to serve its political ends (as informed by *raison d'état*), and humanitarian concerns as they developed since the late 19th century. This paper also identified a related historical continuity with regards to the language of the 'standard of civilisation' and argued that state-determined distinctions of 'civilised' and 'barbarian' continue to inform protections afforded by IHL.

Indeed, it was argued here that as evinced by a number of the quotes above, the de-humanising of enemy combatants via the language of the 'standard of civilisation', continues to remain an informant of who should be afforded protections by IHL, and in turn, a concept by which we can continue to understand the gulf between the (universal) humanitarian underpinnings of IHL, and violations of the laws of war. Importantly, none of this is to argue that IHL is either redundant, nor that it offers little to no protection for civilians or civilian objects during conflict; rather, it is to provide a *via media* interpretation of IHL that lies between somewhat naïve expectations of 'humanitarian war' and conflict with restraint.

Filling the Gaps: The Expansion of International Humanitarian Law and the Juridification of the Free-Fighter

Amanda Alexander

Abstract

This article traces the expansion of international law from the Hague Conventions, where only a state's soldiers had legal status, to the contemporary understanding that international law governs all participants in conflict. This can be seen as a humanitarian shift that diminishes state power. This article, however, argues that the Hague Conventions only established a limited sphere of formal law because delegates deliberately left free-fighters outside the law, to be governed by their own will and moral code. In doing so, delegates echoed a philosophical tradition that situates true freedom outside the state. As this article shows, the expansion of law to include such fighters required the replacement of such alternative codes with a renewed and extended range of formal legal criteria. As such, the expansion of international law to the realm outside the state has led to a reaffirmation of that law which is synonymous with the state.

Keywords

international humanitarian law – juridification – irregular combatants – history of international law

 | DOI:10.1163/9789004712478_006

1 Introduction

In 1899, 27 governments met at The Hague to 'seek the most effective means of ensuring to the peoples a lasting peace, and of limiting the progressive development of military armaments'.[1] These aims may not have been realised, but the Peace Conference did produce the Hague Convention II, which laid down the laws and customs of war. These laws were shaped to govern a certain form of war – a war between civilised states. The laws themselves were characteristic of a particular form of law: formal, neutral and modern. James Turner Johnson described this as non-ideological law – a doctrine which was stripped of beliefs about justice and referred back to 'reasons of state'.[2] These features are made most clear in the provisions governing combatant status. Combatant privileges were limited to those fighting in a state's army; only those in uniform, disciplined, law-abiding and under effective command would fall within the law's regime.

These requirements left many people outside the law – in particular, the 'uncivilised' and the 'savage'. They were denied what legal protection existed; their struggles were not regarded as real wars or conflicts. In 1927, Colby listed an array of legal opinions that insisted that 'the rules of International Law apply only to warfare between civilized nations, where both parties understand them and are prepared to carry them out.'[3] Savage tribes were incapable of waging war in the sense of international law – 'barbarous and loosely organized bands are incapable of attaining a status of belligerency.[4]

The fact that so many people and incidents fell outside the law led, as has been rightly noted, to some horrific political and ethical consequences as well as an array of practical problems.[5] As a result, there were repeated, if slow, attempts to fill the gaps in international law. The *1949 Geneva Conventions*

1 James Brown Scott, *The Proceedings of the Hague Peace Conferences: Translation of the Official Texts: The Conference of 1899* (Oxford University Press 1920) 7.

2 James Turner Johnson, *Ideology, Reason, and the Limitation of War: Religious and Secular Concepts 1200–1710* (Princeton University Press 1975) 11, 262.

3 Elbridge Colby, 'How to Fight Savage Tribes' (1927) 21 Am J Int'l L 279, 280, citing the British Manual of Military Law, 1914, p. 235, par. 7.

4 ibid 280, citing an argument before the Court of Claims of the US: *Marks v. U. S.*, 28 Ct. Cl. 147.

5 Frédéric Mégret, 'From 'Savages' to 'Unlawful Combatants': A Postcolonial Look at International Law's 'Other' in A Orford (ed) *International Law and its Others* (Cambridge 2006) 271; Sibylle Scheipers, *Unlawful Combatants: A Genealogy of the Irregular Fighter* (Oxford University Press 2015) 170–182; Emily Crawford, 'Regulating the Irregular: International Humanitarian Law and the Question of Civilian Participation in Armed Conflicts' (2011) 18(1) U.C. Davis Journal of International Law and Policy 163, 165.

brought partisans within the law and the *1977 Additional Protocols* extended combatant status to some guerrilla or irregular fighters. In more recent years, despite opposition from some states, it has generally been accepted that all participants in a conflict are now covered in some way by international humanitarian law.

This expansion of the laws of armed conflict can be seen as a triumph of humanitarianism over the traditional, state-centred, laws of the Hague and Geneva.[6] Alternatively, it can be regarded as a political triumph – or defeat – that undermined the traditional framework of law.[7] In this paper, however, I will argue that while the expansion of the law might have been influenced by ethical or political considerations,[8] the fundamental nature of the law was not changed. If anything, the same kind of law – the law that Johnson described as stripped of value and tied to the competence of the state – was extended rather than diminished. As the law extended its reach, an array of conflicts and participants, which were previously considered to belong to a realm of justice or ethical contest beyond the state, became part of the state's legal domain.

I show this effect by looking first at the creation of the Hague and Geneva Conventions. The delegates at the Hague would not extend legal protection to irregular belligerents; they considered such fighters as heroic, autonomous, persons who could not be contained within the law. In much the same way, the delegates at Geneva would not bring autonomous groups or individuals within the law – no matter how just their cause. Law could only regulate the actions of states and their armies. I argue that this understanding echoes and reaffirms deep seated philosophical and cultural ideas about the state and modern law. In these narratives, formal, non-ideological law is considered to be synonymous with the state. At the same time, these narratives express, to varying degrees, some regard for the free-fighter outside the state and ambivalence towards the legal power of the state.

In the following section, I show how this ambivalence towards state and law grew in the second part of the twentieth century, as revolutionary writers

6 See, eg Claude Pilloud et al, *Commentary on the Additional Protocols of 8 June 1977 to the Geneva Conventions of 12 August 1949* (M Nijhoff Publishers 1987) 1324; George H Aldrich, 'Guerilla Combatants and Prisoner of War Status' (1981–1982) 31 Am U L Rev 871, 872; Boyd van Dijk, 'Internationalizing Colonial War: On the Unintended Consequences of the Interventions of the International Committee of the Red Cross in South-East Asia, 1945–1949' (2021) 250 Past & Present 243, 280; Sandesh Sivakumaran, 'Re-envisaging the International Law of Internal Armed Conflict' (2011) 22 EJIL 219, 219–220.

7 See, eg Geoffrey Best, *War and Law since 1945* (Clarendon Press 1994) 259.

8 See Amanda Alexander 'International Humanitarian Law, Postcolonialism and the 1977 Geneva Protocol I' (2016) 17 Melb J Intl Law 15.

and movements outlined the possibilities of different forms of violence against the state. The Diplomatic Conferences to draft the Additional Protocols provided an opportunity to extend the law to these forms of violence and, perhaps, even to recognise the just struggle of irregular fighters. Law, for a moment, appeared the tool of a political struggle. Yet, while the Additional Protocol I extended the law to areas that were previously extra-legal, it did not change the formal, neutral, non-ideological character of the law. Rather it reasserted and multiplied the same form of legal criteria. Moreover, as I show in the final section, even attempts to adjust or reject these rules led to more law and more legal work. Despite the attempts by some states to maintain a category of combatants outside the law, the law has continually reasserted itself, becoming ever more complex and ubiquitous. Thus, the expansion of international law has not overturned the formal law of the state with ethical or political objections; rather the formal law, which is synonymous with the state, is continually reaffirmed.

2 The Free-Fighter and the Law of Nations at the Hague

The 1899 and 1907 Hague Conferences laid down a set of laws for war in a society of civilised states.[9] The civilised state and its laws are almost a tautology in Western political philosophy and sociological thought. The early liberal political philosophers described the state as a pacified realm, governed by a sovereign's laws. They juxtaposed this against an uncivilised, natural world which was free and violent and lawless – a war of every man against every man.[10]

In social contract theory, men are drawn (or tricked, according to Rousseau[11]) into accepting the laws that shape a pacified society. In doing so, they choose security and certainty over the freedom, but violence, of the natural state. For other liberal thinkers, the move to a civilised state is more of a gradual development; the state becomes stronger and its purposes and agents more differentiated. War becomes the preserve of a particular group of citizens.[12]

9 See, eg Antonio Cassese in Paola Gaeta and Salvatore Zappalà (eds), *The Human Dimension of International Law: Selected Papers of Antonio Cassese* (Oxford University Press 2008) 105, 119; Best (n 7) 174.

10 Hobbes, *Leviathan* (Wordsworth Editions 2014) 97.

11 Jean-Jacques Rousseau in Susan Dunn (ed), *The Social Contract and the First and Second Discourses* (Yale University Press 2002) 125.

12 Mark Neocleous, 'O Effeminacy! Effeminacy!' War, Masculinity and the Myth of Liberal Peace' (2013) 19(1) *European Journal of International Relations* 93, 97.

These philosophical accounts, especially the social contract ones, might seem like a story or, as Peter Fitzpatrick argues,[13] a myth about the development of the civilised state. There is certainly much in these models of the sovereign state and the free state that can be regarded as romanticisation or reification. Yet, this is a story about the nature of modern law that is repeated again and again, in both more 'scientific' and more irrational forms, until it has come to produce a definition of law and the state that has had great significance for international law and relations. Max Weber's enormously influential, sociological account of the modern state and modern law, reaffirms and cements this understanding. Weber's definition of the state in *Politics as a Vocation* as a 'human community that (successfully) claims the monopoly of the legitimate use of physical force within a given territory',[14] is widely accepted as the definition of the state. Weber considered this type of political community as a product of evolution. First, *ad hoc* warrior groups solidified into a more stable warrior community, which owned their weapons and lived off the plunder of war.[15] Then, gradually, a political community might gain control over the warrior group and their violence – whether through pacification, disintegration of the warrior group or the imposition of political control.[16] The modern state is established when the political community achieves control over the legitimate use of force.

When this happens, the state controls its own army which is a mass, disciplined group. Discipline, according to Weber, means that the obedience of a plurality of men is rationally uniform.[17] Discipline is impersonal and neutral; it places itself at the disposal of every power that claims its service and knows how to promote it.[18] In this way, the soldiers of the modern state do not fight for individual or group causes, nor do they follow personal motivations or values. They simply obey and represent the state. As Weber writes, 'Discipline puts the drill for the sake of habitual routinized skill in place of heroic ecstasy, loyalty, spirited enthusiasm for a leader and personal devotion to him, the cult of honor, or the cultivation of personal fitness as an art'.[19]

The state's monopoly on force requires, according to Weber, continuous administration, the control of the material goods needed for violence, and an

13 Peter Fitzpatrick, *The Mythology of Modern Law* (Routledge 1992).

14 Max Weber, 'Politics As A Vocation' in Max Weber (ed), *Essays In Sociology* (H H Gerth And C Wright Mills trs, OUP 1946) 4.

15 Max Weber in Guenther Roth and Claus Wittich (eds), *Economy and Society: An Outline of Interpretive Sociology* (University of California Press 1978) 906.

16 ibid 908.

17 ibid 1149.

18 ibid 1149.

19 ibid 1149.

associated administrative staff that is separated from the material means of violence.[20] Alongside the creation of this bureaucratic state, societies develop a legal system with a formal, "rational" character.[21]

Moreover, when violence belongs only to the state, this right to use violence, to dominate men, must rest on some form of legitimation.[22] This distinguishes it from the violence of the warrior group, which required no legitimation or normativity.[23] In the modern state, the most characteristic form of legitimation is domination 'by virtue of "legality", by virtue of the belief in the validity of legal statute and functional "competence" based on rationally created *rules*'.[24] Thus, there is a link between the modern state's monopoly on violence, and the idea of a formal rule of law, also characteristic of the modern civilised state.

The laws of the Hague seem to render, almost perfectly, this Weberian concept of modern law and the modern state. The Hague Conventions made it clear that the state could use force to achieve its aims. There was no need for an ethical assessment of those aims; their legitimacy was derived from the facts of statehood and law. As Johnson points out, the emphasis on military necessity in the Hague Conventions meant that any inquiry into the legitimacy of the use of force could be answered by 'reasons of state'.[25] Moreover, the Conventions made it clear that *only* the state could use force. They laid down strict, precise conditions on belligerents to ensure this. Lawful combatants had to be members of armies, militias or volunteer corps that were commanded by a responsible person. They had to bear a distinctive emblem, carry arms openly, and conduct their operations in accordance with the laws and customs of war. As President Martens stated, the goal of the Conference was to ensure that forces were, above all, 'organised and disciplined'[26] – a realisation of Weber's disciplined modern soldier. The one exception was the *levée en masse,* when a population rose up spontaneously against an invader. In such a situation, if the population can act as the state, before the state has succumbed, it will have some rights. Once, however, the invading state has achieved control, any individual actions against it will fall outside the law.

Yet, while such fighters had no legal status, this is not to say that they had no legitimacy at all. All the delegates agreed that patriots, fighting for their

20 Max Weber, 'Politics as a Vocation' (n 14) 80, 82.
21 Max Weber, 'Economy and Society,' (n 15) 809.
22 Max Weber, 'Politics as a Vocation' (n 14) 78.
23 Max Weber, 'Economy and Society,' (n 15) 905.
24 Max Weber, 'Politics as a Vocation' (n 14) 79.
25 Johnson (n 2) 262.
26 Scott (n 1) 547.

country, had a great deal of moral legitimacy. Patriotism was described as a higher morality, a virtue that could inspire admirable heroism. Switzerland and Belgium, in particular, extolled the higher morality of those who fought for their soil.[27] Colonel Künzli pointed to historical examples, glorious epochs, when not only able-bodied men but also old men, children and women took part in the battles.[28] There was a sacred right for a population to act in such a way; but it was not a legal right.

This was made clear when the Swiss and British delegations suggested amendments that would give more rights to the population of an occupied country that resisted invaders. Russia, Germany and the Netherlands strongly opposed these suggestions, holding that the draft was already too liberal in recognising 'non-soldiers'.[29] Martens, speaking as President but also representing Russia, responded that it was not the aim of the conference to prescribe laws for heroes or to curb the impulses of patriots.[30] This was a point that Martens repeated a few times. He said that neither the Conference of Brussels of 1874 nor that of the Hague could accomplish an impossible task, namely to codify the heroic acts of individuals or populations.[31] Martens explained:

> The Brussels Conference, therefore, by no means intended to abolish the right of defense, or to create a code which would abolish this right. It was, on the contrary, imbued with the idea that heroes are not created by codes, but that the only code that heroes have is their self-abnegation, their will and their patriotism. The Conference understood that its duty was not to try to formulate a code for cases which cannot be foreseen and codified, such as acts of heroism on the part of populations rising against the enemy … They have left the doors open to the heroic sacrifices which nations might be ready to make in their defense; a heroic nation is, like heroes, above codes, rules, and facts.[32]

In this way Martens, while expressing his admiration for heroism, states that it must necessarily take place outside the Hague's law. This outcome was reinforced, if somewhat hidden, by Martens' next words, which state that while the Conference could not agree on every case, belligerents would remain

27 Scott (n 1) 551.
28 Scott (n 1) 551.
29 William I Hull, *The Two Hague Peace Conferences* (Ginn and Company 1908) 220.
30 Scott (n 1) 551.
31 Scott (n 1) 551.
32 Scott (n 1) 547.

under 'the protection and empire of the principles of international law, as they result from the usages established between civilized nations, from the laws of humanity, and the requirements of the public conscience.'[33]

This principle, which came to be known as the Martens clause, eventually succeeded in quieting the debates on this matter. It was placed in similar terms in the Preamble to the Hague Conventions, alongside other aspirational statements. As Antonio Cassese notes, the clause was ambiguous and evasive, whether intentionally or unwittingly.[34] This ambiguity encouraged the various Parties to hope that they might argue for their interpretations in the future.[35] Certainly, the references to laws of humanity led some international lawyers in later years, particularly in the 1990s, to argue that the Martens Clause supports a broad and humane interpretation of the laws of war.[36] Yet, despite these hopeful interpretations, more authoritative statements continued to read the Martens clause as simply saying that customary law continues to exist alongside treaty law.[37] This is a reading that adds little to the accepted understanding of international law; it does not allow a lawyer to posit new laws or to 'build castles out of sand'.[38]

As such the Martens clause, however comforting, did not bring irregulars inside the law.[39] If anything, it allowed the stricter position to continue in law and practice.[40] Irregulars would not necessarily be considered unethical or illegitimate. They might be admirable. But they would simply be something outside the law and, therefore, beyond the protection of the law. As Mr Rahusen of the Netherlands said:

> It is optional with the population as to whether or not it conforms to the conditions which constitute the status of a belligerent, but it will have to bear the consequences of not doing so.[41]

33 Scott (n 1) 548.
34 Antonio Cassese, 'The Martens Clause: Half a Loaf or Simply Pie in the Sky? (2000) 11(1) *European Journal of International Law* 187, 189.
35 ibid 198.
36 See Theodor Meron, 'The Martens Clause, Principles of Humanity, and Dictates of Public Conscience' (2000) 94(1) *The American Journal of International Law* 78, 80; Cassese (n 34) 196–200.
37 Meron (n 36) 87–88.
38 Meron (n 36) 88.
39 Cassese (n 34) 198.
40 Cassese (n 34) 198.
41 Scott (n 1) 553

The Hague delegates' belief that heroism is admirable, but something beyond law, echoes another aspect of the narrative of the modern state. For even the most liberal of the political philosophers felt some admiration for the idealised figure of the free-fighter, the warrior or savage of the world before the state and they regretted the loss of martial virtues.[42] Mark Neocleous argues that these philosophers considered that the process of pacification had come at a cost – it had separated the citizen from the warrior[43] and taken from men the chance to realise their humanity in combat.

The idea that the liberal, juridified state necessarily excludes freedom and warrior values is seen in other accounts of the modern state. It takes one of its most extreme forms in Nietzsche, who describes the essence of civilisation as turning man from a beast of prey into a domesticated animal.[44] For Nietzsche the 'tame' modern man is a wretched and unedifying worm compared to the fearsome warriors – the blonde beasts – of the past.[45] The modern, uniformed and 'uniform' soldier is nothing like these warriors.[46] For Nietzsche, escape from uniformity, mediocrity and pacification can only come with the end of the state, and the creation of an individual's own law.[47]

Nietzsche's work can be seen as an extreme reaction to liberal thought. Yet, Weber, in his own account of the development of the modern state, was influenced by Nietzsche's romanticism of the hero.[48] In *Economy and Society*, Weber describes the superseded warrior society as a fraternity of men with free access to women (stolen or purchased),[49] whose only work is the waging of war and the care for their weapons. Weber does not provide a gloss on this commentary nor any judgement on these privileges, but he does place it in stark contrast to the asceticism of modernity. The asceticism and self-control of Protestantism, Weber says, is aimed against one thing – the spontaneous enjoyment of life and all that it has to offer.[50]

---

42 Fitzpatrick and Neocleous describe this in detail: Neocleous (n 12); Fitzpatrick (n 13).

43 Neocleous (n 12) 93, 97 referring to Ferguson.

44 Friedrich Nietzsche, *On the Genealogy of Morals* (Michael A Scarpitti tr, Penguin Books 2013) 30.

45 ibid 30–31.

46 Friedrich Nietzsche, *Thus Spake Zarathustra* (Algora Publishing 2003) 35.

47 ibid 38, 48.

48 Stephen A Kent, 'Weber, Goethe, and the Nietzschean Allusion: Capturing the Source of the "Iron Cage"
Metaphor' (1983) 44 Sociological Analysis 297, 301.

49 Franz zu Solms-Laubach, *Nietzsche and Early German and Austrian Sociology* (De Gruyter 2007) 78; Bryan S Turner, 'Max Weber and the Spirit of Resentment: The Nietzsche Legacy' (2011) 11 Journal of Classical Sociology 75, 76.

50 Max Weber, *The Protestant Ethic and the Spirit of Capitalism* (Talcott Parsons tr, Charles Scribner's Sons 1930) 167.

Thus, these varied accounts of the modern state see the state and its law as inimical to a particular kind of freedom, represented by an idealised autonomous warrior. They all show a degree of respect, or nostalgia, for the warrior who necessarily exists outside law. This regard for heroism outside law is shown in the debates at the Hague. Patriotism and heroism were seen as virtues to be admired. The idea that law might weaken these virtues was a widespread concern. Ultimately, however, it was agreed that these virtues could not be provided for by law. Individuals or groups acting autonomously could be admirable, could be heroes, but they would clearly be acting outside the law.

3 The Geneva Conventions and the Neutrality of Law

This understanding of the nature and limitations of law was reiterated at the conference to draft the Geneva Conventions in the 1940s. Delegates once again considered whether partisans – understood as those in occupied territory who take up arms against the occupying power[51] – should have some kind of belligerent status.

The Draft Convention, approved by the XVIIth International Red Cross Conference and known as the Stockholm text, repeated the *levee en masse* provision for citizens of a non-occupied country. It then added a provision covering partisans in an occupied territory:

6)Persons belonging to a military organization or to an organized resistance movement constituted in an occupied territory to resist the occupying Power, on condition:

(a) That such organization has, either through its responsible leader, through the Government which it acknowledges, or through the mediation of a Party to the conflict, notified the occupying Power of its participation in the conflict.

(b) That its members are under the command of a responsible leader; that they wear at all times a fixed distinctive emblem, recognizable at a distance; that they carry arms openly; that they conform to the laws and customs of war; and in particular, that they treat nationals of the occupying Power who fall into their hands in accordance with the provisions of the present Convention.

51 International Committee of the Red Cross, *Report on the Work of the Conference of Government Experts for the Study of the Conventions for the Protection of War Victims* (14–26 April 1947) 108.

This provision makes it clear that the ICRC expected partisans to resemble ordinary combatants and to distinguish themselves. They were also expected to be under the command of a government or, at least, a responsible leader, and to act in a disciplined, legal manner, following the laws of warfare and the Convention.

Some delegations – notably Denmark, the USSR and Israel – wanted civilians to have more scope to fight in an occupied territory. They argued that when there was an illegal war, a war of aggression, waged in an illegal manner against civilians, those civilians should be able to act in self-defence. Mr Cohn, representing Denmark, suggested an amendment that would recognize the right of civilian persons to defend themselves when their life, their health or their means of livelihood were threatened.[52]

Major Steinberg for Israel supported this amendment, pointing out that wars no longer only involved combatants. When, as in the Second World War, a belligerent Power was manifestly bent on exterminating a whole people, massacring women and children in cold blood, should a people not rightly and dutifully seek to defend itself? Persons attacked in this manner were surely entitled to be treated as prisoners of war when they fell into enemy hands.[53] General Slavin for the USSR also supported the Danish proposal, stating that civilians who took up arms in defence of the liberty of their country should be entitled to the same protection as members of armed forces.[54]

Other delegations, however, would not accept that civilians, seeking to defend themselves from illegal acts, should be considered to be prisoners of war. It would be inapplicable in practice, the US said, or it would weaken the Prisoners of War Convention, which applied to members of regular armed forces and others of an analogous character.[55] Miss Gutteridge for the UK stated:

> The Danish amendment would have the effect of abolishing the distinction between combatants and non-combatants. To accept the amendment would be tantamount to rejecting the principles generally accepted at the Hague, and recognized in the Prisoners of War Convention. It was essential that war, even illegal war, should be governed by those principles.[56]

52 Final Record of the Diplomatic Conference of Geneva of 1949, Vol. II Section A (Federal Political Department, Berne) 425.

53 ibid 426.

54 ibid 426

55 ibid 426.

56 ibid 426.

According to this approach, the formal legal rules that restrict belligerency to the disciplined representatives of state parties had to be maintained even in the face of clear injustice or violence against civilians. Individual or unorganised acts by civilians could not be countenanced by the law; they would undermine it completely.

Indeed, some delegations were concerned that even the Stockholm text would not guarantee that partisans were properly organised and under 'effective command'.[57] As Sir Robert Craigie of the United Kingdom stated, militia and volunteer corps would obviously be under effective command, but resistance movements were a new situation.[58] It was essential, Craigie insisted, to establish a clear distinction between such movements and 'small groups of snipers'.[59] The United Kingdom and Belgium therefore suggested other amendments that would ensure that partisans were really under effective command. One suggestion was a requirement that resistance groups should be organised in military formations, and that the organised resistance movement must be in proper control of its formations and subordinate units.[60] The United Kingdom also wanted to ensure that those in command of partisans should be in a position to receive communications and to reply to them.[61] This communications requirement was not something that was required of regular armed forces. Mr Gardner, however, explained that this was because it was assumed that a belligerent Power could always be communicated with. That assumption was not applicable in the case of irregulars who were not responsible to any government recognized by the adverse belligerent.[62]

Therefore, imposing a communications requirement would make it more likely that the resistance movement would be attached to a government, even if that government was in exile. It would also require a headquarters, with commanders who could give orders and ensure they were complied with. Again, this would mean that the resistance movement belonged to a state and looked like disciplined regular forces.

A number of delegations agreed with these requirements, but others were concerned that additional conditions might be arbitrarily interpreted by an Occupying Power. These disputes, however, were defused by an acknowledgement that the real concern was that a resistance movement might be independent – that it might not have to depend formally on a Party

57 ibid 422.
58 ibid 428.
59 ibid 428.
60 ibid 422.
61 ibid 562.
62 ibid 242–3.

to the conflict.[63] The delegates found a new way to resolve this concern – by including the resistance movements in the provision concerning militias and other volunteer corps.[64] This ensured that partisans would have to be commanded by a State, that they would have to follow the rules of warfare, and that they would be disciplined and controlled.

In this way, the Geneva Conventions reconfirmed that the law of war was a law of nation states. It would only regulate and protect state parties. It also reconfirmed that it was the kind of law that belonged to modern states – it was formal, objective and distinct from notions of justice or ethics.

4 Just War against the State

Liberal political philosophers, like the delegates at the Hague, might have felt some ambivalent nostalgia for an age of heroes and warriors. For the most part, however, they valued the benefits that the state provided: law, certainty, that realm of pacification. More critical thinkers, however, disregarded or questioned these benefits and described the ostensible lawfulness of the state as a particular form of oppression. Right from the early days of social contract theory, Rousseau described the idea of law and government as a trick. What seemed like a benign proposal simply:

> gave new fetters to the weak and new power to the rich; irretrievably destroyed natural liberty, fixed forever the laws of property and inequality; changed an artful usurpation into an irrevocable right; and for the benefit of a few ambitious individuals subjected the rest of mankind to perpetual labor, servitude, and misery.[65]

This idea that apparently liberal law institutionalises inequality and oppression, as well as diminishing humanity in the manner described above, was further developed by Marxists, fascists and critical thinkers from the nineteenth century and achieved a widespread reach in the twentieth century.[66] In these critiques, law and civilisation are based on violence and violence always lies below the surface. The Marxist perspective, in its mid-twentieth century form, is put forward by Maurice Merleau-Ponty:

---

63 ibid 410.

64 ibid 410.

65 Rousseau (n 11) 125.

66 Francois Furet, *The Passing of an Illusion: The Idea of Communism in the Twentieth Century* (Deborah Furet tr, University of Chicago Press 1999) 171.

> Communists reply that in democracies cunning, violence, propaganda, and realpolitik in the guise of liberal principles are the substance of foreign or colonial politics and even of domestic politics. Respect for law and liberty has served to justify police suppression of strikes in America; today it serves even to justify military suppression in Indochina or in Palestine and the development of an American empire in the Middle East. The material and moral culture of England presupposes the exploitation of the colonies. The purity of principles not only tolerates but even requires violence. Thus there is a mystification in liberalism, fudging from history and by everyday events, liberal ideas belong to a system of violence of which, as Marx said, they are the "spiritual point".[67]

The argument that liberal law and society are based on and perpetuate violence made violence a justifiable and ethical tactic for these Marxist and fascist political movements.[68] As Merleau-Ponty writes: 'for the moment the question is not to know whether one accepts or rejects violence, but whether the violence with which one is allied is "progressive" and tends toward its own suspension or toward self-perpetuation.'[69]

By the 1960s, there was a well-established doctrine for practising this kind of 'progressive' violence through revolutionary people's wars. The work of revolutionaries like Lenin, Mao and Fanon laid down the strategy and principles for a new form of just ideological war, fought against imperial states that were agents of violence and oppression.[70] Frantz Fanon undertook a complex analysis of the different forms of violence that the colonised are subjected to: physical violence; material depredation; and psychological damage. He also identified the inherent violence of a lawful imperialist order – 'that peaceful violence that the world is steeped in'.[71]

Violence and war was necessary to end this violence.[72] Fanon wrote that the only cure for the violence of colonisation is violence from the colonised; this is the only way for the colonised man to find his freedom.[73] Fanon described

---

67 Maurice Merleau-Ponty, *Humanism and Terror: An Essay on the Communist Problem* (John O'Neill tr Beacon Press 1969) xiii.

68 Furet (n 66) 171.

69 Merleau-Ponty (n 67) 1.

70 Mao Tse-tung in Samuel B Griffith USMC (ed), *On Guerrilla Warfare* (Praeger Publishers 1961) 68–9; Vladimir Lenin in Todd Chretien (ed), *The State and Revolution* (Haymarket Books 2014) 44.

71 Frantz Fanon, *The Wretched of the Earth* (Constance Farrington tr, Penguin Books 1967) 81.

72 Lenin (n 70) 57; Mao (n 70) 65.

73 Fanon (n 71) 86.

violence as a cleansing force that 'frees the native from his inferiority complex and from his despair and inaction; it makes him fearless and restores his self-respect.'[74] It also brings a people together, 'since each individual forms a violent link in the great chain, a part of the great organism of violence which has surged upward in reaction to the settler's violence in the beginning.'[75] Indeed, the struggle against colonialism 'belongs in the general process of man's liberation'.[76]

Fanon's description of revolutionary violence envisages a very different form of violence to that of the obedient soldier, governed by the Hague and Geneva conventions, who acts as an instrument of the modern state. For Fanon, violence is a form of psychological regeneration of an individual and a people. For Mao Tse-Tung, and those in his tradition,[77] violence is part of a political regeneration. A revolutionary war had to be based on a politically awakened people:[78]

> The essence of Comrade Mao Tse-tung's theory of army building is that in building a people's army prominence must be given to politics, i.e., the army must first and foremost be built on a political basis. Politics is the commander, politics is the soul of everything. Political work is the lifeline of our army. True, a people's army must pay attention to the constant improvement of its weapons and equipment and its military technique, but in its fighting it does not rely purely on weapons and technique, it relies mainly on politics, on the proletarian revolutionary consciousness and courage of the commanders and fighters, on the support and backing of the masses.[79]

A politically awakened people would form a people's army, which famously disavowed the differentiation between soldier and citizen, which characterises the modern state and is codified in the Hague and Geneva Conventions. As Mao writes:

---

74 ibid 94.

75 ibid 93.

76 Frantz Fanon, 'The Algerian War and Man's Liberation' in *Towards the African Revolution: Political Essays* (Haakon Chevalier tr, Grove Press 1967) 145.

77 See, eg Lin Piao, *Long Live the Victory of People's War!* (Foreign Languages Press 1967) 30; General Võ Nguyên Giáp, *People's War, People's army* (The Gioi Publishers 2004) 28.

78 J Bowyer Bell, *The Myth of the Guerrilla* (Knopf 1971) 21–2.

79 Lin Piao (n 77) 30.

> [T]here are those who say: "I am a farmer," or, "I am a student"; "I can discuss literature but not military arts." This is incorrect. There is no profound difference between the farmer and the soldier. You must have courage. You simply leave your farms and become soldiers. That you are farmers is of no difference, and if you have education, that is so much the better. When you take your arms in hand, you become soldiers; when you are organized, you become military units.[80]

The dissolution of the civilian/combatant distinction, like other aspects of guerrilla warfare, did not comply with the laws of war. Revolutionary writers, however, made no apology for this. Mao wrote, 'We should honestly admit the guerrilla character of the Red Army. It is no use being ashamed of this. On the contrary, this guerrilla character is precisely our distinguishing feature, or strong point, and our means of defeating the enemy'.[81]

Indeed, rather than excusing guerrilla tactics, revolutionary writers emphasised the heroism, bravery and self-sacrifice of guerrilla fighters.[82] The guerrilla fighter emerged as an idealised fighter, the warrior undiminished by the state or the law. The guerrilla's wars became, as Fanon stated, fights for man's liberation.[83]

5 The Juridification of the Free-Fighter

In 1977, the Additional Protocol I extended the reach of international law to these wars of liberation and the guerrillas who fought in them. For the first time in the modern history of international law, the state's monopoly on legitimate violence seemed to be broken.

I have discussed this change in more detail elsewhere, but when the ICRC brought States together in 1974 to 'reaffirm and develop' international humanitarian law, it provided a forum for Third World states to press for new approaches to international law – approaches that drew on the revolutionary principles discussed above.[84] In particular they argued that national liberation

---

80 Mao (n 70) 73.

81 Cited in J L S Girling, *People's War: The Conditions and the Consequences in China and in South-East Asia* (Allen and Unwin 1969) 77.

82 Piao (n 77) 27–8; Mao (n 70) 85–86; Giáp, (n 70) 22, 47–8.

83 Fanon (n 76) 145.

84 Alexander (n 8).

conflicts should be recognised as international conflicts,[85] and that the 'freedom fighters' who fought in them should have combatant privileges – even when they did not distinguish themselves.[86] Some states advocated for these changes by referring to the justice of these wars, and calling for a distinction in the law between just and unjust wars.[87]

Many Western states and commentators were horrified by these suggestions. Like their predecessors at Geneva, they considered the resurrection of just war thinking as completely inimical to the established law of war.[88] Baxter, who represented the United States, wrote that separate bodies of law for just and unjust wars could bring down the whole fragile fabric of the humanitarian law of war.[89] International law was meant to be neutral – blind to causes or values or politics.[90] It had, as Israel stated, 'its own origins and methods of work, characterized by a high degree of neutrality, objectivity and discretion … '[91]. Reference to the justice of wars, Sir Colin Crowe (United Kingdom) argued, was dangerous and 'totally alien to all the principles of international humanitarian law.'[92] He went on to say it 'struck at the very heart of the Geneva Conventions and the philosophy of equality of rights and non-discrimination which inspired them.'[93]

Even when the Third World's suggestions were not framed within a just and unjust war dichotomy, they were still seen as subjective politics – a failure to

85 Michael Bothe, Karl Josef Partsch and Waldemar A Solf, *New Rules for Victims of Armed Conflicts: Commentary on the Two 1977 Protocols Additional to the Geneva Conventions of 1949* (Martinus Nijhoff Publishers 1982) 40.

86 See, eg *Official Records of the Diplomatic Conference on the Reaffirmation and Development of International Humanitarian Law Applicable in Armed Conflicts, Geneva (1974–1977)* (Hein 1981) vol 5, 147: Mr Boudjakdji (Algeria) at 38, Mr Plaka (Albania) at 146, Mr Dugersuren (Mongolia) at 191.

87 ibid: see, eg Ould Dada (Mauritania) at 13, Mr Mishra (India) at 198, China at 119–120.

88 David P Forsythe, 'The 1974 Diplomatic Conference on Humanitarian Law: Some Observations' (1975) 69 The American Journal of International Law 77, 80; Richard Baxter, 'Humanitarian Law or Humanitarian Politics? The 1974 Diplomatic Conference on Humanitarian Law' (1975) 16 Harvard International Law Journal 1, 17; Capt John F DePue, 'The Amended First Article to the First Draft Protocol Additional to the Geneva Conventions of 1949 – Its Impact Upon Humanitarian Constraints Governing Armed Conflict' (1977) 75 Military Law Review 75, 97.

89 Richard Baxter, 'The Geneva Conventions of 1949 and Wars of National Liberation' in Detlev F Vagts (ed), *Humanizing the Laws of War: Selected Writings of Richard Baxter* (Oxford University Press 2013) 285.

90 *Official Records of the Diplomatic Conference* (n 86) vol 6, 41: Mr Hess (Israel).

91 ibid vol 5, 177.

92 ibid vol 5, 134: Sir Colin Crowe (United Kingdom).

93 ibid.

understand international law or legal reasoning.[94] This was the case even with issues that, while having significant political implications, could be supported by legal reasoning. For example, today, the war of a colonised people against a foreign imperial state can look objectively like an international conflict; the 1970s insistence that this interpretation is nothing but subjective politics is a little hard to understand. David Forsythe, however, explains the contemporary Western perspective. He states that the core Western argument was based on 'geomilitary scale'.[95] That is, only a war between the 'regular troops' of two states could reach the level of violence that made for an international armed conflict. This, and this alone, was considered an objective indicator. If the 'objective' indicator of statehood was not present, then it meant referring to a normative judgement about the cause of the fighting which was 'alien to the *jus in bello* and traditional humanitarian law'.[96] This explanation shows the degree to which 'real' law was considered synonymous with the state.

Yet, while Western states remained uneasy about the 'political' language and demands of the Third World, they ultimately gave in to 'politics' – international politics, the politics of the forum, and the politics of their domestic constituencies.[97] The number of states supporting national liberation conflicts meant that the amendment to recognise them as international conflicts was eventually passed in committee, with 70 in favour, 21 against, and 13 abstentions.[98] This issue had seemed so fundamental to Western states' view of law that it was feared, for a moment, that they might abandon the Conference over the vote.[99] This did not, however, come to pass. The Western states decided not to destroy the Conference over a point that would have little real effect, now that the decolonisation movement was essentially over.[100] Nor, Mantilla suggests, did they want to appear racist.[101] The most they were prepared to do was to abstain, citing their concerns about the neutrality and clarity of international law.

The question of combatant status, however, required more negotiation and compromise. Some Third World states argued that members of national

94 Forsythe (n 88) 87–88.
95 ibid 80.
96 ibid 80.
97 Giovanni Mantilla, *Lawmaking under Pressure: International Humanitarian Law and Internal Armed Conflict* (Cornell University Press 2020), 150.
98 Bothe, Partsch and Solf (n 85) 43.
99 Charles Lysaght, 'The Attitude of Western Countries' in Antonio Cassese (ed), *The New Humanitarian Law of Armed Conflict* (Editoriale Scientifica 1979), 354.
100 ibid 354.
101 Mantilla (n 97) 150. Hays Parks makes much the same argument: W Hays Parks, 'Air War and the Law of War' (1990) Air Force Law Review 1, 79.

liberation movements should have combatant privileges without having to distinguish themselves from civilians.[102] Indeed, North Vietnam argued that the 'new law of the people's war' was that the lives of national liberation armies were inseparable from the civilian population.[103]

Most Western states, however, wanted to keep the traditional requirements of the Hague and Geneva Conventions.[104] As Mr Reed (US), said:

> In our view, a combatant who deliberately fails to distinguish himself from other civilians while engaging in combat operations has committed such an extraordinary violation of the laws of war and so prejudices the protection for civilians that he loses his entitlement to be a prisoner of war, and, along with it, any immunity from punishment he may have had for acts of violence against the adversary.[105]

The US position, however, softened. Mr Aldrich, the head of the US delegation, later wrote that to ask a guerrilla to distinguish himself at all times is like telling him to go around with a bull's eye pinned to his chest.[106] At the Conference, Aldrich worked hard to find a compromise between the Western adherence to traditional requirements and the revolutionary insistence that guerrillas should never have to distinguish themselves. The result was Article 44, which stated that combatants had to distinguish themselves from the point of deployment. This removed the strict delimitation of combatant status, allowing people to move between civilian and combatant status. Article 43 preserved the traditional requirement that combatants should be organised forces belonging to a party – but now a party could be a national liberation movement – not just a state.

Many Western delegations remained uneasy about the new provisions. They acknowledged their misgivings about the article when they voted and referred to it as a compromise.[107] Nevertheless, once again, they found it more

102 *Official Records of the Diplomatic Conference* (n 86) vol 14, 344, 324, 531: North Vietnam, Nigeria, North Korea, Pakistan, Ghana and Lesotho.

103 *Official Records of the Diplomatic Conference* (n 86) vol 14, 466.

104 *Official Records of the Diplomatic Conference* (n 86) vol 14: see, eg the US at 475, Brazil at 507, Switzerland at 508, Federal Republic of Germany at 515, Australia at 525, UK, Israel and the Netherlands at 526. Belgium was an exception.

105 *Official Records of the Diplomatic Conference* (n 86) vol 14, 477: Mr Reed (US) speaking.

106 Aldrich (n 6) 872.

107 *Official Records of the Diplomatic Conference* (n 86) vol 15, 177, 180, 182, 185.

politically feasible to abstain than to vote against the new rule.[108] As a result, the provisions were adopted by 66 votes to 2 with 18 abstentions.[109]

These provisions went a long way towards bringing the kind of movements and people that were traditionally outside the law into the law. This result might seem like a triumph for the advocates for a new, just law of war. Yet the extension of the law was just that – an extension and amplification of the same kind of legal language and framework that had been used at the Hague and Geneva. Article 44 may, as the ICRC acknowledged, have been designed to deal with a form of guerrilla warfare that had always been outside the law.[110] Yet it made no mention of guerrilla warfare,[111] nor did it suggest the values or voice of a revolutionary movement. Rather, the Article is expressed in legalistic language, which is ostensibly objective, yet deliberately obfuscatory. It continues to assess combatant status using external, neutral criteria – distinction from the point of deployment. 'Deployment', however, was a term that was known at the time to be open to different interpretations. Indeed, Aldrich said that it was chosen because its very ambiguity made it acceptable to more delegations.[112] The provision, therefore, creates a foundation and a new set of parameters for ongoing legalistic argument about how formerly extra-legal figures would be governed by international law. The free-fighter, the hero who seemed to only exist outside law, could now be assessed through legal forms.

This legalistic yet ambiguous provision also provided the basis for the Additional Protocol I's definition of the civilian – the first definition of the civilian in international law. Article 50 states that civilians are those who were not covered by Article 43 or Article 4 of the Third Geneva Convention. This 'negative' definition,[113] like the definition of the combatant, is ethically neutral, lacking substantive content. Moreover, because of its reliance on Article 43, it shares the ambiguity inherent in the provisions on combatant status. Thus, although the civilian has become the moral centre of international humanitarian law,[114] the definition reaffirms and extends a particular form of legal reasoning and contestation.

108 Mantilla (n 96) 161.

109 Brazil and Israel voted against. NZ, Nicaragua, Spain, Thailand, UK, Uruguay, Argentina, Australia, Bolivia, Canada, Chile, Colombia, Denmark, Guatemala, Holy See, Ireland, Italy, Japan abstained from the vote: *Official Records of the Diplomatic Conference* (n 86) vol 15, 155.

110 Pilloud (n 6) 520.

111 ibid 520.

112 Aldrich (n 6) 878–879.

113 Pilloud et al (n 6) 610.

114 See, eg Nils Melzer, 'Direct Participation in Hostilities: Operationalizing the ICRC's Guidance' (2009) 103 American Society of International Law Proceedings 299, 299.

This ambiguity is only further increased by Article 51, another fundamental provision in international humanitarian law.[115] Article 51 states that civilians will enjoy general protection unless and for such time as they take a direct part in hostilities. As the next section shows, this provision opened up a new field of legal criteria and argumentation that, eventually, brought every participant and every conflict within the law.

6 Universal Law

The complexity and political implications of these provisions meant that many states, especially military powers, refused to ratify the Additional Protocol I for a long time. As the political landscape changed, however, acceptance of the Additional Protocol grew. From the 1990s onwards, more states ratified Additional Protocol I and it became more common to see it referred to as customary international law.[116] There were, however, still some objectors to the new legal regime; the most conspicuous were the United States and Israel. These objections became particularly noticeable at the beginning of the 21st century when the US became involved in the 'war on terror'. This was a transnational war, fought against combatants who did not belong to a state and who rejected international humanitarian law.[117] As Sean Murphy wrote, they operated 'in a free-wheeling manner unmoored from the constraints of being a sovereign entity.'[118]

The United States presented this argument in legal terminology, defining such fighters as 'unlawful combatants'.[119] As they were neither civilian nor lawful combatant, their treatment was not regulated by law. Moreover, the United States argued that the entire conflict with Al Qaeda fell outside the law. As it was not an international conflict between states, it was not governed by common article 2 of the Geneva Conventions. Nor, the United States maintained, could it be covered by common article 3, which provided

115 Pilloud et al (n 6) 615.

116 Amanda Alexander, 'A Short History of International Humanitarian Law' (2015) 26 European Journal of International Law 109, 137.

117 Sean D Murphy, 'Evolving Geneva Convention Paradigms in the War on Terrorism: Applying the Core Rules to the Release of Persons Deemed Unprivileged Combatants' (2007) 75 George Washington Law Review 1105, 1112.

118 ibid 1112.

119 Ryan Goodman, 'The Detention of Civilians in Armed Conflict' (2009) 103 Am. J. Int'l L. 48, 62.

minimum protection in 'conflict not of an international character', as the conflict with Al Qaeda was 'international in scope'.[120]

Some critics, horrified by the United States' position and the subsequent internment of combatants in the 'legal black hole'[121] of Guantanamo Bay, accused the United States of creating a condition of extra-legality, a Schmittian state of exception in which law is suspended.[122] Other commentators, however, considered that the United States had exploited a real gap in the traditional laws of armed conflict – laws which did not regulate the new, transnational conflicts.[123] War, they recalled, had historically been perceived and governed as a relationship between states, fought by their regular armies.[124] Christopher Greenwood argued that the law of armed conflict expected both parties to have the capacity to wage war, and he explained that capacity to wage war is not the same as the ability to use force. Capacity to wage war requires the apparatus of the state: territory, a legal system, armed forces.[125]

As Al Qaeda did not have the apparatus of a state, it could not legally make war.[126] Since it was not a state, and could not legally make war, it had 'no armed forces as such' and no right to take life.[127] As such, any 'act of war' which Al-Qaeda committed would be a criminal act.[128] In this traditional, if tautologous, explanation, legal war is synonymous with the state.

Common article 3, these commentators agree, only extended the reach of the law a little way beyond international conflicts. It had been drafted, they

---

120 Marko Milanovic, 'Lessons for Human Rights and Humanitarian Law in the War on Terror: Comparing Hamdan and the Israeli Targeted Killings Case' (2007) 89 International Review of the Red Cross 373, 377.

121 Johan Steyn, 'Guantánamo Bay: The Legal Black Hole' (2004) 53(1) The International and Comparative Law Quarterly 1.

122 Fleur Johns, *Non-Legality in International Law: Unruly Law* (Cambridge University Press 2013) 69; Joshua Comaroff, 'Terror and Territory: Guantánamo and the Space of Contradiction' (2007) 19 Public Culture 381, 383; Simon Reid-Henry, 'Exceptional Sovereignty? Guantánamo Bay and the Re-Colonial Present' (2007) 39 Antipode 627, 630. These works all discuss this approach, but all find it unsatisfactory as a description of a realm that seems to have been created by a certain form of politico-juridical power.

123 See, eg Geoffrey S Corn, 'Hamdan, Lebanon, and the Regulation of Hostilities: The Need to Recognize a Hybrid Category of Armed Conflict ' (2007) 40 Vanderbilt Journal of Transnational Law 295, 296; Murphy (n 116) 1112.

124 Murphy (n 117) 1113; Christopher Greenwood, 'War, Terrorism, and International Law' (2003) 56 Current Legal Problems 505, 511.

125 ibid 511–2, 529.

126 Jordan J Paust, 'Post-9/11 Overreaction and Fallacies Regarding War and Defense, Guantánamo, the Status of Persons, Treatment, Judicial Review of Detention, and Due Process in Military Commissions' (2004) 79(4) Notre Dame Law Review 1335, 1340.

127 Greenwood (n 124) 529.

128 ibid 528–9.

argue, to deal with a civil war within a state – something like the Spanish Civil War.[129] In these cases, the insurgent group needs to have the semblance of a state: a government; an organised, disciplined, military force; and control of significant portions of territory as their own.[130]

Whether the United States had suspended an existing law or exploited a legal lacuna, the law soon reasserted itself to fill any gaps. A series of court cases refused to accept that the inmates of Guantanamo fell outside the law. In *Hamdan*, the Court rejected the US argument that the conflict with Al Qaeda was not covered by the Geneva Conventions. The Court held that the term 'conflict not of an international character' in common article 3 was used in contradistinction to a conflict between nations.[131] This broad interpretation suggested that common article 3 would cover *all* conflicts between a state and individuals not associated with a state.[132] It certainly, the Court held, covered Hamdan and it meant that he could not be kept outside the law. Common article 3 required that Hamdan be tried by a 'regularly constituted court affording all the judicial guarantees which are recognized as indispensable by civilized peoples.'[133] The Rule of Law, the Court stated, would prevail here and it would extend to Hamdan.[134] Hamdan, and his fight, were thereby gathered beneath the umbrella of the law.

The Israeli Supreme Court established the ubiquity of law even more thoroughly in *The Public Committee Against Torture in Israel* (*PCATI*) *v Israel* ('*Targeted Killings Case*'). The PCATI brought the case, arguing that the Israeli government's policy of preventative strikes, or targeted killings, against terrorists was illegal under domestic and international law. The PCATI first argued that the laws of war could not apply to Israel's actions in the occupied territories. This was because, the PCATI explained, the laws of war deal primarily with international conflicts and the armed conflict between Israel and the Palestinians was not an international conflict.[135] Alternatively, the PCATI suggested that Israel could not act in self-defence against an occupied territory. The appropriate legal regime, therefore, would be the rules of policing

129 Murphy (n 117) 1115; Milanovic (n 119) 379.
130 Paust (n 126) 1341.
131 *Hamdan v Rumsfeld* 548 US 557 (2006) 630.
132 Murphy (n 117) 1138.
133 *Hamdan v Rumsfeld* 631–2.
134 *Hamdan v Rumsfeld* 635.
135 *Israel Supreme Court: Public Committee Against Torture in Israel v Israel* ('*Targeted Killings Case*') [December 16, 2006] (2007) 46 ILM 375 [4].

and law enforcement that apply in an occupied territory, rather than the laws of armed conflict.[136]

The Government's position, however, was that the laws of war did apply, even if this was not a conventional conflict. It argued that:

> [T]he laws of war apply not only to war in the classic sense, but also to other armed conflicts. International law does not include an unequivocal definition of the concept of "armed conflict". However, there is no longer any doubt that an armed conflict can exist between a state and groups and organizations which are not states. That is due, inter alia, to the military ability and means which such organizations have, as well as their willingness to use them.[137]

The Court agreed:

> Our starting point is that the law that applies to the armed conflict between Israel and the terrorist organizations in the area is the international law dealing with armed conflicts … the fact that the terrorist organizations and their members do not act in the name of a state does not turn the struggle against them into a purely internal state conflict … Indeed, in today's reality, a terrorist organization is likely to have considerable military capabilities. At times they have military capabilities that exceed those of states … It should be noted that even those who are of the opinion that the armed conflict between Israel and the terrorist organizations is not of international character, think that international humanitarian or international human rights law applies to it.[138]

In this way, the Court made it clear that the laws of armed conflict would cover a range of conflicts; the conflict did not take place in a 'normative void'.[139]

The PCATI also argued that, if the laws of war did govern the conflict, the targets were immune because they were civilians.[140] The Israeli government, in response, argued that the targets were terrorists, who were 'unlawful combatants'. This argument, like the United States' argument, would put the targets outside the law. In the alternative, the Government described the targets

136 ibid [4].
137 ibid [11].
138 ibid [21].
139 ibid [17].
140 ibid [5].

as civilians who were taking a direct part in hostilities and had, therefore, lost any legal protection.[141]

President Barak rejected the argument that international law contained a third category of 'unlawful combatants'.[142] International law, he said, only recognised two categories: lawful combatants, as defined in Article 4 of the Third Geneva Convention, and civilians. Yet those two categories covered everyone in a conflict. There are, President Barak said, 'no black holes' in international law:[143]

> Every struggle of the state – against terrorism or any other enemy – is conducted according to rules and law. There is always law which the state must comply with ... Indeed, the State's struggle against terrorism is not conducted "outside" of the law. It is conducted "inside" the law, with tools that the law places at the disposal of democratic states.[144]

Since the terrorists in this case were not, President Barak said, lawful combatants, they must be civilians. This classification of terrorists as civilians was not, as Vice-President Rivlin said, an obvious one.[145] They were, however, civilians who, for such time as they might take a direct part in hostilities, would lose the protection owed to civilians. To establish who fell into this category, President Barak undertook a legal analysis of what 'hostilities' meant, what a 'direct part' meant, and what 'for such time' meant. He also examined the meaning and assessment of proportionality in response to such actions.

President Barak noted that there was no consensus about the meaning of 'direct' or the term 'for such time'.[146] He pointed to the Commentary on the Additional Protocols that said that the determination of 'direct' would require 'some margin of judgement'. As such, 'without a comprehensive and agreed upon customary standard, there is no escaping going case by case, while narrowing the area of disagreement'.[147] President Barak proceeded to do this, considering a variety of hypothetical examples.

When this examination was applied to the facts, it meant that targeted strikes would be legal if they complied with an intricate legal analysis of a large

141 Eric Christensen, 'The Dilemma of Direct Participation in Hostilities' (2010) 19 J. Transnat'l L. & Pol'y 281, 301.
142 *Targeted Killings Case* [28].
143 ibid [61].
144 ibid [61].
145 Ibid [2].
146 ibid [34], [39].
147 ibid [34].

number of apparently formal, but intrinsically unstable, legal terms. This is shown in President Barak's conclusion:

> The result of that examination is not that such strikes are always permissible or that they are always forbidden. The approach of customary international law applying to armed conflicts of an international nature is that civilians are protected from attacks by the army. However, that protection does not exist regarding those civilians "for such time as they take a direct part in hostilities" (§51(3) of The First Protocol). Harming such civilians, even if the result is death, is permitted, on the condition that there is no other less harmful means, and on the condition that innocent civilians nearby are not harmed. Harm to the latter must be proportionate. That proportionality is determined according to a values based test, intended to balance between the military advantage and the civilian damage. As we have seen, we cannot determine that a preventative strike is always legal, just as we cannot determine that it is always illegal. All depends upon the question whether the standards of customary international law regarding international armed conflict allow that preventative strike or not.[148]

The law was never silent, President Barak insisted, the law could speak to every person and every part of conflict.[149] But what does the law say here? Nothing very clear about justice or even the rights of war. The only thing it seems to say is that a particular, and indeterminate, form of legal argumentation can and must apply in every situation. What the law really states here is its victory over alternative forms of action and thought. Indeed, President Barak makes this clear, stating that 'the State's fight against terrorism is the fight of the state against its enemies. It is also law's fight against those who rise up against it'.[150]

The link between the law and the state was shown again in the Court's conclusion, which found that the law, ubiquitous and universal, could countenance the practice of targeted killings. The state's war against all of its enemies was now embedded in the law of armed conflict. Thus, the *Targeted Killings Case* expanded the law; it juridified the state's actions, but it did not restrain them.

148 Ibid [60].
149 ibid [61].
150 Ibid [62].

This result inspired a concerned ICRC to begin its own investigation, led by Nils Melzer, into the meaning of direct participation in hostilities.[151] The aim and the result of this investigation was to define 'direct participation in hostilities' in a way that *would* restrain state action, by making it easier to move between civilian and combatant status and by limiting the way states could respond to direct participation in hostilities.[152] These changes were controversial; many international lawyers refused to support them.[153] Nevertheless, the ICRC published its report as the *Interpretive Guidance on the Notion of Direct Participation in Hostilities under International Humanitarian Law* ('the Guidance').[154]

Despite some opposition to the Guidance as an ICRC publication, it may have some important influence on the development of international humanitarian law.[155] An international law influenced by the Guidance might become more humanitarian, more protective of 'unlawful' combatants by placing them within legal categories. But it could only do so only by even further enmeshing the individual, unlawful, combatant in a juridical web. For example, the Guidance provided the following guide to when an act would constitute a direct participation in hostilities:

1. the act must be likely to adversely affect the military operations or military capacity of a party to an armed conflict or, alternatively, to inflict death, injury, or destruction on persons or objects protected against direct attack (threshold of harm), and 2. there must be a direct causal link between the act and the harm likely to result either from that act, or from a coordinated military operation of which that act constitutes an integral part (direct causation), and 3. the act must be specifically designed to directly cause the required threshold of harm in support of a party to the conflict and to the detriment of another (belligerent nexus).[156]

---

151 W Hays Parks, 'Part IX of the ICRC Direct Participation in Hostilities Study: No Mandate, No Expertise, and Legally Incorrect' (2010) 42 N.Y.U. J. Int'l L. & Pol. 769, 788–9.

152 ibid 797. See also Damien van der Toorn, 'Direct Participation in Hostilities': A Legal and Practical Road Test of the International Committee of the Red Cross's Guidance through Afghanistan' (2010) 17 Australian International Law Journal 7, 18.

153 Michael N Schmitt, *Essays on Law and War at the Fault Lines* (TMC Asser Press 2012) 514.

154 Nils Melzer, *Interpretive Guidance on the Notion of Direct Participation in Hostilities under International Humanitarian Law* (ICRC 2009).

155 Damien van der Toorn, '"Direct Participation in Hostilities": A Legal and Practical Road Test of the International Committee of the Red Cross's Guidance through Afghanistan' (2010) 17 Australian International Law Journal 7, 17.

156 Melzer (n 153) 46.

Each of these terms is then elaborated upon further. For example, threshold of harm, is explained as follows:

> The qualification of an act as direct participation does not require the materialization of harm reaching the threshold but merely the objective likelihood that the act will result in such harm. Therefore, the relevant threshold determination must be based on "likely" harm, that is to say, harm which may reasonably be expected to result from an act in the prevailing circumstances.[157]

The Guidance, like the *Targeted Killings Case,* uses a range of hypothetical examples to try to demonstrate the application of these rules. Yet, as the Guidance warns, these examples are not conclusive; they 'cannot replace a careful assessment of the concrete circumstances prevailing at the relevant time and place.'[158] In this way, the Guidance sets out an expanded set of legal terms that must be interpreted, argued, balanced and applied through legal reasoning, just as the Israeli Supreme Court did in the *Targeted Killings Case.* Moreover, just as in the *Targeted Killings Case*, these legal terms might look formal and neutral, but their application will always be indeterminate. Thus, the *Guidance* might have tried to skew the law further away from the prerogatives of the State, but it has done so by further extending and intensifying that legal reasoning that is, as was said in the *Targeted Killings Case,* the State itself.

7 Conclusion

I have retold a well-known story about the expansion of the laws of armed conflict, from a law that only applied to states and their armies to a law that covers every conflict and every participant – a law that is ubiquitous and universal. People who were considered irregulars, uncivilised, terrorists, or free-fighters – those fighting for personal or political reasons outside the state and outside the law – were gradually gathered within the law. This story could be (and often is) read as the history of a legal achievement and a moral accomplishment – a story in which the growing reach of the law is seen as an unfolding umbrella of humanitarian protection.

Yet, juridification, or the spread of law into spheres that were previously regarded as outside of law, is a phenomenon that is often viewed as

157 ibid 47.
158 Ibid 10.

problematic in other areas. As discussed above, a wide range of theoretical approaches consider the expansion of law to be synonymous with modernity and the consolidation of the state – a process which necessarily diminishes some aspect of human freedom or authenticity. Jürgen Habermas, drawing on those Weberian and Marxist critiques of law, described juridification as an ambivalent process. It was a means for colonising and distorting a 'life world', which had its own system of meaning,[159] with formal legal reasoning.[160] As such, it creates rights, but it also reduces freedom.[161]

Habermas' work focused on areas like the family and education. Nevertheless, for those who subscribe to the idea that there is some special freedom represented by the autonomous, stateless warrior or a distinctive oppression associated with the state, Habermas' conclusion should appear particularly apropos to the expansion of the law of armed conflict. This expansion has created a new set of rights, but it has done so by absorbing a range of combatants, conflicts and considerations that fell outside the state. Even for someone, like myself, who is more dubious about the idealised warrior and the supposed freedom that lies outside the law, it is certainly worth noting the degree to which the expansion of international law has replaced other forms of legitimacy and value. The juridification of all conflict has translated the heroism of the free-fighter, the just cause of the revolutionary fighting an imperial state, into a belligerent nexus and a chain of causation.

As these terms show, this is formal, non-ideological law in its most idiosyncratic form. The inclusion of new participants in the law did not create a new law. There is nothing here that speaks to justice, or even politics. Rather, there has only been a multiplication of legal criteria – criteria that rely on external, empirical details and apparently neutral legal terms and principles that need to be 'weighed' and 'balanced' interminably. In this way, the extension of the law simply expanded a sphere of specifically legal argumentation. As critical legal scholars have shown, this kind of legal reasoning is indeterminate in a variety of ways; it can lead to different outcomes, including, occasionally, humane outcomes. Overall, however, it tends to serve the interests of an

159 Jürgen Habermas, *The Theory of Communicative Action Volume 2: Lifeworld and System: A Critique Of Functionalist Reason* (Thomas McCarthy tr, Beacon Press 1987) 357; Gunther Teubner, 'Juridification – Concepts, Aspects, Limits Solutions' in Gunther Teubner (ed), *Juridification of Social Spheres: A Comparative Analysis in the Areas Of Labor, Corporate, Antitrust and Social Welfare Law* (De Gruyter 2012) 3–7.

160 Teubner (n 159) 7.

161 Jürgen Habermas, 'Law as Medium and Law as Institution' in Gunther Teubner (ed), *Dilemmas of Law in the Welfare State* (De Gruyter 1985) 211–212; Teubner (n 159) 4.

existing political system, which in international law is the state.[162] As the *Targeted Killings Case* demonstrated, this expansion of law can be understood as a victory over those who rise up against the law and the state.

How this victory is understood will depend on the observer. This retelling does not necessarily disturb the humanitarian or progressive accounts of the growth of international law. It simply notes that this growth takes place through the development of a particular language, a language that creates some silences as it speaks. It also suggests that this progress should not just be seen as a battle between international law and the state, or a triumph of humanitarian values over the state's reasons. Rather, it needs to be seen as a process of furthering these interlinked interests through the language of law.

162 Gary Minda, 'The Jurisprudential Movements of the 1980s' (1989) 50(3) Ohio State Law Journal 599, 616; David Kennedy, 'International Human Rights Movement: Part of the Problem?' (2002) 15 Harvard Human Rights Journal 101, 119; Dale A Herbeck, 'Critical Legal Studies and Argumentation Theory' (1995) 9 Argumentation 719, 719; Chris af Jochnick and Roger Normand, 'The Legitimation of Violence: A Critical History of the Laws of War' (1994) 35 Harvard International Law Journal 49, 74.

Another Look at the Gendered Constitution of the Laws of War

Semantic Fields, Hegemonic Masculinities and the Reproduction of Heteronormativity

Frédéric Mégret

Abstract

This article argues that the gendered constitution of the regulation of war runs even deeper than typically understood. Instead of merely the laws of war's internal categories being gendered, it is the entire apparatus of war's regulation as expressed in various versions of its denomination that manifests different shades of gender. Specifically, the article shows how the laws of war emerged as the hegemonic masculine synthesis between different conceptions of manhood, from the most unconstrained to the most chivalrous. As that compromise has been challenged by more 'feminine' approaches, this has triggered repeated reassertions of the regulation of war's inherently masculine character. The article speculates about the staying power of the masculine script of war through law at the intersection of misogyny, racism and the politics of legal expertise. It concludes by reflecting on what it might mean to transcend the implicit heteronormativity of the regulation of war by queering its categories.

Keywords

laws of war – gender – masculinity – critical theory – international humanitarian law – human rights – necessity – humanity

 | DOI:10.1163/9789004712478_007

1 Introduction

The gendered constitution of the laws of war has been analyzed from a variety of angles. Most notably, it has been envisaged as excluding, minimizing and neglecting the impact of war on women, particularly in terms of sexual violence. The gendered analysis of war in that context has consisted mainly in a complex discussion of the excluded feminine, and the way it is problematically portrayed as requiring protection of chastity, modesty, and honor.[1] The risk, however, is that one may fail to deliver on what has long been the radical promise of feminist insights on international law: not only a defense of the place of women or even an analysis of how the gender of war constitutes women, but as a more fundamental critique of the very categories of international law,[2] including as they contribute to perpetuating a culture of war. A more ambitious move has thus consisted in problematizing the very operation of the laws of war from a gendered perspective. Helen Kinsella, the leading contemporary representative of that effort, has focused on the extent to which the operation of the regulation of war is *internally* gendering through the deployment of the principle of distinction.[3] More recently, Boyd van Dijk has enriched our understanding of the gendered nature of the Geneva Conventions at large.[4]

In this article, I seek to contribute to the further renewal of the gendered analysis of the regulation of war in order to 'disrupt and make visible the masculinized, militarized, sexualized and classed dynamics through which war operates,'[5] by foregrounding law's regulation. In this I draw on a feminist tradition of thinking about international law that has long been less interested in merely 'inclusion' of women, than in the fundamentally disruptive potential of gendered analysis on a structural level.[6] As will be seen, the gendered critique of the laws of war ultimately requires one to move from sex to gender,

1 Judith G Gardam and Michelle J Jarvis, *Women, Armed Conflict and International Law* (Brill 2021).
2 Hilary Charlesworth and Christine Chinkin, *The Boundaries of International Law: A Feminist Analysis* (Manchester University Press 2000).
3 Helen M Kinsella, *The Image before the Weapon: A Critical History of the Distinction between Combatant and Civilian* (Cornell University Press 2011). See also Griffin Ferry, 'Oppression Through Protection: A Survey of Femininity in Foundational International Humanitarian Law Texts' (2017) 35 Minnesota Journal of Law & Inequality 57.
4 Boyd van Dijk, 'Gendering the Geneva Conventions' (2022) 44 Human Rights Quarterly 286.
5 Krista Hunt and Kim Rygiel (eds), *(En)Gendering the War on Terror: War Stories and Camouflaged Politics* (Routledge 2016) 3.
6 Hilary Charlesworth and Christine Chinkin, *The Boundaries of International Law: A Feminist Analysis* (Manchester University Press 2000).

from female to male, and from feminism to queer theory. I propose do so through the combination of three moves.

First, the article will argue that the role of gender is even more constitutive of the laws of war than has typically been thought so far. Rather than operating only at the level of the law's internal categories (for example in producing the combatant/non-combatant distinction),[7] I want to suggest that it is the very categories of the regulation of war (i.e.: the laws of war as a distinct branch and its relation to other branches) within the broader architecture of international law which, themselves, expresses a peculiar, gendered sensitivity. The gendering of war through law is thus also *externally* constituted through a series of stylized postures that compete against alternatives and against each other. In a sense, even the notion that there ought to be a specific, largely self-contained regime dedicated to the regulation of war naturalizes certain expectations about war and law. The protection of that self-sustaining, largely autarchic legal regime, then, becomes a condition of the possibility of its perpetuation.

Second, I contend that the regulation of war is specifically premised on a discursive tug-of-war between different semantic fields ('laws of war', 'international humanitarian law' ('IHL'), 'laws of armed conflict' ('LOAC'), 'human rights' etc.) that compete to capture imaginations about the role of law in war. I argue that the endemic and oft-remarked debates over these labels reflect more than semantic squabbles and are in reality genuine battles for the definition of the regulation of war. More importantly, the key to understanding these dynamics is that they powerfully monopolize and are deeply aligned with gendered imaginaries that systematically oppose a privileged 'masculinized' and a devalued 'feminized' (including women but also subordinate men).[8] Moreover, the labels are fluid but most importantly they are relational and only take meaning, as if within some pre-existing Saussurean semantic grid, in relation each other. Discursive regularities and patterns around the use of certain terms and how they are used contextually and to disqualify other labels, then, are crucial to the constitution of the laws of war as a language and how it channels thinking about its object.[9]

7 Helen M Kinsella, 'Discourses of Difference: Civilians, Combatants, and Compliance with the Laws of War' (2005) 31 Review of International Studies 163; Helen M Kinsella, 'Gendering Grotius: Sex and Sex Difference in the Laws of War' (2006) 34 Political Theory 161.

8 V Spike Peterson, 'Thinking Through Intersectionality and War' (2007) 14 Race, Gender & Class 10.

9 Molly Lewis and Gary Lupyan, 'Gender Stereotypes Are Reflected in the Distributional Structure of 25 Languages' (2020) 4 Nature Human Behaviour 1021.

Third, the article seeks to specifically centre the question of *masculinities* as the key to understanding these gendered semantic dynamics.[10] A limitation of earlier feminist work on the laws of war is, despite the occasional gesturing at the existence of a 'male norm,'[11] a tendency to avoid a genuine problematization of masculinities in war (as Michael Kimmel once put it, 'as if gender applied only to women'[12]), even as feminism provides the very tools for that enterprise.[13] This seems to conspicuously skirt the central role of normal 'military masculinities,' which has since become such a productive axis of research.[14] This risks leaving largely intellectually unattended the crucial 'man question' not as some sort of niche and otiose curiosity for macho subcultures but as one of the keys to unravel the morbid compromises at the heart of law, war, and the laws of war.[15]

By contrast, this article, drawing on my previous work on the international constitution of a masculine laws of war[16] as well as an interest in a more all-encompassing understanding of gender,[17] suggests that the critical study of masculinities provides a key conceptual entry point to illuminate centuries of debates on the laws of war. The law is a key site of gender 'essentialization' because of the way it lastingly embeds certain coded gendered expressions. Of particular interest here will be 'European' or 'white' masculinity which has historically proved central to the constitution of the regulation of Westphalian warfare,[18] and whose domestic ascendancy has often translated into global hegemony under the banner of sexual and civilizational superiority. However, this article will not discount the claim that 'the gendered character of warfare

10 Jane L Parpat and Marysia Zalewski (eds), *Rethinking the Man Question: Sex, Gender and Violence in International Relations* (Bloomsbury Publishing 2008).

11 Helen Durham, 'International Humanitarian Law and the Protection of Women' in Helen Durham and Tracey Gurd (eds), *Listening to the Silences: Women and War* (Brill 2005) 97.

12 Michael S Kimmel, *The Gendered Society* (Oxford University Press 2000) 6.

13 On the relationship between feminism and the study of masculinities in international relations, see Adam Jones, 'Does "gender" make the world go round? Feminist critiques of international relations*' (1996) 22 Review of International Studies 405; Terrell Carver, Molly Cochran and Judith Squires, 'Gendering Jones: Feminisms, IRs, Masculinities' (1998) 24 Review of International Studies 283.

14 Hannah C Hale, 'The Role of Practice in the Development of Military Masculinities' (2012) 19 Gender, Work & Organization 699.

15 Raewyn Connell, *Masculinities* (2nd edn, Routledge 2020).

16 Frédéric Mégret, 'The Laws of War and the Structure of Masculine Power' (2018) 19 Melbourne Journal of International Law 200.

17 Helen Durham and Katie O'Byrne, 'The Dialogue of Difference: Gender Perspectives on International Humanitarian Law' (2010) 92 International Review of the Red Cross 31.

18 Shula Marks, 'White Masculinity: Jan Smuts, Race and the South African War', in *Proceedings of the British Academy* 117 (Oxford University Press 2001).

is extraordinarily consistent across human cultures,'[19] and the possibility that understandings of masculinity have provided the linchpin of the regulation of war in many cultures (albeit with different results).

Indeed, whatever else it may be, war has been a place of intense socialization among men and production of expectations about masculinities.[20] The law, then, is called upon to both express and arbitrate such expectations.[21] Behind their apparent neutrality and universality, the laws of war involve recurring and even obsessive conversations about the place of manhood (with men as an evident proxy) in society and the subtle and not-so-subtle crafting of masculine domination. Drawing on Michael Kimmel's idea of 'classical social theory as a hidden meditation of manhood,'[22] the article thus hopes to make a contribution to how the gendered semantics of the regulation of war are a crucial terrain of war's constitution, and hence to our understanding of masculinity in war/masculinity as war. Methodologically, it will pay attention to rhetorical structures in the law that can be understood to be gender-coded, even when they are not gender explicit and manifest an underlying structural misogyny and homophobia. In the process, it will show the fluid construction of masculinity-through-war and war-through-masculinity to be part of an ongoing gendered 'performance' of law in war.

In the next section, I begin by sketching the fundamental process by which the contemporary regulation of war has emerged on the basis of a contestation between different ideal-regulatory-types of masculinity and war. In the third section, I show how this basic masculine consensus about the regulation of war has in turn increasingly been challenged by efforts at reorienting it in directions that are understood as more feminine, prompting strong resistance. In the fourth section, I question more broadly the endurance of the masculine script for war's regulation, highlighting some reasons for its puzzling staying power. I conclude by considering what it might mean to challenge hegemonic masculinities in the regulation of war in an age of gender fluidity.

---

19 Joshua S Goldstein, 'War and Gender' in Carol R Ember and Melvin Ember (eds), *Encyclopedia of Sex and Gender: Men and Women in the World's Cultures* (Springer US 2004).

20 Suzanne Hatty, *Masculinities, Violence, and Culture* (Sage Publications 2000).

21 Ann-Dorte Christensen and Morten Kyed, 'From Military to Militarizing Masculinities' (2022) 17 International Journal for Masculinity Studies 1.

22 Michael S Kimmel, 'Masculinity as Homophobia: Fear, Shame, and Silence in the Construction of Gender Identity', in Mary M Gergen and Sara N Davis (eds), *Toward a New Psychology of Gender* (Routledge 1997) 225.

2 Spectra of Masculinity and the Genesis of the Regulation of War

Failure to tackle masculinity in the regulation of war head on has tended to reproduce a sort of implicit deference to the dominance of masculinity as the gender of reference. It also risks essentializing masculinity as homogeneous and monolithic, where masculinity is very much a contested, fluid concept, and where the domination of masculinity is, more often than not, also the domination of certain forms of masculinity over others. Problematizing masculinity, then, requires adopting a non-essentializing vision, seeing it as a set of gender relations that are fundamentally contested and constructed, notably through the needs of militarism and war themselves.[23] Masculinity is nothing more than an ongoing competition whose central stake is obtaining the upper hand in defining masculinity; in vying to express, so to speak, 'hegemonic masculinity.'[24]

The dynamics of that struggle over the meaning of masculinity are fraught, fundamentally anxious and, potentially, violent. Far from being merely a cultural or aesthetic exercise, they crystalize fundamental relations of power and dominance over the conduct of war through its regulation. They also contribute to establish social hierarchies of prestige, honour and merit between men and women but also between different kinds of men ('sorting the men from the boys'). And they are part of an attempt at closing off the regulation of war to potential 'feminine' interlopers, manifested in the intensely self-referential nature of the military institution and its 'demarcation' from surrounding fields.[25] In short, there is no mistaking the fact that the regulation of war is directed at *both* war and masculinity as co-constituted categories that render each other 'both intelligible and acceptable as a social practice and institution.'[26]

In this context, it is traditionally asserted that the entire arc of the regulation of war is defined by a tension between 'necessity' and 'humanity,' which provides the field with some of its structuring dichotomies, even as it acts as a major source of both its indeterminacy and dynamism. The two, as it happens, barely conceal their roles as signifiers for gendered positionalities: it has been said that '"humanity", rightly or not, is associated with women

23 Maya Eichler, *Militarizing Men: Gender, Conscription, and War in Post-Soviet Russia* (Stanford University Press 2011).

24 Raewyn Connell and James W Messerschmidt, 'Hegemonic Masculinity: Rethinking the Concept' (2005) 19 Gender & Society 829.

25 Hatty (n 20) 170.

26 Kimberly Hutchings, 'Making Sense of Masculinity and War' (2007) 10 Men and Masculinities 389.

more than with men,'[27] whilst 'necessity' clearly signals a realist 'masculine' outlook on 'what needs to be done.' The underlying challenge of the regulation of war, then, is realizing that synthesis in ways that do not forfeit and, in fact, express and prolong dominant forms of masculinity, including by 'taking necessity seriously' as the 'keystone of the arch,' and ensuring that '[w]hatever restraints the law imposes [...] accommodate themselves to military necessity and regulate around its margin.'[28] As will be seen, not all historical attempts at this synthesis have historically or analytically fared equally, but all can be understood as discursive variations on some concept of masculinity.

2.1 *'Kriegsraison': Toxic and Hyper-Masculinity*

The doctrine of Kriegsraison emerges in 19th Century Prussia as an appeal to the need to emancipate oneself from the normal rules that would apply in warfare. Field Marshal von Moltke argued for 'short wars', claiming that 'all means not absolutely reprehensible must be used to accomplish this end.'[29] Kriegsraison thus idealizes necessity, and proclaims the rejection of all restraint. It has echoes even in Francis Lieber's preference for harsh but short wars.[30] It imagines men as uniquely suited to make the decisions that impose themselves for the survival of the nation. It is not exclusive of a law of war but compliance with such law is subject to the ultimate decision of the commander in the field. War is imagined as always potentially a total exercise in violence that knows no bounds. It manifests in its purest form what Henry James, himself a pacifist but committed to understanding the military ethos, described as a fundamental 'contempt for softness.'[31]

The tradition of Kriegsraison, then, can be read in light of modern understandings of toxic masculinity. Toxic masculinity has been particularly highlighted in prisons as involving domination by men of other men through violence and the suppression of 'feminine' weakness as a way of coping with harsh conditions. It can be understood as 'the constellation of socially regressive male traits that serve to foster domination, the devaluation of women, homophobia and wanton violence.'[32] Its significance specifically in

27 Christopher Coker, *Humane Warfare* (Routledge 2001) 88.

28 David Luban, 'Military Necessity and the Cultures of Military Law' (2013) 26 Leiden Journal of International Law 315, 322–328.

29 Daniel Hughes, *Moltke on the Art of War: Selected Writings* (Random House Publishing Group 2009) 24.

30 Richard Salomon, 'The Unsuspected Francis Lieber' (2018) CUNY Academic Works.

31 William James, *The Moral Equivalent of War* (Read Books 2015).

32 Terry A Kupers, 'Toxic Masculinity as a Barrier to Mental Health Treatment in Prison' (2005) 61 Journal of Clinical Psychology 713, 714.

the military as an obstacle to change has been highlighted.[33] Toxic masculinity in war underpins a vision of men as the only decision-makers and as the only ones capable of the harshness necessary in war.

There is arguably a direct filiation between Kriegsraison and fascism, going all the way to the fanatical masculinity of the SS and the Einsatzgruppen. This was preceded by the radicalized masculinity of the Freikorps and its fantasies of expunging rather than simply dominating the feminine.[34] On the margins of the Holocaust, drinking rituals were central to the elaboration of a certain kind of 'performative masculinity', focused on sexual and physical violence, in a context where heavy drinking was associated with rites of passage and male prowess.[35] In Dachau, the notion that 'tolerance means weakness' was evoked against the background of ideas about militarism and masculinity.[36] It is also worth noting that the imaginary of Kriegsraison was projected onto the Japanese military during the Second World War. Echoes of Kriegsraison and the importance of ruthlessness can be heard to this day in the suggestion that 'fiercer, angrier, most-blood-lusting force will win wars.'[37]

Interestingly, however, already embedded within Kriegsraison was an implicit fragility. To begin with, Kriegsraison was not entirely without its own appeal to humanitarian values, as it expressed itself in an insistence that brief wars were likely overall to be less harmful. That appeal was limited, but it at least narrowly steered Kriegsraison away from nihilism. Bizarrely, moreover, even the Nazis saw this untrammelled masculinity as ultimately unsustainable, if not particularly problematic morally. Whilst witnessing mass executions, Himmler was addressed by a General who insisted that 'these men are finished for the rest of their lives. What kind of followers are we training here? Either neurotics or savages!'[38] The pursuit of untrammelled warfare seemed to

33 Joseph E Webster, *Resisting Change: Toxic Masculiniity in the Post Modern United States Armed Forces, (1980s-Present)* (University of Central Oklahoma 2019).

34 Klaus Theweleit, *Male Fantasies, Vol. I: Women, Floods, Bodies, History* (University of Minnesota Press 1989); Klaus Theweleit, *Male Fantasies, Vol II: Male Bodies: Psychoanalyzing the White Terror* (University of Minnesota Press 1989).

35 Edward B Westermann, 'Drinking Rituals, Masculinity, and Mass Murder in Nazi Germany' (2018) 51 Central European History 367.

36 Christopher Dillon, '"Tolerance Means Weakness": The Dachau Concentration Camp S.S., Militarism and Masculinity' (2013) 86 Historical Research 373.

37 Stephanie Gutmann, *The Kinder, Gentler Military: Can America's Gender-Neutral Fighting Force Still Win Wars* (1st edn, Scribner 2000) 275.

38 Peter J Haas, *Morality After Auschwitz: The Radical Challenge of the Nazi Ethic* (Wipf and Stock Publishers 2014) 87.

ultimately impugn a dimension of self-respect in masculinity but also point to the psychological limits of all masculinity in harsh conditions.[39]

2.2 *'Chivalry': Noblesse Oblige and Gentlemanliness*

Kriegraison itself arose against the background of what was imagined to be the chivalrous pursuit of war, inherited from the European Middle Ages. Within the chivalrous tradition, limitations in war were framed by an honor code that referred back to manly virtues. Men were to not do what was 'dishonorable' because of the way it might indict their masculinity. War was imagined primarily as a game played by men between themselves and in which it was essential that conditions of fair play be respected, but in ways that were largely oblivious to how that 'game' might impact its surroundings.

In this context, for example, there was honor in resorting to 'stratagems' but shame in resorting to 'perfidy.' Stratagems, according to Vattel are 'consistent with good faith' and 'have often constituted a great share of the glory of the most celebrated commanders.' It was therefore 'really more commendable to succeed in this way than by a bloody siege or the carnage of battle.'[40] By contrast, the characteristic offence under a chivalric code was perfidy, understood as obtaining an undue military advantage through an unfair ruse. Specifically, perfidy is defined by Article 37(1) of Additional Protocol I as a form of 'betrayal of confidence.' In other words, perfidy abuses the honor and righteousness of those it tricks and is a failure to behave according to chivalrous men's honor code. Perfidy is also sometimes conveniently identified with women as in the case in which 'an ostensibly pregnant woman lured three American soldiers to their deaths by pretending to be in distress at a checkpoint and then detonating concealed explosives,'[41] and at any rate associated with fantasies about feminine deviousness corrupting the *entre-soi* of military men.[42] One of the inspirations for prohibiting perfidy, then, is a fundamental sense of division of labor in war between combatants (masculine) and non-combatants (feminine) and an underlying sense that each should very much adhere to the role assigned to them by the legal/gender script.

---

39 See, in the colonial context, Warwick Anderson, 'The Trespass Speaks: White Masculinity and Colonial Breakdown' (1997) 102 The American Historical Review 1343.

40 Emer de Vattel and M P Pradier-Fodéré, *Le droit des gens ou principes de la naturelle appliqués a la conduite et aux affaires des nations et des souverains*, book 3, chaper 10 (Guillaumin 1863).

41 Neal A Richardson and Spencer J Crona, 'Make Iraqis Pay for Acts of "Perfidy"' *Los Angeles Times* (8 April 2003) <https://www.latimes.com/archives/la-xpm-2003-apr-08-war-oerichardson8-story.html>.

42 Jerry Lembcke, *Hanoi Jane: War, Sex, and Fantasies of Betrayal* (1st edn, University of Massachusetts Press 2010).

Chivalry posits an ideal of masculinity that is in some ways the polar opposite of Kriegsraison. Knights were also characterized by their piety, largesse, magnanimity and manners, in addition to military prowess, courage, forbearance and hardihood. Léon Gautier's Ten Commandments of Chivalry exemplify that tension: 'Thou shalt not recoil before thine enemy' but also 'Thou shalt respect all weaknesses, and shalt constitute thyself the defender of them.' In fact, the ideal of chivalry was encouraged by the Church as a way of reforming and guiding knights away from disorderly, martial and chauvinistic manifestations of masculinity.[43] The courtly ideal of knights, moreover, gestured at a certain gender 'schism' which saw the masculine coexist with a significant dose of the feminine,[44] sometimes cutting a remarkably androginous figure.[45]

At the same time, chivalry was largely fictitious, the stuff of romances. Even in its idealized form, it was rife with exclusive undertones that still made it a classic manifestation of hegemonic masculinity. Its obsession with the pursuit of honor also went hand in hand with a conception of violence as the privilege of men. Its emphasis on protecting widows and orphans left little doubt about its domineering tendencies. The point of chivalry, moreover, was that it bound only a certain kind of upper-class men into a certain mutual male self-respect that it did not grant to others. Its courtly love of and devotion to women was part of a rigid division of gender roles. 'Chivalry', then, illustrates a kind of elite masculinity in war that made restraint uniquely dependent on manly virtues, and therefore uniquely fragile and increasingly hard to justify under conditions of modernity and nationalism.

2.3 *The 'Laws of War': Restraint and Manliness*

Contra traditions that emphasize the untrammelled power of men or the implausibly restrained chivalry of the knight, the central, hegemonic tradition that emerges in the 19th Century is that of 'the laws of war.' The laws of war operate a kind of grand synthesis between military 'necessity' and 'humanity' in modernity, essentially extending the chivalrous restraint to the entire battlefield but normalizing and secularizing it as part of the growth of modern states. From Kriegsraison, the laws of war keep the realist recognition of a certain underlying ruthlessness even as the concept of necessity is reframed as a limitation rather than a licence of violence; from chivalry, they borrow

43 Richard Kaeuper, *Chivalry and Violence in Medieval Europe* (Oxford University Press 2001).

44 Timothy Morris, 'Chivalric Schism: The Man Who Occupies the Masculine and the Feminine 2014' (2014).

45 Michele F Cooper, 'Chretien de Troyes' Perceval: Androgynous development of the hero' (1991).

the sense of masculine *noblesse oblige* but without the tenderness, piety and homoeroticism of the courtly-Christian tradition.

In that, however, as I have shown, the laws of war do not depart from a fundamentally masculine script; in fact, they reinforce and embody it by playing on old ideas of dominant masculinity as, in fact, *restrained* masculinity.[46] The origin of masculinity as restrained maleness lies in Roman ideals about *virilitas*, understood as the ability to be simultaneously sexually 'assertive' and 'level-headed, vigorous yet deliberate, courageous yet restrained.'[47] These ideas have significantly shaped modern ideas of masculinity, all the way to the 19th Century and notions of Victorian gentlamanliness. They can be traced specifically to gendered archetypes mentioned in the canonical literature on the laws of war that idealized manly virtues.[48] They fundamentally underscore the process of masculine domination in war in that they make 'men at war' the only arbitrators of violence. They also highlight Western masculinity as qualitatively different, in its very restraint, from the untrammelled violence of the 'savage.'[49]

In that respect, manliness, is not primarily contrasted with femininity, at least the imagined femininity of women, any more than the laws of war's main gripe is with pacifism: it almost goes without saying that manliness is not feminine. Rather manliness emerges at a precarious distance from two intimately competing masculine ideal types: the hyper-masculine brute, and the effeminate man. The hyper-masculine brute is, essentially, unreformed maleness without the benefit of manly restraint, a model that appears increasingly outdated and intolerable, particularly after the horrors of the Second World War; the 'sissy' is the man who has adopted excessively feminine characteristics and is either incapable of engaging in war due to a lack of basic masculine ruthlessness, or only capable of a perfidious war, again a model that activates strong societal anxieties about male inadequacy.[50]

It is vis-à-vis these familiar masculine alter egos that the 'narcissism of small differences' manifests itself with most intensity.[51] It is also here that notions

---

46 Mégret, 'The Laws of War and the Structure of Masculine Power' (n 16).

47 Alain Corbin, Jean-Jacques Courtine and Georges Vigarello, 'Preface' in Alain Corbin, Jean-Jacques Courtine and Georges Vigarello (eds), *A History of Virility* (Columbia University Press 2017) xiii.

48 Mégret, 'The Laws of War and the Structure of Masculine Power' (n 16).

49 Helen M Kinsella, 'Settler Empire and the United States: Francis Lieber on the Laws of War' (2022) 117 American Political Science Review 629.

50 Stephen Ducat, *The Wimp Factor: Gender Gaps, Holy Wars, and the Politics of Anxious Masculinity* (Beacon Press 2005).

51 Anton Blok, 'The Narcissism of Minor Differences' (1998) 1 European Journal of Social Theory 33.

of gender hierarchy within masculinity allow us to make sense of the process by which the domination of the laws of war as a peculiar model of regulating armed violence is performed. Therein, in fact, lies the unique opportunity to assert a vision of restrained masculinity 'in the middle,' or at least very close to it. The 'middle' here is not an androgenous middle between the masculine and the feminine, but rather a manly middle between hypermasculinity and humanitarian masculinity. Manly virtues in war are thus consecrated as embodying 'toughness without callousness, authority with as little criminal cruelty as possible, and painful work done cheerily because the duty is temporary.'[52] Restrained masculinity is not only the ideal the laws of war seek to articulate; it is also a crucial vector of their authority, somewhere between apology and utopia.[53]

3 Crises of Masculinity: the Feminization of War and Virile Backlash(es)

If defining, upholding and privileging masculinity has been the underlying stake of much regulation of war, then these efforts exist against the background of and have to contend with opposite efforts that may be described as having as their main thrust what can be understood as the attempted 'femininization' of the regulation of war. The point of the latter is not that they are deliberately feminine/feminist or indeed necessarily voiced by women (although they may certainly also be), but rather that they intervene in the struggle over the regulation of war as so many attempts to shift its center of gravity in ways that are coded as feminine, typically understood here as more humane. These efforts have been undertaken with some success and have long been argued to have begun changing the fundamental character of the regulation of war.[54]

In turn, however, the perception that this is indeed an effort at femininization has triggered powerful reassertions of masculine dominance that seek to bring the regulation of war back to its imagined masculine centre of gravity, essentialize women in order to reassert manhood, and promote a rigid

52 James (n 31).

53 Frédéric Mégret, 'Thinking About What International Humanitarian Lawyers "Do": An Examination of the Laws of War as a Field of Professional Practice' in Wouter Werner, Marieke de Hoon and Alexis Galán Ávila (eds), *The Law of International Lawyers; Reflections on the Work of Martti Koskenniemi* (2017).

54 See, e.g., Theodor Meron, 'The Humanization of Humanitarian Law' (2000) 94 The American Journal of International Law 239.

defense of gendered roles.[55] This is all the more so that masculinity is *already* understood as an ongoing compromise between untrammelled manhood and contained manliness on masculinity's own terms. The notion of 'brittle' or 'fragile' masculinity[56] here may be useful to describe the process involved. It describes men who find themselves in situations of being unable to fully build their masculinity and who, as a result, are tempted by over-demonstrative masculine bravado and the repression of feminine inclinations. It has been used, for example, to describe late 19th Century imperial men who grew up between rigid fathers and the affections of nannies, mothers, and sisters but who would end up being torn between their desire for homosocial sexual companionship and considering all affection unmanly.[57] The term has been more recently popularized by Timothy Snyder to describe the Trumpian *fin de règne*.[58]

The suggestion is that, far from being merely dominant, masculinity is in fact also deeply precarious and, as a result, tempted to lash out. In a context where war is 'the sole remaining domain of men [...] which makes them feel powerful and strong and offers them the intoxicating cocktail of masculine superiority,'[59] its continued cultural production feeds on persistent anxieties about manhood in late modernity, notably in the pursuit of military affairs where men's monopoly has been steadily eroded. This then 'threatens the boundedness of the military institution and the separation of men and women' and thus 'dilutes the masculine character of the institution, erodes the solidarity of the body of fighting men, and introduces confusion and conflict to the system of loyalties' to the point of 'destabiliz[ing] or even pollut[ing] the military machine.'[60] That fear, fed by and translating as it does into homophobia, sissyphobia, and misogyny, is powerfully reinforced by in-group

55 Katerina Agostino, 'The Making of Warriors: Men, Identity and Military Culture' (1998) 3 Journal of Interdisciplinary Gender Studies 58.

56 Maryam Kouchaki, Keith Leavitt, Luke Zhu and Anthony C Klotz, 'Research: What Fragile Masculinity Looks Like at Work' (*Harvard Business Review*, 26 January 2023) <https://hbr.org/2023/01/research-what-fragile-masculinity-looks-like-at-work>; Sarah H DiMuccio and Eric D Knowles, 'The Political Significance of Fragile Masculinity' (2020) 34 Current Opinion in Behavioral Sciences 25.

57 John Beynon, *Masculinities and Culture* (McGraw-Hill Education 2001) 47–49.

58 Timothy Snyder, 'Don't underestimate the harm "brittle masculinity" can do to the world' *The Guardian* (20 April 2017) <https://www.theguardian.com/commentisfree/2017/apr/20/dont-underestimate-harm-brittle-masculinity-do-world>.

59 Constantina Safilios-Rothschild, 'The Negative Side of Development Interventions and Gender Transitions: Impoverished Male Roles Threaten Peace' in Ingeborg Breines and others (eds), *Male Roles, Masculinities and Violence: A Culture of Peace Perspective* (UNESCO Publishing 2000) 92.

60 Hatty (n 20) 170.

peer dynamics, notably in militarized environments but also across borders as a manifestation of the transnational solidarity of men at arms even in a culture of extreme nationalism.

The scenario that plays out in various successive reassertions of masculinity, then, is one in which masculine performances are deployed to marginalize certain non-gender conforming visions of the regulation of war and, specifically, to exorcise 'deeply held fears and anxieties about the literal loss of masculinity in warfare.'[61] Excessive sensitivity, squeamishness or idealism in relation to the regulation of war thus make one easily disqualifiable as a serious (manly) participant in discussions therein. The regulation of war is always at risk of lapsing into an imagined 'femininity,' thus prompting reassertions of its intrinsic masculinity. A series of dichotomies highlight the fortitude of certain men at the intersection of the toxicity and weakness of others: 'violent/virile/effete', 'brute/man/boy,' 'toxic man/real man/wimp,' 'war criminal/officer/conscript,' etc. In this section, I review three ways in which the laws of war have been subjected to efforts that can be understood as disrupting the 'manly consensus,' prompting furious corresponding efforts to reassert the basic virile script.

3.1 *'International Humanitarian Law,' Between Male Weakness and Male Decentering*

The shift to the more gender ambiguous vision of the regulation of war is revealed in a first major inflexion in the terminology of the laws of war, namely the idea expressed in the very first Geneva Convention of 1864 that this treaty concerns itself primarily with the protection of the wounded, the sick and the shipwrecked. The humanitarian sensitivity, for the first time, highlighted men not as brutes, chivalrous knights or even the site of virile restraint but as *themselves* victims of violence and it is not only dehumanizing but specifically demasculinizing impact. It is hard to underestimate the extent to which this foundational image of suffering men destabilized dominant Victorian concepts of stoic masculinity in war, even though it continued to coexist with more conventional masculine scripts.[62]

For example, in '*Un souvenir de Solferino*', the origin of war-humanitarianism lies in the almost feminine empathy for the suffering male body. Beyond the bravado of arms, Henry Dunant finds only moaning wounded bodies rescued by caring Italian nurses. From Florence Nightingale's activities in the Crimean

61 Hatty (n 20).

62 Adrian Caesar, *Taking It Like a Man: Suffering, Sexuality, and the War Poets: Brooke, Sassoon, Owen, Graves* (Manchester University Press 1993).

war to the post First-World War emergence of the Red Cross movement,[63] the humanitarian effort has been conceived as saving suffering men, men who therefore could not be reduced once and for all to their warlike exploits but must endure the indignity of being rescued and slowly nurtured back into civilian life. At a certain level, it is the entire dominant concept of manhood that stood to be derailed, as post-Crimean war narratives increasingly emphasized 'acts of mercy' over sheer ruthlessness, as well as the particular proclivities of gentle 'military men of feeling.'[64]

At any rate, this newfound emphasis on suffering bodies, was soon joined by the humbled, exposed and feminine bodies of those who, as prisoners of war ('POWs'), had been captured and were suspected of finding themselves in a state of passivity that 'conjure[d] up a feminised condition.'[65] The First World War and the emergence of a generation of 'shell-shocked' young men 'unable to exercise the power of will over fear' in turn 'implied a major revision of nineteenth-century discourses about manliness.'[66] The theme of 'emaciated or emasculated' white masculinity in war, notably in representations of Australian POWs at the hands of the Japanese making 'a symbolic journey from one gendered sphere to another, where the masculine world of action is left behind for the more culturally feminine site of containment,' uprooted expectations about masculine and white superiority in battle.[67] In short, these developments focused the internationalist gaze on war's sorry aftermath rather than war's heroics. It made the point that even a chivalrous war was an unseemly sight once fighting had ceased. This more 'feminine' humanitarian sensitivity, in threatening to excessively expose masculinity as fragile and in need of feminine succour marked a significant inflexion point on the way to the redefinition of the laws of war as a form of international *humanitarian* law: suffering bodies of warriors, expressing a sort of bare humanity, were on some level indistinguishable and certainly no more meritorious than the suffering bodies of civilians, thus powerfully contributing to the normalization of manhood.

---

63 Bertrand Taithe, '"Cold Calculation in the Faces of Horrors?" Pity, Compassion and the Making of Humanitarian Protocols' in Fay Bound Alberti (ed), *Medicine, Emotion and Disease, 1700–1950* (Palgrave Macmillan 2006).

64 Holly Furneaux, *Military Men of Feeling: Emotion, Touch, and Masculinity in the Crimean War* (Oxford University Press 2016).

65 Stephen Garton, *The Cost of War: War, Return and the Re-Shaping of Australian Culture* (Sydney University Press 2020) 210.

66 Michael Roper, 'Between Manliness and Masculinity: The "War Generation" and the Psychology of Fear in Britain, 1914–1950' (2005) 44 Journal of British Studies 343, 344.

67 Christina Twomey, 'Emaciation or Emasculation: Photographic Images, White Masculinity and Captivity by the Japanese in World War Two' (2008) 15 The Journal of Men's Studies 295, 299.

But this revelation of masculine weakness was open to brutal reassertions of masculine dominance. The initial focus on assistance and ensuring that armies had access to sanitary services in the field, for example, was soon taken over by men ('professional' doctors as opposed to well-meaning but 'amateur' nurses).[68] Indeed, as Henry Dunant put it, after extolling the "saintly" virtues of female nurses, what would have really been needed in Solferino "was not only weak and ignorant women, but, with them and beside them, kindly and experienced men, capable, firm, already organized." (footnote to Henry Dunant, A Memory from Solferino (2013) 121). This was followed by a much more militaristic emphasis on the proper conduct of hostilities rather than assistance to the wounded. This was illustrated by the Oxford Manual and its rules of warfare which reinstated a sensitivity more characteristic of the traditional 'laws of war.'[69] In foregrounding the rules that apply to men between themselves, the laws of war emphasized the homo-erotic dimensions of its practice on the battlefield and the centrality of men's sadomasochistic consent to the violence they inflict on each other.[70]

Subsequently, however, the use of the term 'international humanitarian law' manifests a further recalibration of gender norms and underlying conception of masculinity. IHL, a label that becomes dominant after the Second World War and arguably even more so in the final decades of the 20th Century,[71] shifts the gaze away from men at arms altogether (even the wounded) to civilian victims of armed conflict as the principal victims of war, thus displacing the original core focus of the laws of war. As Hersch Lauterpacht famously put it:

> We shall utterly fail to understand the true character of the law of war unless we are to realize that its purpose is almost entirely humanitarian in the literal sense of the word, namely to prevent or mitigate suffering and, in some cases, to rescue life from the savagery of battle and passion. This, and not the regulation and direction of hostilities, is its essential purpose.[72]

---

68 Michael Brown, '"Like a Devoted Army": Medicine, Heroic Masculinity, and the Military Paradigm in Victorian Britain' (2010) 49 Journal of British Studies 592.

69 *The Laws of War on Land* (Institute of International Law 1880).

70 Margot Weiss, 'Rumsfeld!: Consensual BDSM and "Sadomasochistic" Torture at Abu Ghraib' in Ellen Lewin and William L Leap (eds), *Out in Public: Reinventing Lesbian/Gay Anthropology in a Globalizing World* (Blackwell Publishing 2009).

71 Amanda Alexander, 'A Short History of International Humanitarian Law' (2015) 26 European Journal of International Law 109.

72 Hersch Lauterpacht, 'The Problem of the Revision of the Law of War' (1952) 29 British Year Book of International Law 360, 363.

On one particularly influential reading, then, the new term 'represented [...] not just a shift in terminology but also a fresh approach to the jus in bello.'[73] Where the 'laws of war' were still principally concerned with regulating the behavior of parties to armed conflict in relation to each other (the 'conduct of hostilities' on the battlefield, essentially a modality of socialization between men), IHL was to be primarily about protecting civilian victims from the ravages of war, as if war's collaterality (the killing of civilians) was henceforth more important than its function (killing men).

On some level, this significantly decenters men. Men at war are at risk of not being the leading characters in their own martial pantomime, their pursuit of violence against each other tolerated but hampered by the risks that it poses, henceforth, to civilians (traditionally understood as women and children), an unacceptable distraction in the otherwise single-minded pursuit of military necessity. It is true that 'virile' states have not always bought into the project and sometimes simply protested the fact that IHL has unjustifiably veered towards excessive humanitarianism (as the US has long done in relation to Protocol I).[74] Indeed the 'international humanitarian law' term has continued to face barely veiled gendered resistance, as expressed for example by one senior US military lawyer who is on the record as 'declin[ing] to refer to the law of war as "international humanitarian law"' on account of the fact that 'combat is a brutal experience.'[75] But even the reconstructed masculinity that emerges is, in the best of cases, complex and manifests significant resistance to fundamentally rewriting the underlying masculine script. On at least three levels, in fact, the humanitarianization of the laws of war remains a very imperfectly realized experience in gender decentering.

First, the broader cultural production of even IHL tends to continue to rely on and reinforce problematic gender tropes. In particular, the law sets up the conditions for a deep, foundational division between norms regulating how 'men' ought to relate to each other (Hague law) and how 'men' ought to relate to their feminine 'other' (Geneva law, the more humanitarian version). As such, it reinforces a sense of male exceptionalism, of rules allowing for a much higher degree of violence between men at war than would ever be tolerated, not only in peace conditions but in war conditions governing the rapport

73 Alexander (n 71).

74 Abraham D Sofaer, 'The Rationale for the United States Decision Not to Ratfiy Protocol I' (1988) 82 The American Journal of International Law 784.

75 W Hays Parks, 'Part IX of the ICRC Direct Participation in Hostilities Study: No Mandate, No Expertise, and Legally Incorrect Forum: Direct Participation In Hostilities: Perspectives on the ICRC Interpretive Guidance' (2009) 42 New York University Journal of International Law and Politics 769, 828.

to civilians. In safeguarding a space for normalized and privileged violence between men (seen as crucial by many LOAC practitioners, see below), the law is part and parcel of the perpetuation of a model that cements the centrality of masculinities to the life of nations and that has historically been a foundation for further privileges.

Second, as has been argued elsewhere,[76] IHL contains a kind of moral trap in that even as it more clearly foregrounds humanitarian concerns particularly as they affect the vulnerable, the very essence of the war compact is consequently not challenged. Some feminist writers have since the 1990s invested considerable energy in highlighting sexual violence in war, for example, but in ways that may have taken the edge off much more radical feminist pacifist projects wary of war's 'civilization.'[77] Although on some level men are designated as culpable for war's ongoing violence against civilians, they have also historically gained considerable social and symbolic gendered capital from their continued ability to engage in war on their own masculine terms, 'in exchange' for their restraint. Even as succouring feminity is valorized, moreover, it is also consigned to a stereotypical 'maternal' role that limits the disruption to gendered hierarchies and simultaneously 'assign(s) men the public sphere responsibility of defending and protecting feminized dependents.'[78]

Third, and more specifically, the 'international humanitarian law' framing of the regulation of war, even as it seeks to further restrain masculinity, constitutes an umptieth version of its ascendancy in that it frames men, henceforth, as guardians of the law's humanitarian character. Men in combat are the constant object of attention as decision-makers (for others). To be sure, men who fail to honor their humanitarian obligations will be vilified but at no point, from that specifically humanitarian standpoint, is there an opening to challenge the fact that men at war should be the ones making complex decisions about who lives or dies. Instead, one encounters a strong masculine insistence that their decisions in that field should enjoy 'broad discretion and deserve significant deference,' not to be second-guessed by outside parties.[79]

3.2 *'Humanization' and the Anxiety of Effeminacy*

The general public has sometimes tended to view even actions allowed *stricto sensu* under IHL as potentially wrong, describing any killing of civilians as *ipso*

76 Mégret, 'The Laws of War and the Structure of Masculine Power' (n 16).

77 Dianne Otto, 'Power and Danger: Feminist Engagement with International Law through the UN Security Council' (2010) 32 Australian Feminist Law Journal 97.

78 Peterson (n 8) 17.

79 Luban (n 28) 326.

facto a war crime.[80] This in turn has prompted reassertions of the necessarily violent *status quo* of men at war against the apparent squeamishness of mere 'civilians' not socialized in the usages of armed violence. For example, after the public was shocked that Danish soldiers had set up an ambush for Afghans who were recovering unexploded bombs, the Danish Minister of Defence insisted:

> Ambushes by Danish soldiers contribute to saving lives and demoralise the enemy. Of course, it comes across as incredibly violent when I say this, and it may sound cynical. But war is violent, and part of being in an armed conflict is that you get shot at and that you will shoot at the enemy.[81]

This of course merely restates the obvious, namely that the laws of war sanction inter-combatant violence; but it also reaffirms a baseline of violence that takes exception from many of the assumptions of civil society and its attempt to intrude on that domain. Behind such gendered performances, arguably lie not so much (yet) fear of a female takeover as chronic anxieties about effeminacy[82] in the ongoing constitution of masculinity[83] and, in particular, what the orientation towards a 'gentler' or more 'caring' approach to war might portend.[84] This is especially in a context of male fraternity and bonding (including, presumably, among military lawyers) that has long been suspected of homoeroticism.[85]

Particularly strongly worded affirmations of the 'virile' status quo have been evident in response to attempts to steer the laws of war in a more humane direction. The humanization of the laws of war, a term pioneered by Theodor Meron,[86] describes a series of efforts to shift the centre of gravity towards what may be seen as relatively more 'humanitarian' – and hence invariably coded

---

80 Frédéric Mégret, 'Overheard Amidst the Bombs' (*Opinio Juris*, 28 May 2021) <http://opiniojuris.org/2021/05/28/overheard-amidst-the-bombs/>.

81 See Rikke Ishøy, 'Humanity and the Discourse of Legality' in Camilla G Cooper, Gro Nystuen and Kjetil Mujezinović Larsen (eds), *Searching for a 'Principle of Humanity' in International Humanitarian Law* (Cambridge University Press 2012).

82 Which have often been shown to trump homophobia. See Niall Richardson, '"Whether you are gay or straight, I don't like to see effeminate dancing": effeminophobia in performance-level ballroom dance' (2018) 27 Journal of Gender Studies 207.

83 Michèle Cohen, '"Manners" Make the Man: Politeness, Chivalry, and the Construction of Masculinity, 1750–1830' (2005) 44 Journal of British Studies 312.

84 Gutmann (n 37).

85 Judith Butler, 'Contagious Word: Paranoia and "Homosexuality" in the Military' in Iain Morland and Dino Willox (eds), *Queer Theory* (Bloomsbury Publishing 2017).

86 Meron (n 54).

as 'feminine' – understandings of the laws of war. One notorious example is provided by the International Committee of the Red Cross's ('ICRC') 2009 Interpretative Guidance on Direct Participation in Hostilities which opted for a regime of civilian participation that is considered by some to be excessively protective, much to the chagrin of a chorus of commentators who argued instead that civilians endorsing combat functions should be assumed to have forfeited civilian protections.[87] At stake is not only the fact that civilians who directly participate in hostilities can reclaim their more protective civilian status at a moment's notice as it were, but also the sheer gendered perfidy of their ability to move back and forth through the revolving doors of combatancy (gendered male) and civilian status (gendered female). LOAC lawyers, through a sort of masculine argument from authority,[88] were clear in their dismissiveness of the Guidelines as 'fatally flawed' and as reflecting 'a troubling ignorance of the realities of 21st Century battlefield combat'[89] as well as 'setting forth a normative paradigm that states that actually go to war cannot countenance.'[90]

A related relatively recent example is provided by the 'wound rather than kill and capture rather than wound' debate as it emerged in the wake of the ICRC Guidelines. Gabriela Blum[91] and Ryan Goodman[92] have argued that we should depart from the dominant view that combatants can be subject to any amount of lethal force unless they are surrendering. Instead, Goodman claims that 'in certain well-specified and narrow circumstances, the use of force should instead be governed by a least-restrictive means' analysis such that one seeks to capture rather than wound, wound rather than kill and injure lightly rather than injure gravely enemy combatants. This general formula is then defended as consonant with a particular reading of the history of the laws of war. The debate has involved a detailed and prolonged exegesis of Article 35 that is interesting on its own terms, but this is not the place to

87 See, e.g., Michael N Schmitt, 'Deconstructing Direct Participation in Hostilities: The Constitutive Elements' (2009) 42 New York University Journal of International Law and Politics 697.

88 Khameiel Al Tamimi and John Fields, 'A Gendered Analysis of the Role of Authority in Argumentation' (2011) OSSA Conference Archive 9.

89 Michael N Schmitt, 'Deconstructing Direct Participation in Hostilities: The Constitutive Elements' (2009) 42 New York University Journal of International Law and Politics 697, 739.

90 Michael N Schmitt, 'The Interpretive Guidance on the Notion of Direct Participation in Hostilities: A Critical Analysis' (2010) 1 *Harvard National Security Journal* 5.

91 Gabriella Blum, 'The Dispensable Lives of Soldiers' (2010) 2 Journal of Legal Analysis 115.

92 Ryan Goodman, 'The Power to Kill or Capture Enemy Combatants' (2013) 24 European Journal of International Law 819.

discuss whether that approach is indeed grounded in law or not in a context where the law is indeterminate and controversies are also settled through the weight of gendered expertise. Rather, I am interested in how the intensity of the response to it can only be understood as part of gendered anxieties that seeks to reassert a model of manly fortitude in war.

One would think that more protections for men would appeal to masculinist sensitivities; yet exactly the opposite seems to have happened, particularly in the eyes of elite LOAC lawyers prompt to assume the perspective of the shooter rather than the target, and therefore irked by the extra layer of scruple such a reading would impose on armed forces' operational freedom. In that respect, those who responded to the ICRC or Goodman not only asserted that his claim was 'flawed,' but also specifically that it was 'a dangerous misinterpretation of the legal limitations applicable to targeting in armed conflict.'[93] They insisted that the need to defeat the enemy meant that all combatants were *ipso facto* targetable merely based on their status as members of the armed forces and that such a rule was 'axiomatic.' They argued that the 'prohibition on unnecessary' suffering could not possibly be held to include a prohibition on 'unnecessary killing.' Proportionality, if at all, applied only in relation to civilians as victims of incidental injury from otherwise lawful attacks.[94]

The debate was at no point explicitly framed in gendered terms, but its underlying politics point to the continuing relevance of a peculiar masculine fixation with the necessary lethality of war. For example, a stark distinction was drawn between the (hard) rule of military necessity and the (soft) principle of humanity, leaving little doubt about which should prevail.[95] The implicit point, beyond the interpretative quarrels, was that the 'wound rather than kill' rule was fundamentally at odds with the nature of war as an activity necessarily premised on a degree of violence between combatants (men) that could only be feminized up to a point. As one response put it, emphasizing the centrality of the perspective of men at war in a not-so-subtle attempt to disqualify feminine interventions (typically presumed to not be battle-hardened, although many military lawyers are not either):

> Anyone who has ever had to carry a loaded weapon into hostilities, contemplate the duty to kill inherent in military service, order the employment

93 Robert Chesney, 'Corn, Blank, Jenks, and Jensen Respond to Goodman on Capture-Instead-of-Kill' (*Lawfare*, 25 February 2013) <https://www.lawfareblog.com/corn-blank-jenks-and-jensen-respond-goodman-capture-instead-kill>.

94 ibid.

95 Schmitt, 'The Interpretive Guidance on the Notion of Direct Participation in Hostilities: A Critical Analysis' (n 90).

> of combat power against enemy personnel, or train and advise them on the legal parameters applicable to such actions understands just how operationally impractical a capture rather than kill obligation would be to implement.[96]

In particular, Goodman was criticized for 'Confusing what the law is with what one might believe it should be [...] especially when doing so undermines the clarity and initiative central to the effective execution of combat operations against enemy belligerents, can result in deadly consequences for those called upon to fight and win our wars.'[97] The framing of the response, including for example the need to 'recapture the concept of necessity,'[98] suggested the crucial importance of not ceding ground on this issue.

In short, whilst superficially civil, the controversy over the 'least violent means' foregrounded intense argumentative practices and the more 'realist' position of those presented as having experience in the field. These moves barely concealed assumptions about masculinity, including that 'voicing concerns about the number of casualties in the enemy's armed forces, imagining the suffering of the killed and wounded young men, is out of bounds.'[99] The ICRC's guidelines and Goodman's overture, then, whatever their historical pedigree and interpretative plausibility, tapped into and triggered a rich reservoir of anxieties about the necessarily violent nature of (masculine) warfare, bizarrely threatened by an intemperate desire to neuter men at war.

3.3 *Human Rights Approaches to War and the Reactivation of Misogyny*

Humanization of the regulation of war on the laws of war's own terms may lead a dead end in the face of reassertions of traditional tropes about the necessity of certain violence in war. Some seeking to humanize the laws of war have, however, gone further and even more explicitly sought to incorporate an element of international human rights law ('IHRL') in their effort to challenge the LOAC paradigm.[100] Indeed, IHRL has become more generally a potentially alternative paradigm to address violence, notably in situation of non-international armed conflict, prolonged occupation or peacekeeping but also,

96 Chesney (n 93).

97 ibid.

98 Jens D Ohlin, 'Recapturing the Concept of Necessity' (2013) Cornall Legal Studies Research Paper No. 13–90 <https://papers.ssrn.com/abstract=2230486>.

99 Carol Cohn, 'Wars, Wimps, and Women: Talking Gender and Thinking War' in Miriam Cooke and Angela Woollacott (eds), *Gendering War Talk* (Princeton University Press 2014) 232.

100 Jens D Ohlin, 'The Duty to Capture' (2012) 97 Minnesota Law Review 1268.

potentially, when it comes to the core of the laws of war, namely the conduct of hostilities in international armed conflicts.[101]

There is nothing necessarily feminine about this effort except that its simultaneously principled and normalizing orientation can be understood as an attempt to rein in masculinity run amok and that it can be easily culturally coded as 'feminine'. More pointedly, the attempt to rule war through human rights is premised on a sort of 'domestic analogy' and, ultimately, the denial that there is anything 'exceptional' about war that would justify that it be regulated by unique and highly anomalous (masculine) norms.[102] That theoretical claim also has all the appearances of a collapsing of the public and private spheres (of the international system and the state, respectively) that leaves very little room for a kind of 'boys club' approach to the regulation of war. Contra mere 'humanization' at the margins, it proposes a less oblique and potentially more radical alternative to the virile humanitarian compact rooted in assumptions about equality. As a frontal challenge to a certain kind of masculine dominance of war's ordering, then, it has activated a rich repertoire of underlying misogyny and 'flight from the feminine'[103] at the heart of the military/war compact.[104]

This has manifested itself, in turn, in a furious defense of the continuation of the project of the laws of war as necessarily as project of chronic adaptation to the unavoidable violence of men. That reaction and its particular intensity, again, may say more about masculine anxieties about war's regulation than about the debate on the place of human rights itself. For example, Yoram Dinstein has decried 'the unpleasant phenomenon of human rights-niks who, hoisting the banner of human rights law, are attempting to bring about a hostile takeover of LOAC.'[105] For such authors, it is not that human rights do not have their place in the regulation of war, but that they should operate on the margins of the traditionally virile domain of the 'conduct of hostilities.' *Lex specialis derogat generalis*, then, can be understood as literally a claim to the perpetuation of masculine exceptionalism, against 'an encroachment that we

---

101 Kenneth Watkin, 'Controlling the Use of Force: A Role for Human Rights Norms in Contemporary Armed Conflict' (2004) 98 American Journal of International Law 1.

102 Gabriella Blum, 'The Paradox of Power: The Changing Norms of the Modern Battlefield' (2019) 56 Houston Law Review 745, 765.

103 Kimmel (n 22) 229.

104 Ben Wadham, 'Violence in the Military and Relations Among Men: Military Masculinities and "Rape Prone Cultures"' in Rachel Woodward and Claire Duncanson (eds), *The Palgrave International Handbook of Gender and the Military* (Palgrave Macmillan 2017); Genevieve Lloyd, 'Selfhood, War and Masculinity'in Carole Pateman and Elizabeth Grosz (eds) *Feminist Challenges* (Routledge 1986).

105 Yoram Dinstein, 'Concluding Remarks: LOAC and Attempts to Abuse or Subvert It' (2011) 87 International Law Studies 20, 488.

must stoutly resist.'[106] Of course, all the doctrinal arguments on the difficulty of delineating the '*specialis*' and the '*generalis*' are apposite here, but even more so in a context where, more often than not, normality ends up being ruled from the exception (or at least the possibility of the exception).

Indeed, the increasing forays of IHRL into the regulation of armed conflict are typically seen as an attempt at femininization that is and ought to be resisted as such by those who believe that '[t]he law of war has always been, and should continue to be, within the province of, and from the perspective of, the warrior.'[107] One author, US Major Michelle Hansen, devoted an entire article in 2007 to the need to, quite literally and graphically, 'prevent [...] the emasculation of warfare' by 'halting the expansion of human rights law into armed conflict.'[108] For Hansen, as explained in a non-ironic footnote, the use of the term 'emasculation' is deliberate, reflects the significance of gendered-discourse in international law and is based on the idea that human rights law 'is ill-equipped for the harsh realities of war.'[109] That literal[110] and metaphorical fear of metaphorical castration is evident, then, in much masculinist protestations against human rights as, essentially, a 'regime change [...] making hostilities impossible to engage in effectively'[111] and thus profoundly questioning manhood as a signifier of the ability to define war.[112]

Several concerns animate this backlash against human rights. Some have to do with the notion that human rights approaches will improve the protection

106 ibid.

107 Scott R Morris, 'The Laws of War: Rules by Warriors for Warriors' (1997) Army Law 4, 13.

108 Michelle A Hansen, 'Preventing the Emasculation of Warfare: Halting the Expansion of Human Rights Law into Armed Conflict' (2007) 194 Military Law Review 1. The metaphor of emasculation in debates on how the laws of war are threatened by excessive pusillanimity is older. See Georg Schwarzenberger, 'Functions and Foundations of the Laws of War' (1958) 44 Archiv für Rechts-und Sozialphilosophie 351, 353. Also A P V Rogers, *Law on the Battlefield* (Manchester University Press 1996) 2. ("the less technologically advanced states sometimes see the law of war as an instrument for emasculating the mighty").

109 Hansen (n 108) 4.

110 Linsey Robb and Juliette Pattinson, *Men, Masculinities and Male Culture in the Second World War* (Palgrave Macmillan 2018).

111 Dinstein (n 105) 492.

112 To be fair and as perhaps testimony to the embededness of the metaphor, the image of 'emasculation' is also routinely used by those who argue that the laws of war are not humanitarian enough. See Richard L Fruchterman Jr, 'Enforcement: The Difference between the Laws of War and the Geneva Conventions' (1983) 13 Georgia Journal of International and Comparative Law 303, 304. Although seemingly counter-intuitive, it bears underlining, again, that restraint (including since at least Roman times, sexual restraint as a sign of virtue and self-control) is constantly and precariously balanced against licence as a potent symbol of manliness.

of civilians and victims in war at the expense of warriors themselves, while others bemoan the complexity of the resulting approach. In characteristic paternalistic fashion, the probability of 'perverse effects' is emphasized, notably the risk that excessive humanization of war will ('in the real world (as distinct from the dreamworld of human rights-niks)'[113]) actually prolong violence and in the end that civilians will pay the price.[114] One underlying question is 'who owns the rules of law in today's post-Cold War?,' a question that is not of course addressed in explicitly gendered terms, but which is answered by neatly opposing the uncertain legitimacy of the 'liberal internationalism' of non-governmental organizations and the United Nations, against revisionist powers China and Russia, forcing the '"good guy" states' to, 'once again [...] take "ownership" ' in the form of, presumably, the indispensable virile synthesis.[115]

To conclude this section, behind the fear of civilianization, human rights-ization and femininization also lies the fear of an androgenous world: a 'civilization' to use the words of French Fascist Pierre Drieu de la Rochelle, that 'no longer has sexes.'[116] This is a 'civilization' in which the precarious identity of one imagined gender cannot be asserted against the other, and in the process the power of patriarchy is significantly threatened through a phasing out of gendered binaries. It is also a 'civilization' that rests on a construct of 'masculinity as homophobia' that constantly activates panics about one's gender-conformity.

4 The Curious Resilience of Masculinity in War

The increasing deconstruction of gender roles, the critique of hegemonic masculinity and beyond it of heteronormativity, as they trickle slowly into the quotidian reality of the military and war, are bound to disrupt some of the laws of war's foundational categories. At the same time, as the previous section has suggested, masculine conceptions of the laws of war remain remarkably resilient in their ability to fend off feminizing challenges. What, in this context, is the secret of masculinity's resurgence amidst its ongoing contestation? How does it maintain itself despite these challenges?

113 Dinstein (n 105) 491.

114 Dinstein (n 105).

115 Kenneth Anderson, 'Who Owns the Rules of War in Today's Post-Post-Cold War' (2018) 56 Houston Law Review 789, 819.

116 Pierre Drieu La Rochelle, *Le jeune Européen: et autres écrits de jeunesse, 1917–1927* (Bartillat 2016).

The homeostatic nature of the regulation of the laws of war is arguably a function of the ability of certain constituencies to capture and constantly reimagine what is presented as the evolving middle ground between military necessity and humanity whilst still, somehow, always *in fine* entrenching masculine domination. This is in line with cultural histories of Western masculinity that note the ability of hegemonic masculinity to constantly refashion itself from opposites, at the intersection of 'anti-heroic' and 'heroic' stereotypes.[117] Although constantly evolving, hegemonic masculinity goes through a series of set equilibria that maintain its ascendancy.

Several factors certainly contribute to masculinity's stability as an implicit signifier of the effort to regulate war. First, its relative invisibility. Masculinity as mentioned in the introduction, is rarely problematized even in feminist readings of the laws of war, except as a sort of implicit reference. Hegemonic masculinity never needs to defend itself precisely because it is hegemonic. It is content with rent seeking, merely interpreting 'doctrinally' texts that it has itself crafted, leaving 'theory,' 'deconstruction' and 'interdisciplinarity' to 'feminine' interlopers. To add to the confusion, the regulation of armed conflict operates in ways that allow for a range of gendered permutation (e.g., feminine combatants and masculine civilian victims) that complicate gender's meaning. War's masculine character, in particular, is evidently not exclusive of some women having so internalized gendered tropes that they goad men into battle to prove their manhood[118] or even are responsible for sexualized violence.[119] Second, masculinity is dynamic and constantly evolving. This makes it hard to pin down the notion as one is constantly faced with an actualized version of its potentialities, including some, as has been seen, already integrating 'feminine' criticism of its toxicity. In that respect, the ongoing polishing of martial discourse has paradoxically made it harder to detect stereotypes that are now constantly denied even as they are constantly re-enacted. Third, masculinity is relational and ambiguous. There is evidently no masculine ontology any more than there is a feminine ontology, as much as ongoing contestations about what masculinity is. Masculinity can only be captured in tension to what it designates as its opposite, something which changes over time.

At the same time, masculinity is also not *that* invisible, dynamic and ambiguous. The constitution of masculinity through the laws of war often

---

117 Sonya O Rose, 'Temperate Heroes: Concepts of Masculinity in Second World War Britain' in Stefan Dudink, Karen Hagemann and John Tosh (eds), *Masculinities in Politics and War: Gendering Modern History* (Manchester University Press 2004).

118 Jean B Elshtain, *Women and War* (University of Chicago Press 1995) 196.

119 Mark A Drumbl, 'She Makes Me Ashamed to Be a Woman: The Genocide Conviction of Pauline Nyiramasuhuko, 2011' (2012) 34 Michigan Journal of International Law 559.

takes a deeply cyclical and recursive, even predictable, form, which follows the following pattern. To begin with, the continued sustenance of strong conceptions of masculinity suggests the possibility of 'men' going to war on their own terms and at a safe distance from 'ill-informed,' 'feminine' attempts to regulate their participation. The Vietnam war, for example, instead of leading to a 'rethink (of) patriarchal ideology', drove many men to 'reassert [...] traditional discourses of male power.' These emphasized at least the possibility of not 'fighting the war with our hands tied behind our backs [...] kow-towing to the lily-livered liberals, peaceniks and doves in Congress who curtailed American bombing.'[120] More often than not, then, the call to arms has been a call to resurgent masculinity, to shed effete manhood, perhaps even to get rid of individual bourgeois manliness for the sake of a collective and cathartic violent masculinity.

This move has a long history that goes back at least Fascism.[121] From the Bush administration to the Trump White House, there is no doubt that masculine reassertion can quickly turn into an exercise in under-cutting masculinity's own precarious standard of restraint. In the 'torture memos,' for example, one witnesses first a US Presidency unconstrained by constitutional moorings, and then the violent field executioners of US policy 'freed' of humanitarian rules.[122] The hyper-masculinization of the state and the hyper-masculinization of the individual go hand in hand. Masculine re-assertion is part of a broader pattern visible throughout the 20th Century through which (certain) men have sought to re-masculinize activities that were increasingly feminized, by reinventing forms of increasingly muscular and closed-off masculinity, not least in the military.[123] Occasionally, this will feed into a sort of 'hysterical masculinity,'[124] all the more theatrical that it is threatened.[125]

Yet every attempt to tilt the laws of war back in a more hyper-masculine direction comes with its own dangers, *even on hegemonic masculinity's own*

---

120 Lynda E Boose, 'Techno-Muscularity and the "Boy Eternal": From the Quagmire to the Gulf', *Gendering war talk* (Princeton University Press 2014) 72.

121 Sandro Bellassai, 'The Masculine Mystique: Antimodernism and Virility in Fascist Italy' (2005) 10 Journal of Modern Italian Studies 314.

122 Bonnie Mann, *Sovereign Masculinity: Gender Lessons from the War on Terror* (Oxford University Press 2013) 183–184.

123 Lori Holyfield et al, 'Masculinity under Attack: Melodramatic Resistance to Women in Combat' (2019) 5 Critical Military Studies 168.

124 Mark Straw, 'Traumatized Masculinity and American National Identity in Hollywood's Gulf War' (2008) 6 New Cinemas: Journal of Contemporary Film 127.

125 'Manning up: Men May Overcompensate When Their Masculinity Is Threatened' (*UW News*, 22 June 2015) <https://www.washington.edu/news/2015/06/22/manning-up-men-may-overcompensate-when-their-masculinity-is-threatened/>.

terms. These include laying bare that regulation's authority and its claim to universality: indeed, why should women, or racialized subjects for that matter, care about the laws of war (and having them if not care at least voluntarily adhere is, very much, one of the project's goals) if they are structurally on the losing end of their operation? Moreover, the loosening of restraints which constituted a certain manly identity also leads the warrior into a gendered *terra incognita*, perhaps that of the 'immature, oversexed men-children'[126] or that of 'deep boyhood.'[127] By exposing a sort of bare violent masculinity, it also sabotages the patient work of masculine obfuscation involved in the laws of war, at the risk, if nothing else, of fundamentally undermining the normative underpinnings of true masculine domination which rests in part on the ability to perform restraint and exact allegiance in exchange.[128]

This may be why the actual *dominants* are prone to appear more level-headed in the face of challenges to their hegemonic masculinity, always hedging their virile protestations with a generous dose of concessions to the ascending femininization of the world. In particular, and true to the fundamental script of the laws of war, the fundamentally protective role of soldierly masculinity is stressed.[129] This is at one with the liberal-martial state and the projection of its (manly) protective aura. Since the 'role for liberal states cannot be one of simplistic domination [...] Instead, it can be cast as chivalrous, self-sacrificing and responsibly masculine in valiantly facing the dangers of the world.'[130]

At any rate, simultaneously, the idea that certain brutish behaviour is 'not worthy of a soldier' in war remains a powerful motif, even in what may otherwise seem to be some of the most depraved armies. As General Manstein wrote in his diary, 'it is not worthy of an officer to witness shootings of Jews.'[131] One is always, it seems, another man's better in that one would not lower oneself to certain extremes. Contra the glorification of extreme violence, defenders of the laws of war such as Bluntschli have long played on the repertoire of upholding civilization through a commitment to virtue: 'toutes les fois que les convoitises et les passions de l'homme sont excitées, sa nature bestiale se réveille, et dès que les liens de la civilisation se relâchent apparaît déchaîné le loup vorace et

126 Grant A G Tracey, *Filmography of American History* (Greenwood Publishing Group 2002) 230.

127 Michael S Kimmel and Michael Kaufman, 'The New Men's Movement: Retreat and Regression with America's Weekend Warriors' (1993) 13 Feminist Issues 3.

128 Mégret, 'The Laws of War and the Structure of Masculine Power' (n 16).

129 Ferry (n 3); Iris M Young, 'The Logic of Masculinist Protection: Reflections on the Current Security State' (2003) 29 Signs: Journal of Women in Culture and Society 1.

130 Victoria M Basham, 'Liberal Militarism as Insecurity, Desire and Ambivalence: Gender, Race and the Everyday Geopolitics of War' (2018) 49 Security Dialogue 32.

131 Mungo Melvin, *Manstein: Hitler's Greatest General* (Macmillan 2011).

lubrique, qui jamais n'avait été entièrement apprivoisé, n'était complètement devenu homme.'[132] In other words, contra untrammelled bestial energies, it is restraint in war that makes man *man*.

In this section, I further reflect on a number of ways in which the dynamics of masculinization remain structuring of the laws of war, at times even as the stereotypes on which they rely have become socially outdated. It is important to note that, just as racism is not only a question of individual moral agency but a systemic property of social, political and legal systems, the 'sexism' involved in the constitution of the laws of war is deeply embedded into international legal structures and thus quite resistant to change. This manifests itself in how masculinity is prolonged intersectionally (4.1), in what it makes unthinkable (4.2), and through the social types it helps sustain (4.3).

4.1 *Masculinity's Peculiar Intersectionality*

It is worth noting that the Western tradition has been haunted by its own ambivalence towards restrained manhood, which has often been overlaid by racist tropes and an identification of manliness with civilization. In the colonial context, the perception was often that that 'black' and 'indigenous' men were more masculine and thus capable of fighting a more ruthless war, one unhindered by the polite restraints of white masculinity. This coexisted with fears among settlers about 'virile "savages."'[133] In the Darwinian climate of the time, moreover, the anxiety was that more virile nations would win the struggle and the more effete would be left by the wayside. 'Overcivilization was endangering American manhood' and leading straight to effeminacy, which meant that one should reclaim exactly what one had been 'endeavoring to teach the savages to avoid.'[134]

Indeed, this also coincides with a long history of fascination for and ambivalence towards 'Indian warfare.'[135] A whole part of the Western military tradition has long been tempted to follow the imagined 'savages' and engage in 'savage' wars; or at least is only too willing to see the rationality of 'non-manly'

---

132 Johan-Caspar Bluntschli, 'Droit de la guerre et coutume de guerre' (1876) 8 Revue de droit international et de législation comparée 665. English translation: 'Every time the desires and passions of men are aroused, their bestial nature is awakened, and as soon as the bonds of civilization are loosened, the voracious and lustful wolf, which had never been entirely tamed, nor had it completely become a man, appears unchained.'

133 John Lambert, '6 "The Last Outpost": The Natalians, South Africa, and the British Empire' in Robert Bickers (ed), *Settlers and Expatriates: Britons over the Seas* (Oxford University Press 2010).

134 Gail Bederman, *Manliness and Civilization: A Cultural History of Gender and Race in the United States, 1880–1917* (University of Chicago Press 2008) 77–78.

135 Kinsella, 'Settler Empire and the United States' (n 49).

warfare given the terrain and the forces in presence. The temptation of 'going local' in warfare, and not letting one be unduly constrained by one's Western/ virile delicacy in view of the Oriental/feminine ruthlessness of the enemy is omnipresent. It enthusiastically invokes the other's imagined deviancy to better normalize one's own. Theodore Roosevelt could not have been clearer when he asserted that 'Over-sentimentality, over-softness, in fact washiness and mushiness are the great dangers of this age and of this people. Unless we keep the barbarian virtues, the civilized ones will be of little avail.'[136]

The recurring crises of masculinity that have ensued during the First World War and up to the Second have occasionally manifested themselves as an infatuation with 'primal' or 'natural' manhood, a sort of imagined repressed inherent male at the heart of every man, whose savagery ought to be released in battle.[137] They also translated into hatred of black bodies and their perceived over-sexed proclivities in the Rhine by the Germans.[138] Indeed, at the same time the 'savages' imagined 'savagery,' that same savagery that white armies occasionally sought to mimic was reviled as unmanly and thus below them.

In our era, calls to be ruthless on the battlefield have been resurrected by a perception that 'savages' will themselves be ruthless and can thus only be tackled by similar means – that one must fight fire with fire. This leads to aspiration to resurrect hyper-masculinity:

> Do we have the strength of will, as a military and as nation, to defeat an enemy who has nothing to lose? When we face warriors, we will often face men who have acquired a taste for killing, who do not behave rationally according to our definition of rationality, who are capable of atrocities that challenge the descriptive powers of language, and who will sacrifice their own kind in order to survive. We will face opponents for whom treachery is routine, and they will not be impressed by tepid shows of force with restrictive rules of engagement. Are we able to engage in and sustain the level of sheer violence it takes to eradicate this kind of threat?[139]

136 See Jeanne Fox-Friedman, 'The Chivalric Order for Children: Arthur's Return in Late Nineteenth-and Early Twentieth-Century America' in Debra N Mancoff (ed), *King Arthur's Modern Return* (Routledge 2014) 152.

137 Bederman (n 134).

138 Rotem Giladi, 'The Phoenix of Colonial War: Race, the Laws of War, and the "Horror on the Rhine"' (2017) 30 Leiden Journal of International Law 847.

139 Ralph Peters, 'The New Warrior Class' (1994) 24 Parameters 24.

This brutishness-by-mimetism presents the loosening of manly restraints as done grudgingly and tragically: challenged to feminize at home, the military claims that it is 'provoked' into hyper-masculinization abroad. But toxic masculinity is, at any rate, seen as the masculinity of the Islamic 'other.'[140] The warrior is then prone to exorcise his challenged masculinity by lashing back in an attempt to outdo the 'savages' in their ruthlessness, whilst claiming innocence from his transformation. Torture is also a way in which 'a hegemonic white masculinity seeks to impose itself' and, in the process, a certain vision of (male) sovereignty over 'the subordinate Muslim male *homo sacer*.'[141]

One hears echoes of this sort of crepuscular fantasy in the 'long-felt common anxiety that democracy has made us weak and there are no real men anymore' so that 'failing to torture is the sissy's response; only a real man knows what to do.'[142] As a result, however, 'modern civilized "warrior man"' becomes a 'curious throwback to the 'frenzied barbarian' who represent[s] the antithesis of civilization.'[143] At the same time, the Western warrior never ceases to claim the mantel of civilization since, in relation to the hypermasculine/devious Taliban and Iraqi insurgents 'who refuse to play fair [...] the British soldier [...] is the just warrior, respectful of international law and of the rules of fair play.'[144] This has led Yoram Dinstein for example to excoriate 'down to earth' and 'hardheaded' LOAC lawyers for nonetheless being on the defensive against 'barbarians' who invoke the law only to subvert it through lawfare.[145] The figure of the barbarian, both in its brutish and effete versions, then, acts as a constant throwback for visions of redemptive white masculinity. It not only injects masculinity with a particular racial fervour; it also suffuses it with meaning.

4.2 *Feminine Hysteria and the Unthinkability of Pacifism*

Another way of understanding the enduring dynamics of masculine reassertion through the laws of war is as expressing, beyond the narcissism of small masculine differences, a more fundamental contempt for 'feminine' pacifism. Although pacifism is by no means historically only a women's movement, it is one of the few areas in international affairs to have become

140 Elizabeth Pearson, 'Extremism and Toxic Masculinity: The Man Question Re-Posed' (2019) 95 International Affairs 1251.

141 Viola Shafik, Julie A Carlson and Elisabeth Weber, 'Rituals of Hegemonic Masculinity: Cinema, Torture, and the Middle East' in Julie A Carlson and Elisabeth Weber (eds) *Speaking about torture* (Fordham University Press 2012) 162.

142 Darius M Rejali, *Torture and Democracy* (Princeton University Press 2007) 548.

143 Parpat and Zalewski (n 10) 80.

144 Claire Duncanson, *Forces for Good?: Military Masculinities and Peacebuilding in Afghanistan and Iraq* (Palgrave Macmillan 2013) 107.

145 Dinstein (n 119).

over time dominated by women.[146] At any rate, even when pacifism has not been defended by women (there are, needless to say, female warmongers just as there are pacifist men), it has consistently been dismissively *constructed* as feminine.

Prussian Field Marshal von Moltke once dismissed perpetual peace as 'a dream, and not even a beautiful dream. War is an element of the divine order of the world. In it are developed the noblest virtues of man: courage and self-denial, fidelity or duty and the spirit of sacrifice.'[147] For Heinrich Von Treitschke, 'the features of history are virile, unsuited to sentimental or feminine natures. Brave peoples alone have an existence, an evolution or a future; the weak and cowardly perish, and perish justly. The grandeur of history lies in the perpetual conflict of nations, *and it is simply foolish to desire the suppression of their rivalry*. Mankind has ever found it to be so …'[148] During the First World War, feminist 'hysterical peacettes' were portrayed as traitors and as emissaries of the Kaiser or as naïve extremists, even by some fellow women. Men who have identified as peacemakers in war contexts have highlighted a 'dovishness [which] provided a reason for other men … to question [their] competence and responsibility, their understanding of the 'tough' choices that face "real statesmen".'[149] After 9/11, 'those seeking debate and diplomacy were feminized – cast as behaving like cowardly women and undermining US interests by wimping out of military action.'[150]

This designation of pacifism as not only irrelevant to the practice of war but bordering on the treasonous manifests itself in the absolute insistence within the laws of war tradition that *in bello* and *jus ad bellum* concerns be kept apart as foundational condition of the very possibility of regulating war. International humanitarian lawyers portray their discipline as one of pragmatism, drawing an equivalency between aggressor and attacked parties in the name of the fog of war, the difficulty of ascertaining responsibilities and the need for a simplified regime of obligations for warriors. By contrast, *jus contra bellum* concerns are understood as largely irrelevant to the humanitarian pursuit and their potentially radical implications for the *jus in bello* shunned even by the

146 Frédéric Mégret, 'A Look Back at The Women's Hague Peace Conference: What Contribution to International Law Today?' in Jaya Ramji-Nogales and others (eds), *The Oxford Handbook of Women and International Law* (2023).

147 Cited in Brian Bond, *War and Society in Europe, 1870–1970* (McGill-Queen's Press – MQUP 1998) 26.

148 Cited in Jacob Leib Talmon, *Myth of the Nation and Vision of Revolution: Ideological Polarization in the Twentieth Century* (Transaction Publishers 1991) 106.

149 Marysia Zalewski and Jane L Parpart, *The 'Man' Question in International Relations* (Routledge 2019) 100.

150 Peterson (n 8) 18.

(often male) revisionist just war theorists who have come closest to denouncing the moral anomaly of the laws of war.[151]

As has been argued by Dianne Otto, 'the popular palatability of military discourse relies on strongly contrasting images of masculinity and femininity, which serves to marginalize pacifism because it is associated with the feminine.'[152] Where 'women' are imagined as prone to see a world based on love and empathy, only 'men' can see its harsh reality, and therefore the need to regulate war rather than seek to eliminate it. In *The Bostonians*, Henry James described 'the masculine character' as 'the ability to dare and endure, to know and yet not fear reality, to look the word in the face and take it for what it is.'[153] In that respect the feminine utopianism of pacifism is contrasted with the realism of the laws of war: women want to have it all; only men have the ability to accept the tragic.

4.3 *Locating the Humanitarian Warrior Lawyer*

A third way of understanding the persistence of dominant masculine tropes in the regulation of war is as specifically mediated by the practice of militarized lawyers as a further, peculiar synthesis of the different demands on modern masculinity. The position of the military lawyer or even the non-military lawyer seeking recognition among military men is emblematic of masculine gendered hierarchies.[154] Within the military, military lawyers are on the 'feminine' end of the spectrum, more likely to be arguing for restraint in a field that is tempted by brutal reassertions of machismo and therefore 'must at times overcome the suspicion that they are not really part of the band of brothers.'[155] This is compounded by a sense that one is invoking *international* law, a body of law riddled with anxieties about its lack of masculinity.[156] Within the comparatively more 'effeminate' legal field, by contrast, the military lawyer is on the more masculine end of the spectrum as at least in part an apologist for a certain

---

151 Jennifer Kling, 'Engaging in a Cover-Up: The "Deep Morality" of War' in Jennifer Kling (ed), *Pacifism, Politics, and Feminism – Intersections and Innovations* (Brill 2019).

152 Dianne Otto, 'A Sign of "Weakness"? Disrupting Gender Certainties in the Implementation of Security Council Resolution 1325' (2006) 13 Michigan Journal of Gender & Law 113, 125.

153 Henry James, *The Bostonians: Volume II* (Books on Demand 2018) 91.

154 For a similar effort in relation to civilian academics teaching in a military environment, see Huw Osborne, 'Cocked and Ready: The Humanities and Homosociality at the Royal Military College of Canada' in Douglas Higbee, *Military Culture and Education: Current Intersections of Academic and Military Cultures* (Routledge 2010).

155 Luban (n 28) 321.

156 Doris E Buss, 'Queering International Legal Authority' (2007) 101 Proceedings of the ASIL Annual Meeting 122.

inevitability of war, military necessity, etc.[157] The military/humanitarian lawyer is, then, both an insider and an outsider, playing on both fronts as it were, but crucially still in need of asserting his manly credibility simultaneously to two polarized constituencies (neither not masculine enough nor too masculine).

The intensity of the reaction to attempts to further 'humanize' (understood as 'feminize') the laws of war is reinforced by the fact that the lawyer knows, however embedded he may be in the military that, in the pecking order of masculinities, his is a fairly low rank. What precarious status he nonetheless has achieved, he is unlikely to want to give up by being seen as excessively embracing the 'feminine' side of the law, instead making up for his lack battlefield credibility by a competent demonstration of legal virility, defending the imagined core masculinity of the laws of war. This well-worn performance of enabling violence whilst restraining it is increasingly instantiated through bureaucratization and the aura of authority it confers, funnelling masculinity into banal administrative processes.[158] The effect is unmistakably to cement the continuous and structural hold of masculine imaginaries on the law. Incidentally, this further allows men at war to not 'own up' to the masculine archetypes they embody, since these have now been legislated into the core of military activity.

But the reactions to feminizing contenders must also be contextualized in an ongoing struggle over the politics of expertise and anxieties 'relating to the 'loss of monopoly' of military lawyers over the administration of IHL.'[159] More importantly, it involves, despite a cursory recognition of pluralism in the regulation of war, foregrounding 'those with the expertise and experience to fully appreciate the fragile IHL balance between military necessity and humanity' (and notably, a 'grasp [of] the harsh consequences of armed conflict')[160] in a context where the law 'must be handled delicately.'[161] These are typically understood to be 'government experts and States uniquely positioned to evaluate the operational and even strategic costs of legal innovation' rather than 'academics and non-governmental organizations' and some of their

157 Luban (n 28).

158 David Kennedy, *Of War and Law* (Princeton University Press 2006).

159 Eliav Lieblich, 'The Law of Warfare: 1989–2022' in Eyal Benvenisti and Dino Kritsiotis (eds), *International Law Since the End of the Cold War* (Cambirdge University Press, Forthcoming).

160 Michael N Schmitt and Sean Watts, 'The Decline of International Humanitarian Law Opinio Juris and the Law of Cyber Warfare' (2015) 50 Texas International Law Journal 189, 210.

161 ibid 191.

'decidedly unconventional IHL perspectives [that ...] display insensitivity to the realities of battle in favor of interpretative creativity or innovation.'[162]

In this context, it is 'States, *and only States* [that] make IHL' as opposed to civil society (where the former is evidently coded masculine and the latter feminine) since they 'alone enjoy legal competency to interpret international law beyond the confines of a particular case'[163] (i.e., enjoying abstract thought as against 'excessively emotive' and 'impassioned' condemnation of such practices as drone strikes).[164] If need be, further distinctions will be crafted to delineate camps, such as between self-identified 'military' or 'LOAC lawyers' vs. 'humanitarian lawyers.'[165] This reassertion of the authority of 'senior military lawyers' against organizations 'that do not have expertise or experience in combat'[166] simultaneously manages to reverse roles by suggesting that the traditional (masculine) articulators of the laws of war have been overrun by new actors (it is highly unlikely although not impossible that this has already actually happened).

The process of subtle and not-so-subtle otherization at work is, at any rate, a key to understanding the peculiar socio-professional micro-dynamics involved within the field of military law. As part of a recent turn to 'knowledge production' in international law,[167] it can help to understand how gender politics serve to discursively solidify and disqualify expertise, and cement the 'in-group' of 'hard-core' military lawyers operating as agents of state sovereignty against feminine dilettantes. It is not only, then, that expertise in the laws of war is asserted constantly as a series of distinctions between 'lawyers and laymen' and 'dinosaurs' and 'pure academics', as Lianne Boer has argued, but that these polarities serve as barely veiled proxies for gender.[168]

5 Conclusion: Queering the Laws of War?

This article has sought to portray the ongoing constitution of the regulation of war as a tussle between different generic approaches whose underlying stake is

162 ibid.
163 ibid 193.
164 ibid 217.
165 Yahli Shereshevsky, 'Back in the Game: International Humanitarian Lawmaking by States' (2019) 37 Berkeley Journal of International Law 1, 53.
166 Parks (n 75) 795.
167 See notably Lianne Boer, *International Law as We Know It. Cyberwar Discourse and the Construction of Knowledge in International Legal Scholarship* (Cambridge University Press).
168 ibid chapter 5.

masculine domination. One can only understand the intensity of the reaction against human rights or approaches seen as excessively humanitarian, for example, if one sees them as threatening to disrupt subtle and not-so-subtle masculine hierarchies. In the resulting contest, all are constantly at risk of being outflanked by the ultra-masculine (one is always someone else's 'sissy'), and the feminine (one is always someone else's 'brute'). These conversations occur in war, as part of efforts to articulate its regulation, but also within processes of ordinary militarization at home. They involve a constant valorization of the masculine and corresponding devalorization of the feminine, alongside, paradoxically, an increasingly fraught exercise of differentiation between the two.

The conversations canvassed in this article also operate on a continuum of representations of what it means to be a man that goes from the hypermasculine to the feminized male. The imagined 'feminine' provides a sort of backstop to this ongoing struggle, one that is invoked as a reminder of the male's radical 'other,' both idealized and disparaged, even as it never provides more than a convenient temporary prop, especially in light of 'feminity's' own social construction and fluidity. However, particular scorn is reserved in this symbolic ecosystem for gender non-conforming masculinity and departures from its narrow script. This is why I suggested that the fundamental dynamics of the constitution of the laws of war are not merely gendered or, indeed, masculine: they are also specifically and perversely heteronormative, in that they seek to discipline the law's siloed gender construction. Hegemonic masculinity can only exist in a constant struggle against and contempt for its 'lesser' variants, disciplining cis-identification and claiming a monopoly over its identification.

Both feminism and the critical study of masculinity offer paths forward here, somewhere between 'incorrigible beasts,' 'just warriors' and 'beautiful souls.'[169] They certainly bring attention to the sheer destructiveness of masculinity as the dominant referent of Western culture. Hegemonic masculinity is not a uniquely Western problem and armed violence the world over testifies to the complex ways in which gender permutations enable violence.[170] At the same time, masculinity is not as dominant as it seems.[171] It exhibits all the signs of a constantly worsening crisis. 'Men' may even, although this may be neither the most interesting nor the most urgent move, occasionally need to be shielded from blanket mysandry, through a better sense that masculine domination

169 Elshtain (n 118).

170 Ali A Mazrui, 'The Warrior Tradition and the Masculinity of War' (1977) 12 Journal of Asian and African Studies 69.

171 Susan Faludi, *Stiffed: The Betrayal Of The American Man* (Harper Collins 2011).

is always in the end also the domination (including sexual domination) of some men (and some women) over other men (and most women), deeply ratified by inherited legal traditions. The renewed emphasis on male victims of sexual violence,[172] conscientious objectors,[173] non-combatant males,[174] 'cannon fodder',[175] conscripts and prisoners, discrimination within the armed forces,[176] or hazing rituals[177] provides a potentially rich register to connect the pathologies of manhood and their troubling propensity to 'self harm' to the pathologies of militarism and war. The solicitude towards combatants in this context also serves to blur the edges of their maleness by introducing a more complex masculine figure, especially when combined with intersectional analysis that sheds light on how the racialized male underclass (notably in the US and Russia) is easily sacrificed in the name of nationalism and masculine posturing. It is also an opportune reminder of the fact that masculine hegemony is sustained, if at all, through the deliberate and ample shedding of male blood, from the trenches of the Somme to those of Bakhmut, and in the killing fields of Srebrenica.[178]

This does not mean, however, that alternative trajectories are necessarily more appealing and, in this respect, the conventional remedy of further femininization of the laws of war is also a very ambiguous one. For example,

172 Valorie K Vojdik, 'Sexual Violence against Men and Women in War: A Masculinities Approach' (2013) 14 Nevada Law Journal 923.

173 Mark Hussey, 'Clive Bell, "a Fathead and a Voluptuary": Conscientious Objection and British Masculnity' in Brenda S Helt and Madelyn Detloff (eds), *Queer Bloomsbury* (Edinburgh University Press 2016).

174 Adam Jones, 'Straight as a Rule: Heteronormativity, Gendercide, and the Noncombatant Male' (2006) 8 Men and Masculinities 451; Katharine M Millar, 'What Do We Do Now? Examining Civilian Masculinity/Ies in Contemporary Liberal Civil-Military Relations' (2019) 45 Review of International Studies 239.

175 Frédéric Mégret and Raphael Vagliano, '"We Will Not Go to the Trenches!" the "fusillés pour l'exemple," Military Disobedience, and Soldiers' Right to Life' (2021) 47 Peace & Change 97.

176 Kenneth L Karst, 'The Pursuit of Manhood and the Desegregation of the Armed Forces' (1991) 38 UCLA Law Review 499.

177 Anna U Lowry, 'Saving Private Sychev: Russian Masculinities, Army Hazing, and Social Norms' (2008) 52 Berkeley Journal of Sociology 73; Ben Wadham, 'The Dark Side of Defence: Masculinities and Violence in the Military' in Ross McGarry and Sandra Walklate (eds), *The Palgrave Handbook of Criminology and War* (Palgrave Macmillan 2016).

178 Adam Jones, 'Gendercide and Genocide' (2000) 2 Journal of Genocide Research 185. Paradoxically, of course, the ability of men to die for the cause is also what ends up privileging them as 'heroes' to whom 'the nation' owes a debt of gratitude. Evelin G Lindner, 'Gendercide and Humiliation in Honor and Human Rights Societies' (2002) 4 Journal of Genocide Research 137, 151.

it is unclear that strategies to invest in human rights in armed conflict will be broadly emancipatory. Human rights may well merely be the 'emperor's new clothes,'[179] and legitimize very similar degrees of violence, wielding the iron fist of patriarchy in a velvet glove of victim entitlement. In fact, the tendency of international human rights law to abdicate in the face of *jus ad bellum* issues and essentially appropriate the language of humanitarianism has been criticized as a surrender,[180] one merely prolonging humanitarian efforts to launder war. Moreover, the tendency to present combatants as the principal potential victims in more protective understanding of the laws of war (notably in relation to participation in hostilities) or even to emphatically highlight their status as victims of sexual violence in war,[181] whilst key to destabilizing gender scripts, could operate a kind of reversal of victimhood that is reminiscent of the dubious politics of the men's rights movement.[182]

At the same time, the femininization of the military, the ability of Western armies to project an even slightly less masculine and heteronormative image, also helps cement a certain civilizational superiority buttressed by a sense that the powers that be abide by IHL whilst those they are asymmetrically opposed to constantly fail to do so. As early as the 19th Century, the soothing presence of nurses on the battlefield suggested a vision of 'civilized' men and women working hand in hand in war, each within their role, for the greater patriotic and humanitarian good. Today, the presence of women among Western military might be seen as emancipatory domestically, but also as imbricated in reproducing 'a geopolitical dominance in which the ostensible gender equality in the imperial metropole reinforces racial hierarchies in the conquered and occupied colonies and peripheries.'[183] In short, gender is well at work in post-colonial 'civilized' wars, when it suits, against terrorists constructed as simultaneously hyper-violent (masculine) and devious (feminine).

---

179 See, for example, in the context of occupation Aeyal M Gross, 'Human Proportions: Are Human Rights the Emperor's New Clothes of the International Law of Occupation?' (2007) 18 European Journal of International Law 1; Naz K Modirzadeh, 'The Dark Sides of Convergence: A pro-Civilian Critique of the Extraterritorial Application of Human Rights Law in Armed Conflict' (2010) 86 US Naval War College International Law Studies (Blue Book) Series 349.

180 Frédéric Mégret, 'What Is the Specific Evil of Aggression?' in Claus Kress and Stefan Barriga (eds), *The Crime of Aggression: A Commentary* (Cambridge University Press 2016).

181 Leila Ullrich, '"But What about Men?" Gender Disquiet in International Criminal Justice' (2021) 25 Theoretical Criminology 209.

182 Lee Debout, 'Weaponizing Victimhood' in Anthony Nadler and A J Bauer (eds), *News on the Right: Studying Conservative News Cultures* (Oxford University Press 2019).

183 Laleh Khalili, 'Gendered Practices of Counterinsurgency' (2011) 37 Review of International Studies 1471.

More specifically, the femininization of troops can be deployed as a weapon. This is already evident in counterinsurgency struggles in which male soldiers are increasingly required to develop 'softer' and 'gentler' sides and engage in 'non-kinetic' missions, and in which 'female bodies' are deployed as part of 'population centric' rather than 'enemy centric' missions.[184] It has been suggested that drone warfare might, even as it enhances the gender-egalitarian interchangeability of male and female drone operators, lead to a 'gendered cycle of violence' rather than 'prophesy [...] the end of militarized masculinity.'[185] As a result, the transformative potential of gender diversity at the heart of the military institution is typically muted and tends to end up co-opting women or sexual minorities into the dominant masculine mores of the army.[186] Indeed, liberal feminism's own relatively conservative undertones may help cement, a kinder, gentler war for women that does not, ultimately challenge the hold of 'war' on social imaginaries.[187] This certainly cautions against a simplistic 'EDI approach' to the laws of war: the increased socio-professional feminization of IHL will amount to little if it merely translates into the socialization of (elite) women into the mores of the more respectably masculine warrior-lawyers.[188]

It is not obvious, then, that a clearer shift towards a 'feminine way of war' will be an evident blessing, given its own potential for reproduction and the risk of gender essentialization. It is true that some have long argued for the existence of an inherently pacifist feminine streak[189] with potential implications for the *jus in bello*.[190] But suffragettes largely rallied around the hyper-nationalism of the

184 Synne L Dyvik, 'Gender and Counterinsurgency' in Rachel Woodward and Claire Duncanson (eds), *The Palgrave International Handbook of Gender and the Military* (Palgrave Macmillan 2017).

185 Lorraine Bayard De Volo, 'Unmanned? Gender recalibrations and the rise of drone warfare' (2016) 12 Politics & Gender 50, 73.

186 Orna Sasson-Levy, 'Feminism and Military Gender Practices: Israeli Women Soldiers in "Masculine" Roles' (2003) 73 Sociological Inquiry 440.

187 Amin Parsa, 'Images of a kinder and gentler war' (2016) Gender Studies Annual Symposium.

188 Gina Heathcote et al, *The Law of War and Peace: A Gender Analysis: Volume One* (Bloomsbury Publishing 2021) 172–173.

189 Rada Iveković, 'Women, Nationalism and War: "Make Love Not War"' (1993) 8 Hypatia 113; Tove Pettersen, 'Feminist Care Ethics: Contributions to Peace Theory' in Tarja Väyrynen, Swati Parashar, Élise Féron, Catia Cecilia Confortini (eds), *Routledge Handbook of Feminist Peace Research* (Routledge 2021).

190 Lauren Wilcox, 'Gender, Just War, and the Ethics of War and Peace', *Oxford Research Encyclopedia of International Studies* (2010).

First World War,[191] and the women's peace movement collapsed in anticipation of the Second World War.[192] This is not to mention some women's support for the patriarchal way of war, as evident in the 'white feather' movement during the First World War which saw English women shame able bodied males who were not at the front.[193] Women's agency in such episodes as torture at Abu Ghraib cautions against the view that only masculinity is capable of sadistic violence.[194] Nor is it clear that replacing militarized masculinity with the cool-headed competence of governance feminism and its willingness to bomb Afghanistan or Libya in the name of a cosmopolitan sisterhood, impervious to any intersectionality, augurs well of that particular move.[195] Even the brief to combat sexual violence against women in war is not without its own 'othering' and therefore often bellicose undertones.[196] In short, swathes of mainstream feminism may be already too compromised with nationalism, imperialism, racism, and classism (not to mention carceralism) to make much of a dent in the hetero-ordering of war.[197]

In the meantime, a new and worrying synthesis between the masculine and the feminine may already be in the making, one militating for a sort of sacrificial lack of restraint as the ultimate manifestation of manliness. This has long been evident, for example, in the once emblematic Fox TV series 24 with Jack Bauer,

191 Alison S Fell, '"French Women Do Not Wish to Talk about Peace": Julie Siegfried and the Response of the Conseil National Des Femmes Françaises to the First World War' in Alison S Fell and Ingrid Sharp (eds), *The Women's Movement in Wartime. International Perspectives, 1914–1915* (Palgrave Macmillan 2007).

192 Mégret, 'Women, Pacifism and International Law' (n 146).

193 Peter J Hart, 'The White Feather Campaign: A Struggle with Masculinity During World War I' (2010) 2 Inquiries Journal 1.

194 Melanie Richter-Montpetit, 'Militarized Masculinities, Women Torturers, and the Limits of Gender Analysis at Abu Ghraib', in Annick T R Wibben (ed), *Researching War* (Routledge 2016).

195 On "international conflict feminism", see Vasuki Nesiah, 'Lawfare, CVE and International Conflict Feminism' in Lila Abu-Lughod, Rema Hammami and Nadera Shalhoub (eds), *The Cunning of Gender Violence: Geopolitics & Feminism* (Duke University Press 2023).

196 Elizabeth Philipose, 'Feminism, International Law, and the Spectacular Violence of the "Other": Decolonizing the Laws of War' in Renée J Heberle and Victoria Grace (eds), *Theorizing Sexual Violence* (Routledge 2009); Alex Veit, 'Feminism in the Humanitarian Machine. Introduction to the Special Section on "The Politics of Intervention Against (Conflict-Related) Sexual and Gender-Based Violence"' (2019) 13 Journal of Intervention and Statebuilding 401.

197 For a recent critique of some of these limitations, see Heathcote et al (n 188) ch 4. See also Cynthia Enloe, 'Gallipoli, the Somme and the Hague: Feminist Reflections on the Myriad Wars of the First World War' (2014) 21 European Journal of Women's Studies 299.

a CIA operative constantly trying to avert 9/11 repeats as the fundamentally decent man 'forced' to torture by the brutishness of his opponents. This results, in part, from a sense of the exceptionality of the moment and the dangers faced requiring not only supreme sovereign assertion, but also exceptionally ruthless masculinity. That hyper-masculinity takes exception from the normal constraints of virility, perhaps in order to reinstate the possibility of virility against 'governmental agencies and (inter)national laws [that] are feminized bureaucracies and conventions, respectively, out of touch with the field and as such insufficiently adapted for the rapid responses necessitated by absolute dangers.'[198] At the same time, Bauer only rises to the masculine moment because, paradoxically, he is in touch with his feminine side (he cries for his daughter who has been kidnapped).[199] In Bauer, we therefore have the quintessence of the tragic, self-pitying torturer. This emerging liberal monster uses violence without restraint because the virility of his cause (protecting the women at home or saving those abroad) trumps what might have been the virility of his means (exercising restraint to protect non-combatants).

An approximation of this particular conceit in the military context is the sometimes-popular image of the 'shooting and crying' Israeli Defense Force soldier.[200] Such an archetype arguably has a long history as what Marc LiVecche has described as the 'mournful warrior,' a sort of studied callousness that is nonetheless constantly attuned to the sorrow involved in taking lives.[201] Although on one level a Just War ideal, the concept can also easily turn into mere pathological kitsch, as when Himmler addressed SS officers to commiserate with the moral hardships that they had to endure in exterminating Jews. In collapsing any sense of restraint, such figures arguably combine the worst aspects of hyper-masculinity and coopted feminine demands in war. They replace the hesitant, fraternal liberalism of Rousseau by the conquering cosmopolitan liberalism of the neo-cons, one that is ready to inflict any degree of violence on 'their' women, children and men, in order

198 Mike Dillon, 'Bauer Power: 24 and the Making of an American' (2011) 11 Reconstruction: Studies in Contemporary Culture 6.

199 Brenda R Weber and Karolyn Steffens, 'Genre Transvestites: Testosterone Tales and Feminine Textual Bodies on Fox's 24 and The Swan' (2010) 43 The Journal of Popular Culture 860.

200 Gabriel Piterberg, 'Responses to the War in Gaza' (2009) 31 London Review of Books 5.

201 Marc LiVecche, 'The Mournful Warrior' in Marc LiVecche and Timothy S Mallard (eds), *The Good Kill: Just War and Moral Injury* (Oxford University Press 2021).

to protect 'our' women and children. In effect, however, the effeminacy at the heart of the liberal project means it is always ready to unleash violence,[202] especially by 'manly' against 'effeminate' nations.[203]

Contra this *faux queering*, then, the underlying question is nonetheless whether one can transcend rather than merely reproduce 'feminist fables about gender and the military' whose 'heteronormative discourses [...] produce men as masculine and women as feminine and which attribute stereotypical characteristics to each "gender"', including in the military.[204] It has been argued that rather than seeing international law as *regulating* violence, we should see it '*as* violence,'[205] a violence embedded in its self-reproducing heteronormativity and brutally revealed in the practice of war. Masculinity only thrives because it is allowed to constantly prop itself up against an imagined femininity. The practice of war is an ultimate reminder, in what is otherwise a world marked by increased gender fluidity, of 'who calls the shots' given the ever-present possibility of violence. Moreover, one can only have the 'allure' of restraint in war because one has already accepted its violence, both are two sides of the same coin

Queer theory has recently been touted as one possible path to move beyond the sterile heteronormative antinomies of gender in international law and their self-fulfilling tendency to build a world, including a legal world, in their image.[206] Queerness, rather than merely a condition describing a certain group of people, emerges as a transgressive and even subversive way to challenge the rigid gendered role division upon which international law and its regulation – but also its perpetuation – are based.[207] Queering international law means

---

202 Mark Neocleous, '"O Effeminacy! Effeminacy!" War, Masculinity and the Myth of Liberal Peace' (2013) 19 European Journal of International Relations 93.

203 Catriona Kennedy, 'John Bull into Battle: Military Masculinity and the British Army Officer during the Napoleonic Wars' in Karen Hagemann, Gisela Mettele and Jane Rendall (eds), *Gender, War and Politics: Transatlantic Perspectives, 1775–1830* (Palgrave Macmillan 2010).

204 Victoria M Basham and Sarah Bulmer, 'Critical Military Studies as Method: An Approach to Studying Gender and the Military' in Rachel Woodward and Claire Duncanson (eds), *The Palgrave International Handbook of Gender and the Military* (Palgrave Macmillan 2017).

205 Vanja Hamzić, 'International Law as Violence: Competing Absences of the Other' in Dianne Otto (ed), *Queering International Law: Possibilities, Alliances, Complicities, Risks* (Routledge 2017).

206 Dianne Otto (ed), *Queering International Law: Possibilities, Alliances, Complicities, Risks* (Routledge 2017); Gráinne de Búrca, 'Introduction to the Symposium on Queering International Law' (2022) 116 AJIL Unbound 1.

207 Madhavi Menon, *Indifference to Difference: On Queer Universalism* (University of Minnesota Press 2015).

not so much 'extending the existing "normal," normative framework of international law so that it is inclusive of non-heterosexual experience and identities, but otherwise left unaltered' than 'present[ing] a fundamental challenge to the usual way of going about things.'[208]

This it would do by 'making visible the [hetero]sexual ordering that is taken for granted as underpinning of the "normal" system of international law.'[209]

Specifically, an interest in queering the international law on the use of force[210] and, within that, the LOAC,[211] has begun to emerge. Queer theorizing has already helped challenge the central role of hegemonic military masculinities, 'converting the comfortable givens of the well-worn masculinities story into questions.'[212] It might highlight the largely self-serving nature of the military institution as a site of gendered capital accumulation, rather than whatever purpose it explicitly assigns itself.[213] It could, then, disrupt the notion that the laws of war need to be defined both internally and externally by an imagined face-to-face between the 'masculine' and the 'feminine,' and take stock of what is lost in the process, notably the primary role that homophobia at least as much as misogyny continues to play in the constitution of militarism.[214] It

208 Dianne Otto, '"Taking a Break"† from "Normal": Thinking Queer in the Context of International Law', in *Proceedings of the ASIL Annual Meeting* (Cambridge University Press 2007) 119–120.

209 ibid 120.

210 Tamsin P Paige, 'The Maintenance of International Peace and Security Heteronormativity', in Dianne Otto (ed) *Queering International Law: Possibilities, Alliances, Complicities, Risks* (Routledge 2017); Dianne Otto, 'Queerly Troubling International Law's Vision of "Peace"' (2022) 116 American Journal of International Law 22.

211 Matteo Winkler, 'A Queer Eye on the Law of Armed Conflict' (*Lieber Institute West Point – Articles of War*, 2 August 2022) <https://lieber.westpoint.edu/queer-eye-loac/>. The post does focus more ultimately on how LOAC treats queer people than on how 'queering' might function in relation to LOAC.

212 Amanda Chisholm and Joanna Tidy, 'Beyond the Hegemonic in the Study of Militaries, Masculinities, and War' (2017) 3 Critical Military Studies 99; Marysia Zalewski, 'What's the Problem with the Concept of Military Masculinities?' (2017) 3 Critical Military Studies 200.

213 Claire Duncanson, 'Anti-Militarist Feminist Approaches to Researching Gender and the Military' in Rachel Woodward and Claire Duncanson (eds), *The Palgrave International Handbook of Gender and the Military* (Palgrave Macmillan 2017).

214 Diane Warnock, 'June 26, 1983 Militarism, Feminism, and Homophobia', in Robert B Ridinger (ed), *Speaking for Our Lives* (Routledge 2004).

could focus, furthermore, on the price of inclusion not only of women[215] but of non-gender conforming bodies in the military apparatus.[216]

Transcending such gendered constructions might ultimately involve giving up on the regulation of war as too high a price to pay in terms of the ongoing toleration of (gendered) violence in the world (a radical pacifist agenda). It could ask, taking nothing for granted and certainly not massively violent patriarchal conventions, why we need a law of war at all,[217] given the tendency of the two to reinforce each other's violence.[218] Short of that, it could at least thoroughly confuse the gendered script of the laws of war in ways that do not allow it to become an excuse for civilizational violence. For example, it could blur the line between the *jus ad bellum* and the *jus in bello*; external and internal victims of war; international and non-international conflicts; unprotected nationals and protected non-nationals; Hague and Geneva law; in short, all of the many antinomies whose implicit matrix is often nothing more than a coded expression of a binary concept of gender. Specifically, it could also help build a bridge between the study of violence in war and militarism at home, emphasizing the troubling continuum between rape as a 'weapon of war' and cultures of sexual abuse within militaries.[219]

Finally, a queer theorizing of the laws of war could highlight, like feminist theory but perhaps in a more subversive and hesitant way, the extent to which gender and sex do not coincide, opening up space for non-conforming military alignments (manly female warriors, fragile male veterans, etc.), possibly enriched by non-Western traditions of war that have long been more accepting of gendered inversion.[220] Emphasizing how the operative but socially constructed opposition between the two polarities of heteronormativity also serves to exclude constructs of gender in the in-between[221] would help escape

215 Maya Eichler, 'Gendered Militarism' in Caron E Gentry, Laura J Shepherd and Laura Sjoberg (eds), *Routledge Handbook of Gender and Security* (Routledge 2018); Megan H MacKenzie, 'Women in Combat: Beyond "Can They?" Or "Should They?": Introduction' (2013) 1 Critical Studies on Security 239.

216 Dean Spade and Aaron Belkin, 'Queer Militarism?! The Politics of Military Inclusion Advocacy in Authoritarian Times' (2021) 27 GLQ: A Journal of Lesbian and Gay Studies 281.

217 On this radical potentiality in queer theory in relation to international law, see Philipp Kastner and Elisabeth Roy Trudel, 'Unsettling International Law and Peace-Making: An Encounter with Queer Theory' (2020) 33 Leiden Journal of International Law 911.

218 Kennedy (n 158).

219 Caitlin Maxwell, 'Moving beyond Rape as a "Weapon of War": An Exploration of Militarized Masculinity and Its Consequences' (2010) 28 Canadian Woman Studies.

220 Sabine Lang, *Men as Women, Women as Men: Changing Gender in Native American Cultures* (University of Texas Press 2010).

221 Paige (n 210).

a preordained script where men protect women (through *noblesse oblige*, restraint or paternalism) or, at best, women save men (through compassion, an ethics of care or heightened pacifist sensitivity) – and everything else is suspended whilst weapons speak. Just as gender is not constituted by sex, this would belie the notion that the laws of war are the product of war, when it is just as much war that is a product of the laws of war.

Acknowledgements

I am grateful to Helen Kinsella for hosting the first event (Critical, Historical, and Comparative Perspectives on International Humanitarian Law, University of Wisconsin, 21–22 April 2017) where an early version of this article was discussed. The paper subsequently benefited from precious feedback at the "Humanitarianism and the Remaking of International Law: History, Ideology, Practice" organized by Ann Orford (University of Melbourne, 31/05–02/06/2018). All views and mistakes are mine.

The Language of the Protection of Civilians Mandate and the Primary Responsibility of the State: A Legal Norm for Peace and Security

Tamer Morris

Abstract

When the Security Council mandates the protection of civilians mandate in UN peacekeeping missions, it inadvertently forms an obligation on States involved with UN peace missions. To affirm the concept of State sovereignty, the Security Council constantly references 'the primary responsibility of the State to protect' within their resolutions. This developing norm, beginning within the protection of civilians mandate, is an expansion of existing obligations under IHL and IHRL. Within the text of Security Council resolutions there is an obligation that States who are a party to a NIAC are responsible for peace and security. Therefore, force should be used for peace and security, rather than for "triumphing" in the conflict or entrenching power. As such, a State can achieve its obligations under IHL when governments take all reasonable steps to conclude the conflict, for any hostilities within civilian areas by its very nature is a breach of a State's obligation and responsibility to protect their own civilians.

Keywords

Non-international armed conflict – peacekeeping – Security Council – protection of civilians – State obligation

1 Introduction

In 1999 the United Nations' (UN) Security Council mandated the UN Mission in Sierra Leone (UNAMSIL) to use 'all necessary means' to protect civilians under Chapter VII of the UN Charter. Since the creation of UNAMSIL, the Security Council has continuously mandated peacekeeping mission to protect civilians

 | DOI:10.1163/9789004712478_008

using 'all necessary means'. As peacekeepers have been deployed in major internal conflicts, the protection of civilians mandate is developing State practice within non-international armed conflicts (NIACs). The Security Council, as an organ, has contributed and intervened in NIACs more than any other legal person in the international sphere. Since States are bound by decisions of the Security Council under the UN Charter,[1] Security Council resolutions have the ability to influence State behaviour.

For over 20 years, the Security Council has regularly mandated UN peace missions deployed in NIACs to protect civilians without 'prejudice to the primary responsibility of the State'. While the Security Council has inserted this phrase in assurance of State sovereignty, they are incidentally placing an obligation on States derived from the tasks referenced to in the protection of civilians mandate. As the Security Council is mandating peacekeepers to protect civilians in majority of modern NIACs, they are inadvertently forming an emerging obligation on States where UN peacekeepers are deployed.

The implication from the protection of civilians mandate stems from the Security Council's insistence on the primacy of member States' sovereignty. As the UN is founded in the principle of State sovereignty, the peacekeeping function cannot be seen to intervene in domestic affairs without consent of the host State. In respect of State sovereignty the Security Council will ensure that UN peace missions are only deployed with consent of the host State. Moreover, protection tasks mandated to peacekeepers are to be undertaken in 'assistance' or 'support' of the local authorities. Therefore, the protection of civilians mandate is not intended to shift the primary responsibility of the State, but rather is attempting to strengthen that responsibility.

The use of the phrase the 'primary responsibility of the State' is inserted to entrench the principle of State sovereignty in UN peacekeeping, however, the Security Council is inadvertently expanding the interpretation of State responsibility in NIACs. The wording of 'the responsibility of the State' in the protection of civilians mandate implies that the protection owed by the State is an accumulation of the tasks mandated to UN peacekeepers. As peacekeepers are mandated in support of local authorities, the protection of civilians mandate becomes an interpretation of the host State's responsibility in that conflict. Accordingly, as the protection of civilians mandate is premised on halting all violence there is an implication that States have the primary obligation to put an end to the conflict.

1 UN, 'Charter of the United Nations' (1945) 1 UNTS XVI at Article 25.

While the obligations in international humanitarian law (IHL) allow the existence of conflict, the 'primary responsibility of the State' within the protection of civilians mandate implies that the existence of conflict is a violation of the obligation of the State owed to civilians. Therefore, from the protection of civilians mandate the host State's obligation to protect their civilians can only be achieved by halting the conflict. This use of language by the Security Council is developing a norm in NIAC which is intended to clarify the obligations of States when conflict erupts within civilian populated areas. Consequently, from the language of the protection of civilians mandate, a State can adhere to its obligations under IHL, in a NIAC, by governments taking all reasonable steps to conclude the conflict.

This implied norm will be discovered by first discussing the role of Security Council resolutions in international law, then through an examination of the protection of civilians mandate in context of the phrase 'the primary responsibility of the State'. It will be concluded that there is an inherent correlation between the protection of civilians mandate and the Security Council's expectation of the responsibility of the State. Second, from an investigation of the text of the protection of civilians mandate, this responsibility is explicitly connected to armed conflict. Third, the responsibility of the State in peacekeeping resolutions must be compared to existing legal norms, specifically IHL and international human rights law (IHRL). It will be determined that the responsibility mandated by the Security Council goes beyond what is expected by IHL and IHRL, specifically as the protection of civilians mandate finds its roots in the Security Council's role in the maintenance of international peace and security. Finally, as the protection of civilians mandate is founded in peace and security it is implied that States are responsible to ensure peace and security of their populace, and thus, have a duty to ensure that all violence comes to an end.

2 Security Council Peacekeeping Resolutions and the Protection of Civilians

In 1999 the Canadian Mission to the UN, as president of the Security Council, inserted the cross-cutting theme of the protection of civilians in the Security Council agenda.[2] In a positive step to enter the protection landscape, the Security Council adopted their first overarching protection of civilians

2 United Nations Security Council (UNSC), 'Overview of Security Council Meeting Records' (1999) UN Doc S/PV/3980.

resolution, and expressed their 'willingness to consider how peacekeeping mandates might better address the negative impact of armed conflict on civilians.'[3] The protection of civilians mandate became the Security Council's declaration that peacekeepers are no longer passive observers but to use all necessary means to protect civilians under 'threat of physical violence'. With the protection of civilians mandate expanding over 20 years, it has become a cornerstone of UN peacekeeping and a measure of peacekeeping success.[4] As such, the protection of civilians is a prime justification for the deployment of new UN peace missions. Currently, UN peace missions in Mali, Democratic Republic of the Congo (DRC), South Sudan and the Central African Republic (CAR) are all mandated with the primary task to protect civilians. While these UN peace missions continually update their mandates to reflect the change in circumstances, they are still to prioritise the protection of civilians.

Security Council resolutions do not per se create legal obligations, however, within the UN Charter the Security Council is ceded explicit powers that grants them a distinct authority in international law. Predominantly, alongside Article 24, Article 25 of the UN Charter binds all Member States 'to accept and carry out the decisions of the Security Council'. Although Article 25 binds Member States to the decisions of the Security Council, the Security Council has only expressly referenced Article 25 in Resolution 2118.[5] While infrequently used it was decided that Article 25 does not limit Chapter VII, and as suggest by the ICJ that Article 25 applies to all decisions of the Security Council, for 'obligation of states to comply with the decisions of the Security Council under Article 25 of the Charter extends to all decisions of the Security Council, not merely under Chapter VII', moreover, 'to hold otherwise would be deprive this

---

3 UNSC, 'Resolution 1265(1999)' (adopted 17 September 1999) UN Doc S/RES/1265(1999) at operational paragraph 11.

4 Although nearly 30 years have passed, the UN is still haunted that while the UN Assistance Mission for Rwanda (UNAMIR) notified the UN Secretariat of evidence of possible 'extermination' of the Tutsis in Kigali, they were ordered that no 'action, including [a] response to request for protection, should be taken by UNAMIR until clear guidance is received from Headquarters.' (UNSC, 'Report of the Independent Inquiry into the Actions of the United Nations during the 1994 Genocide in Rwanda' (1999) UN Doc S/1999/1257 at para.10) The UN's reluctance to protect civilians was further illustrated with the Srebrenica mass killings occurring the following year, where "at least five written messages were sent on that day, expressing alarm about potential human rights abuses having been committed or that potentially might be committed." (United Nations General Assembly (UNGA), 'Report of the Secretary-General Pursuant to General Assembly Resolution 53/35: The Fall of Srebrenica' (15 November 1999) UN Doc A/54/549 at para.352).

5 UNSC Resolution 2118 (27 September 2013) UN Doc S/RES/2118(2013).

principal organ of its essential functions and powers under the Charter.'[6] Thus, the combination of Articles 24 and 25 awards the Security Council a considerable volume of authority over Member States.

While the Security Council is awarded a significant amount of power, it is suggested that they are still bound to the 'spirit and principles' of international law, and cannot mandate outside the existing legal structure.[7] As the UN is an institution founded in international law, the organisation cannot be above that law,[8] for '[i]t is not logically possible to claim to represent the power and authority of the law, and at the same time, claim to be above the law.'[9] As decided by Sir Jennings in his dissenting opinion in the *Lockerbie* case,[10] Security Council resolutions and decisions cannot override a Member State's obligations under customary international law, especially IHL and IHRL.[11] Therefore, under the traditional view, the Security Council cannot create 'new' legal norms, rather should only clarify already existing obligations in the UN Charter or customary international law.[12] Notwithstanding this theoretical understanding, in practice the Security Council can create procedures that do ultimately affect international law norms. Although the Security Council does not create new legal obligations, they do make decisions that have a substantive legal effect on Member States.[13]

Orthodox legal scholars would insist that the Security Council cannot create law, rather merely make political decisions. Though Security Council resolutions are not law they can still create norms that eventually contribute to customary international law. Security Council resolutions have an ability to influence State behaviour and opinions, although not legal documents within

---

6 *Legal Consequences for States of the Continued Presence of South Africa in Namibia (South West Africa) Notwithstanding Security Council Resolution 276 (1970)* (Advisory Opinion) 1971, ICJ Reports 1971 p.16.

7 Neha Jain, 'A Separate Law for Peacekeepers: The Clash between the Security Council and the International Criminal Court' (2005) 16(2) EJIL 239 at 243.

8 ibid at 243.

9 *Case Concerning Questions of Interpretation and Application of the 1971 Montreal Convention Arising From the Aeria Incident at Lockerbie (Libyan Arab Jamahiriya v United Kingdom)* (Judgment) [1998] at 110.

10 ibid.

11 James D Fry, 'The UN Security Council and the Law of Armed Conflict: Amity or Enmity?' (2006) 38(2) Geo Wash Intl L Rev 327 at 334; Erika de Wet, *The Chapter VII Powers of the United Nations Security Council* (Hart Publishing 2004) at 203.

12 Sufyan Droubi, *Resisting United Nations Security Council Resolutions,* (Routledge Research in International Law 2014) at 2–3.

13 Marko Divac Öberg, 'The Legal Effects of Resolutions of the UN Security Council and General Assembly in the Jurisprudence of the ICJ' (2005) 16(5) EJIL 879 at 881–882.

their own right. However, unlike other 'soft law'[14] instruments, Security Council resolutions have a binding effect on UN member States and therefore, have an ability to change State behaviour. The Security Council themselves have noted that their continuous resolutions do contribute to legal customary norms. For example, with regard to their resolutions on piracy in Somalia, the Security Council has explicitly affirmed that decisions within the resolutions 'shall not be considered as establishing customary international law.'[15]

Furthermore, international organisations and tribunals have also recognised and used Security Council resolutions in evidence of customary international law. For example, the International Committee of the Red Cross (ICRC) in their examination of customary international law, identifies '[s]tate practice at the international level is reflected in a variety of sources, including in resolutions adopted in the framework of the United Nations, in particular by the Security Council…'[16] Further the ICTY recognised that of 'great relevance to the formation of *opinion juris*… are certain resolutions unanimously adopted by the Security Council.'[17]

Regarding NIACs, the Security Council has intervened and made decisions more than any other legal person in international law.[18] Within modern conflict, it would be rare for an NIAC not to involve some resolution or response from the Security Council. Moreover, States who are parties to a NIAC are consistently relying on the decisions of the Security Council, therefore, Security Council resolutions have a significant impact on State behaviour and practice

---

14 For more on soft law and the effects of customary international law and IHL, see Emily Crawford, *Non-binding Norms in International Humanitarian Law: Efficacy, Legitimacy, and Legality* (Oxford University Press 2021).

15 UNSC 'Resolution 2184 (2014)' (12 November 2014) UN Doc S/RES/2184 (2014) at operative paragraph 14; UNSC 'Resolution 2182 (2014)' (24 October 2014) UN Doc S/RES/2182 (2014) at operative paragraph 21; UNSC 'Resolution 2125 (2013)' (18 November 2013) UN Doc S/RES/2125 (2013) at operative paragraph 13; UNSC 'Resolution 2077 (2012)' (21 November 2012) UN Doc S/RES/2077 (2012) at operative paragraph 13; UNSC 'Resolution 2020 (2011)' (22 November 2011) UN Doc S/RES/2020 (2011) at operative paragraph 10; UNSC 'Resolution 1950 (2010)' (23 November 2010) UN Doc S/RES/1950 (2010) at operative paragraph 8; UNSC 'Resolution 1897 (2009)' (30 November 2009) UN Doc S/RES/1897 (2009) at operative paragraph 8; UNSC 'Resolution 1851 (2008)' (16 December 2008) UN Doc S/RES/1851 (2008) at operative paragraph 10.

16 Jean-Marie Henckaerts and Louise Doswald-Beck, *Customary International Humanitarian Law, Volume 1: Rules* (Cambridge University Press 2009) at Introduction p. Iiii.

17 *Prosecutor v Tadić* (*Decision on Defence Motion for Interlocutory Appeal on Jurisdiction*), IT-94-1 (2 October 1995) at 133.

18 Gregory H. Fox, Kristen Boon, and Ian Jenkins, 'The Contributions of United Nations Security Council Resolutions to the Law of Non-International Armed Conflict: New Evidence of Customary International Law' (2018) 67 AULR 649 at 664.

in modern NIACs. As such, with continuous and consistent resolutions, the Security Council has the ability to create norms in customary international law in a NIAC.

As such, the continuous use of language by the Security Council in the protection of civilians mandate in NIAC is developing a norm in customary international law. This paper is not suggesting that the norm has been clearly formed, rather the Security Council's language and decisions have contributed to expanding the interpretation of existing obligations in NIACs, specifically in regards to protection of civilians.[19]

2.1 *The Language of the Protection of Civilians in Security Council Resolutions*

Since its initial insertion, the Security Council has expanded the original language of the protection mandate to intensify its scope and strength. For example, in 2003 the Security Council extended the protection of civilians mandate from the protection against 'physical violence' to 'promote and protect' human rights.[20] As peacekeeping has grown organically in a reactive manner, the Security Council in response has expanded the parameters of the protection of civilians mandate intensifying its reach.

The responsibilities mandated by the Security Council in UN peacekeeping have cultivated organically to reflect the risks and damage occurring to civilians on the ground. As conditions transpire in a UN peace mission, the Security Council will intensify the protection of civilians mandate to rectify the breach in civilian protection occurring within the conflict. As illustrated by the sporadic influx of displaced persons in the vicinity of UN bases in South Sudan, the Security Council amended the UN Mission in South Sudan (UNMISS) mandate to include protections afforded to those provisional camps. As a result, the protection of civilians mandate becomes reflective of the protection that ought to be awarded to civilians within a particular conflict. Therefore, while there are generic tasks mandates throughout UN peace missions, the protection of civilians mandate is intended to mirror the specific threats faced by civilians within the conflict. While this could indicate that the protection of civilians mandate is supplementary to the State's responsibility, the Security Council will reconfirm the 'responsibility of the State' within the text of the mandate and the operative part of the resolution.

19 Further research is needed to articulate State opinion and interpretation of their responsibility in modern NIAC. As such, this paper hopes to begin discussions by examining the text of the Security Council.

20 UNSC 'Resolution 1509 (2003)' (19 September 2003) UN Doc S/RES/1509 (2003).

While the language of the protection mandate has varied, the Security Council has consistently included the protection 'against threats of physical violence'.[21] Consequently, the success of the protection of civilians mandate is measured by the ability of peacekeepers to physically protect civilians using their military presence or the use of force. This presumption is evidenced as UN peace missions are predominately criticised for their inability or unwillingness to use force. As was concluded by the Cruz Report, 'hostile forces do not understand a language other than force. To deter and repel attacks and to defeat attackers, the United Nations needs to be strong and not fear to use force when necessary.'[22] While 'protection from physical violence' is only one of three forms of protection visualised by the UN's 'Draft Operational Concept on Protection of Civilians',[23] in practice, it has become the main consideration and discussion when evaluating the protection of civilians mandate.[24]

As stated in the Secretary-General's report the 'success' of a peacekeeping mission becomes largely dependent on a Mission's 'willingness and capability to act when civilians are threatened.'[25] This was evidenced with the July 2022 protests in the DRC for MONUSCO's alleged failure to protect and create a secure environment.[26] This is further reiterated in the Department of Peace Operations' (DPO) the *Protection of Civilians Handbook*, which only focuses on 'sources of violence' when advising on 'identifying and prioritising' protection

21 In UNSC 'Resolution 1270 (1999)' (22 October 1999) UN Doc S/RES/1270 (1999) the Security Council originally mandated UNAMSIL to 'afford protection of civilians under imminent threat of physical violence.'

22 Carlos Alberto dos Santos Cruz, Willliam R Phillips, and Salvator Cusimano, *Improving Security of United Nations Peacekeepers: We Need to Change the Way We Are Doing Business* (United Nations 2017) at 5.

23 In 2009, DPKO and DFS released the 'Draft Operational Concept on Protection of Civilians'. The document identified that there was no common understanding of what 'protection' is, and also established the still-current three-tier understanding of protection: Tier 1: Protection through political process; Tier 2: Providing protection from physical violence; Tier 3: Establishing a protective environment.

24 Peacekeeping missions are mandated with multiple tasks which varies over the lifespan of the mission. Therefore, the emphasis of physical protection is in the evaluation of the protection of civilians mandate, rather than the entire mission or a other mandated tasks. It is not suggested that all UN missions regardless of their mandate are evaluated the same, rather the success of the mandate to protect is peacekeepers' ability to protect civilians from the threat of violence.

25 UNSC 'Report of the Secretary-General on the Protection of Civilians in Armed Conflict' (13 May 2016) UN Doc S/2016/447 at paragraph 58.

26 Aljazeera, "DR Congo Expels UN Peacekeeping Mission Spokesman After Protests", (*Aljazeera*, 3 August 2022) <www.aljazeera.com/news/2022/8/3/congo-expels-u-n-peacekeeping-mission-spokesman-after-protests.

activities.[27] The emphasis placed on physical protection is a response to the UN's historically publicised 'failures' in Rwanda and Srebrenica. Therefore, while the specific protection tasks have varied within each mission they are premised on the physical protection of civilians when civilians are under threat.

2.2 *The Principle of Consent, State Sovereignty and the Protection of Civilians*

At the creation of the peacekeeping function, the Security Council entrenched all UN peace missions in three principles: consent, impartiality, and the use of force in self-defence and defence of the mandate. While these principles do not originate from the UN Charter or international law, they have long been considered "constitutional" pillars of UN peacekeeping. As stated in the Special Court of Sierra Leone, these principles are 'widely understood as the necessary foundations for a peacekeeping operation.'[28] As such, the Security Council has continually 'reaffirm[ed] the basic principles of Peacekeeping'[29] within the body of peacekeeping resolutions. Although these principles have been diluted in practice within UN peace missions, they are still referenced by the Security Council when mandating UN peace missions.[30]

While questions remain regarding the modern relevance of these principles, the consent principle is nevertheless considered an essential element of UN peacekeeping. As such, the consent of the host State has become a critical component before the deployment of any UN peace mission.[31] The primacy of the consent principle is founded in Article 2(1), that the UN 'is based on the principle of the sovereign equality of all its Members.' Moreover, Article 2(7) of the UN Charter, which affirms that '[n]othing contained in the present Charter shall authorize the United Nations to intervene in matters which are

27 United Nations Department of Peace Operations, *The Protection of Civilians in United Nations Peacekeeping Handbook* (United Nations 2020) at 8.1.

28 Special Court for Sierra Leone *Prosecutor v Issa Hassan Sesay, Morris Kallon and Augustine Gbao* (Judgment) SCSL-04-15-T (2 March 2009) at paragraph 225.

29 UNSC 'Resolution 2625 (2022)' (15 March 2022) UN Doc S/RES/2625 (2022) at operational paragraph 19.

30 For example, UNSC 'Resolution 2605 (12 November 2021)' (2021) UN Doc S/RES/2605 (2021) third paragraph in the preamble.

31 Ralph Mamiya 'A History and Conceptual Development of the Protection of Civilians' in Haidi Willmot, Ralph Mamiya, Scott Sheeran and Marc Weller (eds), *Protection of Civilians* (Oxford University Press 2016) 80. For further discussion regarding the 'constitutional' principles of UN peacekeeping, see John Karlsrud 'The UN at War: Examining the Consequences of Peace-Enforcement Mandates for the UN Peacekeeping Operations in the CAR, the DRC and Mali' (2015) 36 TWQ 40 at 48; Mats Berdal and David Ucko, 'The Use of Force in UN Peacekeeping Operations: Problems and Prospects' (2015) 160 RUSI 6 at 11.

essentially within the domestic jurisdiction of any state…'. While the principles of impartiality and self-defence have arguably been reduced, and at times disregarded,[32] the consent principle is still perceived as an essential component in UN peacekeeping.[33] In consideration of State sovereignty and its foundational role in the UN system, the Security Council cannot be perceived to be interfering in the domestic affairs of sovereign States.

It must be noted that under Chapter VII of the UN Charter, the Security Council is not legally obliged to obtain the consent of the host State before the deployment of a UN peace mission. For while Article 2 emphases the sovereignty of States, the remaining part of Article 2(7) specifies, '…but this principle shall not prejudice the application of enforcement measures under Chapter VII.' Although not a legal requirement, the Security Council has insisted on procuring consent before the deployment of any peacekeeping mission. As the Security Council does not want to be alleged in declaring 'war' against its members, international politics rather than international law, dictates that consent is always sought.

While undoubtably it is questionable at times whether this consent is freely obtained or politically coerced, consent is still sought by the UN. The interpretation of 'consent' came into question in July 2022 with the civilian protests in the DRC and consent of the local population.[34] Although there are calls for the consent principle to encompass the local population,[35] as the UN is founded on the principle of State sovereignty, consent is only sought from the host government. While there are legal questions of the nature and ability of governments to grant consent,[36] nevertheless, no UN peace mission has been deployed without the consent of the host State.

As tangible consent is ingrained in the logistics and politics of deployment, the consent principle is visualised in the language of peacekeeping resolutions

---

32 Tamer Morris, 'The Legal Obligation of the Security Council's Mandate on the Protection of Civilians in UN Peacekeeping' (PhD thesis, University of Sydney 2021).

33 Nicholas Tsagourias, 'Consent, Neutrality/Impartiality and the Use of Force in Peacekeeping: Their Constitutional Dimension' (2007) 11 JCSL 465 at 465–466.

34 Anjali Dayal, 'A Crisis of Consent in UN Peace Operations' (*IPI Global Observatory*, 2 August 2022) <https://theglobalobservatory.org/2022/08/a-crisis-of-consent-in-un-peace-operations/>.

35 For example of some of the discussion, see Jenna Russo, 'Protests Against UN in Eastern Congo Highlight Peace Mission's Crisis of Legitimacy' (*The Conversation*, 31 July 2022) <https://theconversation.com/protests-against-un-in-eastern-congo-highlight-peace-missions-crisis-of-legitimacy-187932>.

36 Consent is an elusive concept in practice, while the Security Council attains consent via political manoeuvring, this 'consent' does not always translate in the field. For more see, Sofia Sebastián and Aditi Gorur, 'U.N. Peacekeeping & Host-State Consent: How Missions Navigate Relationships with Governments' (*Stimson*, March 2018).

when the Security Council confines peacekeeping tasks in assistance to local authorities. To stress that the Security Council is not intervening in domestic affairs with 'robust' missions, peacekeepers are mandated to undertake tasks to 'assist' and 'support' the local authorities. To illustrate this support function, the UN peace mission in Mali (MINUSMA) is mandated '[i]n support of the Malian authorities, to take active steps to anticipate, deter and effectively respond to threats to the civilian population.'[37] This specific reference to 'assistance' or 'support' is crystalised in the protection of civilians mandate as all peacekeeping tasks are caveated to the assistance of local authorities. Consequently, a reading of Security Council's intention is that the protection of civilians mandate is to be undertaken to support and not act independently of the host State.

As such, peacekeepers are envisaged to be deployed to strengthen the protection structures of the host State, rather than working against it. Subsequently, within the field, peacekeepers are reluctant to use force or to intervene into domestic situations without the presence or the express consent of the host State.[38] While UN reports and the DPO documentation insist that the protection of civilians doctrine exists against all sources of violence, practically, peacekeepers have not engaged in protection activities against local authorities.

Currently, only UNMISS is explicitly mandated to protect civilians 'irrespective of the source of such violence'.[39] However, even UNMISS (who is mandated irrespective of assistance of local authorities) is not intended to shift the 'primary responsibility' of the South Sudanese government to protect their own civilians. Nonetheless, outside UNMISS, all other missions are explicitly mandated to protect civilians in 'assistance' or 'support' of the local authorities. The emphasis of the peacekeeping support function is to depart from the Responsibility to Protect (R2P) doctrine, or other humanitarian intervention. This distancing is primarily done as the protection of civilians mandate is not attempting to shift any responsibility away from the host State, but rather strengthen that responsibility.

---

37 UNSC 'Resolution 2584 (2021)' (29 June 2021) UN Doc S/RES/2584 (2021) at operational paragraph 30(c)(ii).

38 For example, as reported in UN Office of Internal Oversight Services Report 'Evaluation of the Implementation and Results of Protection of Civilians Mandates in United Nations Peacekeeping Operations' (7 March 2014) UN Doc A/68/787 at paragraphs 41, 42 and 44.

39 UNSC 'Resolution 2625 (2022)' (n 29) at operational paragraph 3(a)(i); while DPO suggests that all UN peace missions are authorised to use force irrespective of the source of violence, only UNMISS has been expressly mandated to do so.

While the Security Council has seized the protection of civilians agenda, through the lens of State sovereignty, they have continually insisted that the protection is the primary responsibility of the State. Hence, the protection of civilians mandate is envisioned to work in support of local authorities. Explicitly, it is reiterated within the text of peacekeeping mandates that the deployment of a UN peace mission to protect civilians does not shift the primary responsibility of the State. The Security Council is explicit within the text of the protection of civilians mandate that peacekeepers are to protect 'without prejudice to the primary responsibility'[40] of the host State. As such, the deployment of peacekeepers does not alter the primary responsibility of the State to protect their own civilians, nor does that responsibility shift to the Security Council or the UN. UN peacekeepers are not only deployed to protect, but deployed to assist the host State to resume their responsibility to protect their own civilians once peacekeepers have withdrawn.

2.3 *The Primary Responsibility of the State to Protect Within Security Council Resolutions*

The Security Council consistently mandates the protection of civilians 'without prejudice to the responsibility' of the host state, for the State 'has primary responsibility for the welfare and protection of its population.'[41] This 'responsibility of the State' is mentioned both within the preamble and the operative part of UN peacekeeping resolutions. Within the preamble the Security Council explicitly declares that the States "have the primary responsibility to protect the population…",[42] in indication that nothing within the resolution is to supersede the legal responsibility of the State. However, the expression of the responsibility of the State in the preamble is typically limited to specific 'crimes' or 'protections', for instance in the resolution for the UN peace mission in CAR (MINUSCA):

> *Recalling* that the CAR authorities have the primary responsibility to protect all populations in the CAR in particular from genocide, war crimes, ethnic cleansing and crimes against humanity.[43]

---

40 UNSC 'Resolution 2552 (2020)' (12 November 2020) UN Doc S/RES/2552 (2020) at operational paragraph 31(a)(i).

41 Victoria Holt, Glyn Taylor and Max Kelly, *Protecting Civilians in the Context of UN Peacekeeping Operations: Success, Setbacks and Remaining Challenges* (United Nations 2009) at 44.

42 UNSC 'Resolution 2149 (2014)' (10 April 2014) UN Doc S/RES/2149 (2014) at preamble.

43 UNSC 'Resolution 2625 (2022)' (n 29) at preamble.

Accordingly, the Security Council is confirming that the deployment of UN peacekeepers does not permit the host State to forsake its primary obligation to protect – which is entwined with the R2P principles – that is, genocide, war crimes, ethnic cleansing and crimes against humanity. In comparison to the limitation within the preamble, the tasks that are mandated within the protection of civilians mandate goes beyond the principles of R2P. For example, peacekeepers are mandated to 'take concrete measures to mitigate and avoid the use of schools by armed forces, as appropriate, and deter the use of schools by parties to the conflict, and to facilitate the continuation of education in situations of armed conflict.'[44]

In order to intrinsically correlate the protection of civilians mandate with the host State's responsibility the Security Council inserts the 'responsibility of the State' within the mandate. As UN peacekeeping resolutions have developed gradually, the Security Council's reference to the 'responsibility of the State' differs depending on the UN peace mission. For instance, the protection of civilians mandate for MINUSCA states,

> To protect, in line with S/PRST/2018/18 of 21 September 2018, without prejudice to the primary responsibility of the CAR authorities and the basic principles of peacekeeping, the civilian population under threat of physical violence.[45]

In comparison, at the conclusion of UNMISS' protection of civilians mandate, the Security Council, '*reminds* South Sudanese authorities of their primary responsibility to protect civilians in South Sudan.'[46] The above references to the responsibility of State, together with the 'assistance' of UN peacekeepers, indicates a commonality between the protection of civilians mandate and the 'primary responsibility of the State to protect'. As the Security Council is not intending to shift the host States responsibility, the protection of civilians mandate becomes an indicator of the Security Council's understanding of the host State's responsibility to protect their civilians within that conflict. That is to say, as peacekeepers are mandated to assist local authorities, 'to take active

44 ibid at operative paragraph 34(a)(v).

45 UNSC 'Resolution 2625 (2022)' (n 29) at operational paragraph 34(a)(i); Similar in the protection of civilians mandate to MINUSMA the Security Council mandates, 'To protect, without prejudice to the primary responsibility of the Malian authorities, civilians under threat of physical violence' in UNSC 'Resolution 2584 (2021)' (n 37) at operational paragraph 30(c)(i).

46 UNSC 'Resolution 2625 (2022)' (n 29) at operational paragraph 5.

steps to anticipate, deter and effectively respond to threats to the civilian population',[47] it is naturally inferred that the protection tasks mandated are the responsibility of the host State. As the Security Council is making decisions regarding the protection tasks that are owed to civilians within a specific conflict, the mandate assumes that this is the protection that should have been performed by the host State.

This implication is further supported as the UN Secretariat has insisted that peacekeepers are not to replace the role of the government. The DPO has, for example, asserted that the language of the Security Council indicates 'that the mission is not expected to substitute for the role of the host State in protecting the population.'[48] As the Security Council has repeatedly articulated that the protection of civilians mandate does not shift the responsibility of the State, it can logically be concluded that the mandate is the Security Council's expectation of the obligation that is owed to civilians within that conflict. With the consistent use of language by the Security Council, the mandate on the protection of civilians becomes a measure of whether a host State is fulfilling their 'primary responsibility to protect their civilians' within that conflict.

This concept that the State has the primary responsibility to protect is not innovative, for 'protection' as a concept that finds its foundations in the law, and thus 'the duty to protect civilians traditionally belongs first and foremost to the States.'[49] The obligations of the State to protect civilians can be discovered in IHL, IHRL, and refugee law. As asserted by the Secretary-General in his report on the protection of civilians, '[s]tates bear the primary responsibility to protect civilians, and peacekeepers are not a substitute for political engagement to tackle sources of violence.'[50] However, in the context of Security Council peacekeeping resolutions, the 'primary responsibility of the State' is a reference to the responsibilities within the protection of civilians mandate.

As stated earlier, the protection of civilians mandate outlines an expected list of tasks and responsibilities of protection that are owed to civilians during that specific conflict. As peacekeepers are not intended to shift the responsibility of the host State, rather to assist local authorities to be able to undertake these tasks, there is an implication that the protection of civilians *is* the

47 UNSC 'Resolution 2584 (2021)' (n 37) at operational paragraph 30(c)(i).

48 United Nations Department of Peace Operations, *The Protection of Civilians in United Nations Peacekeeping Handbook* (n 27) at 2.1.1.

49 Sylvie Caverzasio (ed), *Strengthening Protection in War* (International Committee of the Red Cross 2001) at 9.

50 UNSC, 'Report of the Secretary-General on the Protection of Civilians in Armed Conflict' (10 May 2017) UN Doc S/2017/414 at para 58.

interpretation of the 'responsibility of the State' to protect in that conflict. In other words, the protection of civilians mandate, with all its expressions, is what the host State is obliged to perform to protect their civilians.

3 Protection of Civilians in Armed Conflict and The Emerging Norm of Peace and Security

While a State's primary responsibility to protect is rather broad and intersects multiple areas of law, the Security Council does constrain the theme of protection to armed conflict. From its first insertion in the UN peace mission to Sierra Leone,[51] the protection of civilians mandate has been continually aligned with armed conflict. For example, the Security Council's overarching resolutions on the protection of civilians is titled 'The Protection of Civilians in Armed Conflict.'[52]

Moreover, protection tasks are confined to civilians 'affected by armed conflict' or 'in armed conflict'.[53] As the Security Council restricts the protection of civilians mandate in times of armed conflict, therefore the primary responsibility of the State to protect is also confined to situations of armed conflict. As UN peace missions are mainly deployed in NIACs, the protection of civilians mandate can be perceived as an indicator of the responsibility of the host State to protect in a NIAC. While the Security Council might not intend to define the legal norm of the State's responsibility to protect in armed conflict, by drafting resolutions with the consistent phrase of 'State responsibility' they are contributing to an emerging norm within NIAC.

As the protection of civilians mandate is linked to armed conflict, this would innately invoke a State's obligations under IHL. However, from the text of UN peacekeeping resolutions, the Security Council is initiating and mandating an obligation of protection that is beyond the traditional view of a State's obligation in a NIAC. For while the Security Council may intend to invoke pre-existing norms, subsequently, the text of the protection of civilians mandate creates an expansive interpretation of the State's responsibility to protect in an armed conflict.

51 UNSC 'Resolution 1270 (1999)' (n 21).

52 For example, UNSC Resolution 2573 (2021)' (27 April 2021) UN Doc S/RES/2573 (2021); UNSC Resolution 1894 (2009)' (11 November 2009) UN Doc S/RES/1894 (2009) at operational paragraph 33.

53 UNSC 'Resolution 2640 (2022)' (29 June 2022) UN Doc S/RES/2640 (2022) at operative paragraph 26(c)(iii).

As the Security Council is using borrowed language from IHL, this intrinsically aligns the 'protection' of the State to their obligations under IHL. UN peace missions deployed under the protection of civilians mandate are generally deployed in a NIAC, therefore, the mandate invokes a State's obligations in a NIAC.[54] While international armed conflicts (IAC) and NIAC are at times considered having similar obligations,[55] in the traditional view, obligations in a NIAC are not as copious as an IAC.[56] Theoretically, obligations of a State in a NIAC should be interpreted and applied through Common Article 3 to the Geneva Conventions and Protocol II. The protection owed to civilians in a NIAC is codified in Article 13 of Protocol II, which states that the 'civilian population and individual civilians shall enjoy general protection against the dangers arising from military operations.'[57] This obligation is given effect by regulating the intent and object of an armed attack, in other words, 'civilian population as such, as well as individual civilians, shall not be the object of attack.'[58]

The theoretical underpinning of the obligations in IHL is to ensure that armed attacks are not directed towards civilians. Further, parties to a conflict are to guarantee that armed attacks do not destroy 'objects indispensable to the survival of the civilian population.'[59] Therefore, the ethical construction of IHL is that 'protection' incorporates parties not specifically targeting civilians, or civilian objects, when implementing their military manoeuvring. Following this line of reasoning, IHL accepts that civilian casualties will and can occur, as long as they are not the target of the attack. This concession can be appreciated when considering that although the use of force was prohibited in 1945, States had also conceded the occurrence of war by negotiating and drafting the regulation of conflict within the Geneva Conventions in 1949. As such, the philosophical obligations under IHL are to guarantee that civilians are not

54 Currently, all protection of civilian mandated missions are deployed in non-international armed conflicts, for example, South Sudan, Mali, DRC and Central African Republic.

55 International Committee of the Red Cross, *How Does Law Protect in War? - Online Casebook* (*ICRC Online Casebook* 2023) <https://casebook.icrc.org> at 'Non-international armed conflict'.

56 For more see Sandesh Sivakumaran, *The Law of Non-International Armed Conflict* (Oxford University Press 2012).

57 Diplomatic Conference on the Reaffirmation and Development of International Humanitarian Law Applicable in Armed Conflicts, 'Protocol Additional to the Geneva Conventions of 12 August 1949, and relating to the Protection of Victims of Non-International Armed Conflicts' (Protocol II) (adopted 8 June 1977, entered into force 7 December 1978) art 13(1).

58 ibid art 13(2).

59 Protocol II (n 57) art 14.

directly targeted, rather than ensuring an end to, and protection against, any and all violence.

Although the protection of civilians mandate relates to armed conflict, the language of the mandate raises differing ethical considerations to that of IHL. Explicitly, the protection of civilians mandate instructs for protection to occur pre-emptively, in deterrence, and does not distinguish between a legal or an illegal attack. In other words, the protection of civilians mandate is not concerned with the legality of the attack against civilians, rather, it mandates protection against all and any 'physical violence'. This is emphasised by the Security Council not mandating against an 'armed attack' or 'armed force' but rather using the language of 'violence', clearly intending a broader understanding than that by IHL. Accordingly, the protection of civilians mandate demands more than what is required or obligated under IHL.

From the language of the protection of civilians mandate, a traditional view of IHL is insufficient to outline the expectation of the Security Council of the host State's responsibility to their civilians. While the reference of 'armed conflict' invokes the obligations of IHL, it is not the only body of law that functions in times of armed conflict. As contended by the International Court of Justice (ICJ) in its Advisory Opinion on *Nuclear Weapons*, human rights law applies alongside IHL, unless a party has lawfully derogated from it.[60] As the Security Council is mandating responsibilities beyond IHL, IHRL may be able to supplement the clarification of the host State's responsibility. As articulated in the 2018 Presidential Statement on the protection of civilians, the Security Council reiterates that the protection of civilians mandate has its foundations in the pre-existing legal framework not only to IHL,

> Stress[es] the responsibility of parties to armed conflict to abide by all their obligations under international humanitarian law, international human rights law, and international refugee law, as applicable and reiterated by relevant Security Council resolutions.[61]

The core of human rights law is to protect individuals from violations committed by their own State. As such, IHRL gives rise to a State's obligation to protect

60 *Legality of the Threat or Use of Nuclear Weapons* (Advisory Opinion) 1996 ICJ Reports 226 at para 25.

61 President of the Security Council, 'Statement by the President of the Security Council – Protection of Civilians in Armed Conflict' (21 September 2018) UN Doc S/PRST/2018/18 at 4.

those rights through their institutional structures.[62] A State is obligated to respect, protect and fulfil the rights of individuals within their control.[63] The obligation to protect requires States to cease any intrusion or obstruction of the individual's rights. This obligation is achieved by offering pre-emptive and remedial avenues to these rights within their administrative mechanisms.

In armed conflict, and specifically within UN peace missions, the most notable human rights in the protection of civilians regime 'include the right to life, the prohibition against torture and ill-treatment, and the freedom from arbitrary detention.'[64] However, the Security Council does not mandate these specific protections, but rather enforces human rights protections by strengthening the host State's structures. As illustrated in the mandate for MINUSMA:

> To assist the Malian authorities in their efforts to promote and protect human rights, in particular in the areas of justice and reconciliation, including to support, as feasible and appropriate, the efforts of the Malian authorities, without prejudice to their responsibilities, to bring to justice without undue delay those responsible for serious violations or abuses of human rights or violations of international humanitarian law...[65]

From the above text, the Security Council replicates the obligation to protect already existing in IHRL, mandating peacekeeping assistance to strengthen the institutional structures of the host State. Therefore, the mandate to protect human rights reconfirms that the host State needs sufficient procedures to safeguard individuals' rights from violations, and significantly, remedial structures when they are violated. While the human rights protections within the Security Council resolutions replicate existing legal obligations, this does not shed light on the Security Council's aggregated language in the protection of civilians mandate, specifically with regards to protection against physical violence.

Whereas the Security Council and the UN echoes that the protection of civilians mandate has its origins in international law, the evolving text of the mandate has incidentally given rise to an expansive interpretation of State obligations in an armed conflict. Regardless of the UN's invocation of international

62 Siobhan Wills, *Protecting Civilians: The Obligations of Peacekeepers* (Oxford University Press 2009) at 112.

63 Henry Shue, *Basic Rights* (Princeton University Press 1980).

64 Haidi Willmot and Scott Sheeran 'The Protection of Civilians Mandate in UN Peacekeeping Operations: Reconciling Protection Concepts and Practices' (2014) 95(891/892) ICRC 517 at 526.

65 UNSC 'Resolution 2584 (2021)' (n 37) at operational paragraph 30(d)(i).

law, the text of the protection of civilians mandate is widening the existing obligations owed to their civilians within the law. As such, the protection of civilians mandate is incidentally broadening the interpretation of protection and the State's responsibility to civilians in NIAC.

4 The Protection of Civilians Mandate and its Foundation in the Maintenance of International Peace and Security

As the protection of civilians mandate encapsulates the Security Council's responsibility for the maintenance of international peace and security, the rationale of the mandate differs from IHL. The Security Council is not explicitly authorised under the UN Charter to deploy peacekeepers, therefore, the Security Council relies on their responsibility under Article 24 of the UN Charter. As Article 24 grants the Security Council the primary responsibility for the maintenance of international peace and security, the protection of civilians mandate must also find its foundations in Article 24.

Since the initiation of the cross-cutting theme of protection, both the Security Council and the Secretary-General have frequently asserted that the protection of civilians is mandated principally in guarantee of international peace and security.[66] Therefore, the protection of civilians mandate finds its legal foundations, and hence its interpretation, through international peace and security.

4.1 *The Maintenance of International Peace and Security*

As the Security Council mandates UN peacekeepers under their responsibility for the maintenance of international peace and security, the protection of civilians mandate's language envisions the discontinuation of conflict and violence against civilians. For example, the Security Council has recognised 'the need to address the gaps and strengthen links between the United Nations peace and security in the field, human rights and development work as a means to address root causes of conflict and threats to the security of women and girls in the pursuit of international peace and security.'[67] Therefore, unlike IHL which intends to govern the conduct of warfare and tolerates civilian casualties, the protection of civilians mandate means to end all violence. The contrasting

66 UNSC 'Resolution 1261 (1999)' (25 August 1999) UN Doc S/RES/1261 (1999) at operational paragraph 16; UNSC 'Resolution 1820 (2008)' (19 June 2008) UN Doc S/RES/1820 (2008) at operational paragraph 1; UNSC *Women and Peace and Security: Report of the Secretary-General* (United Nations 2020) UN Doc S/2009/465 at paragraph 8.

67 UNSC 'Resolution 2122 (2013)' (18 October 2013) UN Doc S/RES/2122 (2013) at preamble.

feature between the two obligations can be demonstrated with the perception on the use of force. While under IHL force is allowed proportionally to the military advantage gained, under the protection of civilians mandate force is utilised for the maintenance of peace and security rather than supremacy on the battlefield. As MONUSCO is mandated to protect,

> in support of the authorities of the DRC… to ensure effective, timely, dynamic and integrated protection of civilians, and to contribute to the objective of reducing the threat posed by armed groups to state authority and civilian security in the DRC and to make space for stabilisation activities, either unilaterally or jointly with the Congolese security forces…[68]

The emphasis on peace and security is further reaffirmed by the Security Council explicitly referencing 'peace and security' in connection to specific tasks of protection. For example, the Security Council '…affirms in this regard that effective steps to prevent and respond to such acts of sexual violence can significantly contribute to the maintenance of international peace and security'.[69]

As the protection of civilians theme finds its beginning in Article 24 of the UN Charter, the protection of civilians mandate's philosophical compass differs from the obligations under IHL. Whereas IHL obligates the mitigation of harm, the protection of civilians mandate obligates the cessation to all violence for the creation of international peace and security. In other words, as the obligations in IHL attempt to regulate conflict to minimise harm to those not participating in hostilities, the obligations under the protection of civilians mandate attempt to create peace and security for all involved. Moreover, while the obligations under IHRL obligates protections within the institutions of the State, the protection of civilians mandate positively obligates the creation of a secure environment in order for those institutions to be developed.

While the divergence of philosophical considerations seems merely theoretical, it does have a practical significance to civilians in the field. For instance, recent protests in the DRC are centred around MONUSCO's inability to protect and stabilise their areas of deployment. As stated by the USA State department, 'MONUSCO plays a critical role in fostering peace and security,

68 UNSC 'Resolution 2612 (2021)' (20 December 2021) UN Doc S/RES/2612 (2012) at operational paragraph 29(i)(e).

69 UNSC 'Resolution 1820 (2008)' (n 66) at operational paragraph 1.

protecting civilians and facilitating delivery of humanitarian assistance.'[70] While under IHL and IHRL there is no obligation in armed conflict to create 'peace and security', the protection of civilians mandate has enabled the international community to invoke a norm of peace and security in a NIAC. As expressed by the DRC in response to the Security Council debates on the July 2022 situation, 'I have heard it said here that it is the primary responsibility of the Democratic Republic of the Congo to protect its own borders and its own population. We agree wholeheartedly…'[71] The reaction of States and the UN to the 2022 incident is evidence that there is an emerging expectation that the protection of civilians is satisfied with the establishment of peace and security, that is, an end to all violence.

4.2 *The primary responsibility of the State and the maintenance of international peace and security*

As the Security Council mandates the protections owed to civilians within specific conflicts, they are incidentally expanding a State's obligation to protect their civilians. This expansion in the language of the Security Council implies that the responsibility of the State in an armed conflict should also be founded in the maintenance of peace and security and the protection of civilians. As the protection of civilians mandate is a list of obligations owed to civilians and those obligations are founded in 'peace and security', there is an emerging obligation on the host State to maintain 'peace and security'. While pre-existing obligations of States under international law allow the existence of an armed conflict, the language of the protection of civilians mandate implies a State's obligation to extinguish that conflict. As such, the Security Council is mandating UN peacekeepers to assist the host State to create peace and security, which is their primary responsibility. Therefore, from the text of the protection of civilians mandate this obligation to create peace and security ultimately is the primary responsibility of the host State.

Part of this philosophical consideration, the Security Council does not merely mandate that the protection of civilians occurs against indiscriminate attacks, rather mandates general protections against all 'physical violence'. For the maintenance of international peace and security, all violence should be obstructed whether or not that violence is legal. Therefore, the Security Council mandates for steps to be taken to anticipate and deter any future

70 Africa News, 'US Urges DR Congo to Protect Peacekeepers After Deadly Unrest,' (*Africa News*, 29 July 2022) <https://www.africanews.com/2022/07/29/us-urges-dr-congo-to-protect-peacekeepers-after-deadly-unrest//>.

71 UNSC, 'Security Council, 77th Year: 9081th Meeting' (29 June 2022) UN Doc S/PV.9081 at 21.

violence. For example, peacekeepers are 'to ensure effective and dynamic protection of civilians under threat of physical violence through a comprehensive and integrated approach, including by anticipating, deterring, and stopping all threats of violence against the populations.'[72] This comprehensive approach to deter all violence is mandated for UN peacekeepers to allow the host State to 'assume' their responsibilities. As emphasised in MINUSMA,

> to take mobile, flexible, robust and proactive steps to protect civilians, including through the set-up of a Mobile Task Force, prioritizing the deployment of ground and air assets, as available, in areas where civilians are most at risk, while expecting Malian authorities to assume their responsibilities in the respective areas.[73]

In other words, the responsibility of the State is to ensure the proactive protection of civilians against any attack or violence from the NIAC, not just from their own military manoeuvring. Moreover, the protection of civilians mandate disregards whether the violence functions as part of a legal attack under IHL. While IHL and IHRL accepts civilian casualties and obligates the protection to minimise harm or implement remedial structures, the protection of civilians mandate on the other hand intends to prohibit any violence as a violation of the duty owed to civilians.

This shift in ethical and theoretical construction implies that local authorities should be using force in order to create a secure environment rather than bolstering their own power. Accordingly, within a NIAC the Security Council is inevitably placing an obligation on States to put an end to the conflict. Therefore, from the text of the Security Council, States should prioritise ending the conflict than 'winning' the war.

5 An Emerging Legal Norm of an Obligation for Peace and Security

While the Security Council is intending to maintain international peace and security, and ensuring the importance of State sovereignty, they are incidentally fashioning a legal norm within NIACs. Subsequently, Security Council resolutions define a State's responsibility to protect their civilians, which is to

72 UNSC 'Resolution 2605 (2021)' (n 30) at operational paragraph 34(a)(iii); another example is when peacekeepers are mandated to 'to take active steps to anticipate, deter and effectively respond to threats to the civilian population' in UNSC 'Resolution 2584 (2021)' (n 37) at operational paragraph 30(c)(ii).

73 UNSC 'Resolution 2584 (2021)' (n 37) at operational paragraph 30(c)(ii).

conclude the conflict in order to create a 'secure environment' and the 'rule of law'. For while the Security Council mandates protection tasks owed to civilians, the purpose of these tasks is the cessation of violence as the fulfilment of the obligation to protect. For example, the Security Council in their mandate to UNMISS:

> Demands all parties to the conflict and other armed actors to immediately end fighting throughout South Sudan and engage in political dialogue, reminds South Sudanese authorities of their primary responsibility to protect civilians in South Sudan...[74]

As the Security Council is mandating tasks striving to conclude all violence, the Security Council is developing a customary norm for States involved in a NIAC. For example, in the recent resolution in the situation in Mali, the Security Council '*emphasizing* that the Malian authorities have primary responsibility for the provision of stability, security and protection of civilians throughout the territory of Mali.'[75] As such, host States within a NIAC have a responsibility to ensure security and stability for their population. From this developing norm, it is implied that military force should only be used to create peace and security. Therefore, it can be implied that States should be taking all reasonable steps to conclude fighting in order to create a secure environment. This is illustrated as one of the major tasks mandated throughout the lifespan of the protection of civilians mandate is the creation of a 'secure environment'.[76]

As stated earlier, while an IAC is highly regulated within the Geneva Conventions, the law in a NIAC relies heavily on customary international law. Therefore, the Security Council has much more influence in effecting and developing norms within a NIAC. This distinction between an IAC and a NIAC can be found in the construction of IHL, as many obligations are premised on the perception of two sovereigns in conflict. That is, these States are permitted

74 UNSC 'Resolution 2625 (2022)' (n 29) at operative paragraph 5.

75 UNSC 'Resolution 2640 (2022)' (29 June 2022) UN Doc S/RES/2640 (2022) at preamble.

76 UNSC 'Resolution 2164 (2014)' (26 June 2014) UN Doc S/RES/2164 (2014) at operational paragraph 13(a)(iv); UNSC 'Resolution 2149 (2014)' (10 April 2014) UN Doc S/RES/2149 (2014) at operational paragraph 30(a)(i); UNSC 'Resolution 2003 (2011)' (29 July 2011) UN Doc S/RES/2003 (2011) at operational paragraph 3; UNSC 'Resolution 2063 (2012)' (31 July 2012) UN Doc S/RES/2063 (2012) at operational paragraph 3; UNSC 'Resolution 2173 (2014)' (27 August 2014) UN Doc S/RES/2173 (2014) at operational paragraph 8(a); UNSC 'Resolution 2155 (2014)' (27 May 2014) UN Doc S/RES/2155 (2014) at operational paragraph 4(a)(ii); UNSC 'Resolution 2304 (2016)' (12 August 2016) UN Doc S/RES/2304 (2016) at operational paragraph 5; UNSC 'Resolution 1856 (2008)' (22 December 2008) UN Doc S/RES/1856 (2008) at operational paragraph 3(e).

to engage in conflict, as long as they are only in conflict with each other. However, this construction has difficulties when there is a conflict between the sovereign State and its people. This theoretical tension between a NIAC and IAC is manifested with the Security Council's language, and their insistence of demanding an end to violence against the populace. As such, the Security Council's language can be perceived as a clarification of the role of the sovereign State in a NIAC, specifically in modern urban warfare.

While in a NIAC, under customary international law a State is obliged to distinguish between civilian and military targets, this traditional view does not consider the growth of urban warfare.[77] As UN peace missions are mandated to protect civilians and are deployed in conflicts within urban and civilian areas, urban conflict becomes an important consideration for the Security Council. With conflict occurring within and amongst the civilian population, from the Security Council's resolutions there is a perception that any conflict within these areas will lead to a breach of civilian protection. For example, the resolution on Sudan the Security Council reaffirms:

> the primary responsibility of the Government of Sudan to protect civilians across its territory… while *expressing concern* that the security situation in some regions of Darfur remains precarious, and underscoring the need to protect peacebuilding gains in Darfur, avoid a relapse into conflict and mitigate the risks for the population posed inter alia by threats against civilians in Darfur, inter-communal violence, human rights violations and abuses, violations of international humanitarian law and continued displacement.[78]

Due to the nature of urban conflict, the Security Council assumes that a 'relapse into conflict' is a threat to civilian protection and violations of international law. As parties to a conflict are to distinguish between civilians and military objects, and to ensure that no destruction occurs of civilian objects indispensable to survival, urban conflict by its very nature can be comprehended as a violation of obligations owed to civilians under IHL. As evidenced in Security

77 To read more about the compatibility of IHL with urban warfare, see Jeroen van den Boogaard, 'Contemporary Urban Warfare: Does International Humanitarian Law Offer Solutions?' in Rob Johnson, Martijn Kitzen, Tim Sweijs (eds) *The Conduct of War in the 21st Century; Kinetic, Connected and Synthetic* (Routledge 2021).

78 UNSC 'Resolution 2524 (2020)' (3 June 2020) UN Doc S/RES/2524 (2020) at preamble.

Council debates over the Tigray conflict in Ethiopia in 2021, Member States have insisted that only a ceasefire and an end to violence would fulfill the obligation to protect civilians in IHL.[79] While not expressly stated by the Security Council, there is a clear implication that only a cessation of violence can satisfy the responsibility owed to civilians, as insecurity and violence threatens the obligations owed to civilians under the law.

As modern NIACs are occurring continuously within civilian areas, it is understandable that the Security Council's interpretation of the obligation to protect encompasses sustaining a secure environment. As host States are parties to the NIAC, by their role within that conflict, the State's use of force will contribute to the insecure environment and hence a violation of their obligations. Within the emerging norm the use of force by the State, unless proportionate to peace and security, would be a breach of their responsibility to protect their civilians and a failure of their sovereignty. Particularly as this force is not against another sovereign State but against the people that they are obliged to protect.

States engaged in a NIAC will find it difficult to adhere to the customary international law principles of distinction, proportionality and precautions in an urban context.[80] While objects such as houses and schools are protected as civilian objects, they lose their protected status when used for military purposes. Therefore, under an obligation of 'peace and security', in modern urban settings the distinction principle, and as a result the proportionality principle, becomes problematic as the 'enemy' and civilians become indistinguishable. As there is no practical way to differentiate between military and civilian objects in modern urban warfare, the use of force will commonly violate a State's obligations under IHL to protect civilians. Therefore, to adhere to the spirit of IHL, the Security Council obligates States to create a secure environment, and therefore attempt to put an end to conflict to protect their civilians. For this reason, the developing obligation for States to create a secure environment and put an end to conflict for the sake of international peace

79 UNSC, 'Security Council, 76thYear: 8812th Meeting,' (2 July 2021) UN Doc. S/PV.8812. As an example, the Member of Vietnam stated '…about the alarming levels of violence and killing of civilians, including women, children and humanitarian workers, as well as the destruction of civilian infrastructure indispensable to the civilian population in Tigray. Those acts of violence are totally unacceptable and run counter to international humanitarian law.'

80 See ICRC, 'Additional Protocol I to the Geneva Conventions (API)' (ICRC, 1977) arts 48, 51 and customary law rules 1 and 7. See Jeanne Marie Henckaerts and Louise Doswald-Beck, *Customary International Humanitarian Law, Volume I: Rules* (Cambridge University Press 2005).

and security, can be suggested not to contradict existing obligations, but rather clarifies the obligations of IHL in modern warfare.

Taken from the theoretical underpinnings of R2P, and applied by the UN General Assembly, State sovereignty, 'today closely carries with it the obligation of a State to protect the welfare of its own peoples and meet its obligations to the wider international community.'[81] As such, when a sovereign State is engaged in a NIAC, they cannot abandon their responsibility to protect their people for the sake of victory. Part of this protection is to ensure a secure environment, and as such, they must attempt to put an end to conflict within urban settings that hinders that security. Therefore, within a NIAC there is an emerging expectation within Security Council resolutions that governments will only engage in conflict to ensure 'security' rather than to cement their own power.

This norm emerging from the protection of civilians doctrine has expanded beyond peacekeeping resolutions and is being emphasized by the UN in their response to other internal conflicts. For example, the UN Human Rights Committee's resolution on the conflict in Syria reiterating 'its urgent call upon the Syrian authorities to put an immediate end to all violence and all human right violations, and to meet its responsibility to protect the Syrian population.'[82] Alternatively, as declared by the Uruguayan delegate to the Security Council in 2017, 'that Côte d'Ivoire is no longer a threat to international peace and security and that the Security Council has transferred all responsibility for achieving sustained peace in the country to its Government.'[83]

Although this emerging norm is an expectation in a NIAC, it is yet to be applied the Security Council to *jus ad bellum*. Majority of writings on *jus ad bellum* focus on the use of force in a foreign territory, rather than on internal *jus ad bellum*.[84] Therefore, internal use of force, is generally discussed as a form of 'hostilities' governed by IHRL and rules within law enforcement. While discussion of the custom of internal *jus ad bellum* is beyond the scope of this paper, the emerging norm is yet to be applied to a State's use of force against their own people before the application of IHL. Theoretically, the obligation for peace and security would not remove the State's ability to use force to impede

---

81 UNGA, 'High-level Panel on Threats, Challenges and Change addressed to the Secretary-General' (6 December 2004) UN Doc. A/59/565 at paragraph 29.

82 UNHRC, 'Situation of Human rights in the Syrian Arab Republic' (17 October 2012) A/HRC/RES21/26 at operation paragraph 5.

83 UNSC, 'Security Council Seventy-Second Year: 7957th Meeting' (2 June 2017) UN Doc S/PV.7957at 9.

84 The term taken from Elav Lieblich, 'Internal Jus Ad Bellum' (2016) 67 Hastings Law Journal 687.

an insurgence, however, the emerging norm would indicate that States should engage in the intense use of force, or the to maintain peace and security. The norm of peace and security does not remove a State's ability to defend itself, rather insists that force is to be used to create a secure environment. In other words, the focus of the government is the protection of its people, rather than its own power.

It must be noted that dissimilar to the doctrine of R2P this emerging norm in the protection of civilians mandate does not intend to shift that responsibility to the international community. The emerging obligation of peace and security is not distorting State sovereignty, rather cementing that sovereignty in clarifying the obligation on States to protect their civilians and ensure security within their territory. As such, this obligation does not give rise to humanitarian intervention, but rather invokes a State's responsibility to respect their sovereignty in protecting their people. As the role of government is to represent their State, therefore, governments are obligated to ensure all attacks are proportionate to overall security of the populace, rather than to sustain their power. Accordingly, government responsibility to protect their civilians is not in conflict with State sovereignty, but rather enforcing it.

6 Conclusion

As the Security Council is consistently mandating peacekeeping missions within a NIAC, they are incidentally affecting State behaviour and opinions of a State's obligations within a NIAC. Since the Security Council is involved in the majority of NIACs, and States are relying on these decisions by the Security Council, these resolutions are developing legal norms and interpretations within NIACs.

When the Security Council is mandating peacekeepers to protect civilians, they are inadvertently forming an obligation on States involved with UN peace missions. By consistently referencing 'the primary responsibility of the State to protect' the Security Council is developing a norm of State responsibility in a NIAC. From the text of the Security Council resolutions there is an expectation that States who are a party in a NIAC have a responsibility to maintain peace and security. Therefore, States should only engage in force proportional to the creation of a secure environment. This expectation means that force will be used for peace and security, rather than "winning" the conflict, or entrenching the power of local authorities. As such, from the language of the Security Council, and other UN agencies commenting on NIACs, there is an interpretation that the obligation for States to protect their civilians can only be achieved by a ceasefire and the conclusion of conflict. This developing norm is an expansion of existing obligations under IHL and IHRL, which allows the existence of an armed conflict. While the traditional view is that the Security Council cannot obligate Member States to violate or contradict existing norms, however, it is suggested that the 'responsibility of the State to protect' expands and clarifies existing obligations rather than contradicts, specifically in consideration of modern urban warfare. In other words, this developing norm is clarifying the role of the State when conflict erupts within civilian populated areas, as any conflict would place civilians at risk. Therefore, according to the protection of civilians mandate, for a State to achieve its obligations under IHL in a NIAC, governments should be taking all reasonable steps to conclude the conflict, for hostilities and force within civilian areas by its very nature is a breach of their obligation and responsibility to protect their own civilians.

Index

#LancsBox 19
9/11 terrorist attacks 144, 153. *See also* War on Terror
24 (television series) 152–53

Abu Ghraib 152
Additional Protocol I 25, 26, 77, 86, 98, 102, 103
  Article 35 132
  Article 37(1) 121
  Article 43 101, 102
  Article 44 101–2
  Article 48 72
  Article 50 102
  Article 51 72–73, 103
  Article 54 76
Additional Protocol II 77, 173
  Article 13 173
Additional Protocols of 1977 8, 15, 17, 18, 25, 27, 30, 60, 70, 71, 74, 76, 85, 86
Al Qaeda 103–5
Alabama Claims Arbitration 11*n*19
Aldrich, Mr (US) 101–2
Alexander, Amanda 4, 25–27, 30, 78, 79
Althusser, Louis 35
AmE06 45, 57
Amnesty International 25
Annan, Kofi 36, 49
Araújo e Castro, Rodrigo 46
'armed conflict' 1, 7, 9, 13–14, 18, 36, 174. *See also* 'law(s) of armed conflict'
'armed conflict between States' 13

Balkans conflict 26, 27, 30
Barak, Ehud 107–8
Baxter, Richard 99
BE06 45, 57
Blum, Gabriela 132
Bluntschli, Johan-Caspar 140–41
BNC 45, 47, 57
Boer, Lianne 147
Brereton Report 81
British National Corpus (BNC) 45, 47, 57
Brussels Conference of 1874 89
Bush, GW 79, 81, 139
Buzan, Barry 61

Cassese, Antonio 77, 90
'ceasefire' 2
Central Intelligence Agency (CIA) 1, 153
'chivalry' 65, 121–22
CIA 1, 153
Civil War (US) 10
Cohn, Mr (Denmark) 93
Colby, Elbridge 64–65, 80, 84
Cold War 65, 137
collateral damage' 2
Conference of Government Experts 16–17, 25
'Contracting Parties' 39–40
'Contracting Powers' 39–40
Convention (II) with Respect to the Laws and Customs of War on Land. *See* Hague Convention II of 1899
Convention (III) Relative to the Opening of Hostilities. *See* Hague Convention III of 1907
Convention (III) Relative to the Treatment of Prisoners of War. *See* Geneva Convention III of 1949
Convention (IV) Relative to the Protection of Civilian Persons in Time of War. *See* Geneva Convention IV of 1949
Convention (IV) Respecting the Laws and Customs of War on Land. *See* Hague Convention IV of 1907
Convention for the Amelioration of the Condition of the Wounded and Sick in Armies in the Field of 1906 68
Convention for the Amelioration of the Condition of the Wounded and Sick in Armies in the Field of 1929 68
Convention for the Amelioration of the Condition of the Wounded in Armies in the Field of 1864. *See* Geneva Convention of 1864
Convention for the Protection of Cultural Property in the Event of Armed Conflict 14
Convention on the Rights of the Child 38

Convention Relative to the Treatment of Prisoners of War. *See* Geneva Convention Relative to the Treatment of Prisoners of War of 1929
'corpus' 18, 27, 36–37, 42–48, 57
corpus linguistics 3, 8, 18–23, 30, 31, 36, 43–48, 57
Craigie, Robert 94
Crawford, Emily 2–3, 41
Crimean War 126–27
Cross, Matthew 73–75
Crowe, Colin 99
Cruz Report 165

Declaration Renouncing the Use, in Time of War, of Explosive Projectiles Under 400 Grammes Weight (St Petersburg Declaration) 10–11, 63, 68–69, 70
Dinstein, Yoram 75, 78, 135, 143
Diplomatic Conference on the Reaffirmation and Development of International Humanitarian Law Applicable in Armed Conflicts. *See* Diplomatic Conferences of 1974–1977
Diplomatic Conferences of 1974–1977 17, 25–27, 77, 86, 98–103
distinction, principle of 41, 60, 71–72, 73, 76, 98, 114–15, 182
Draft Conventions of 1946 13–14, 92
Draft Operational Concept on Protection of Civilians 165
Dunant, Henry 68, 126, 128
  Un souvenir de Solferino (*Memories of Solferino*) 68

Early English Books Online (EEBO) 37
EEBO 37
Einsatzgruppen 120
English School of international relations 61
Ethiopia–Eritrea conflict 29
euphemisms 1–2

Fanon, Frantz 96–98
feminization of war 115, 124–26, 133, 137, 139, 143, 146, 151
Fidler, David 65
'field' 38, 49, 115
First Gulf War 4, 25, 78
First World War 69, 70, 127, 142, 144, 152
Fitzpatrick, Peter 87
Fleck, Dieter 72
Forsythe, David 100
Fowler, Alexander 81
free-fighters 84–112
Freikorps 120

Gardam, Judith 73, 78–79
Gardner, Mr (UK) 94
Gautier, Léon 122
Gaza conflict 1–2
gender 4–5, 43, 113–57
'General Armistice Agreement' 21
General Orders No 100. *See* Lieber Code
'Geneva Convention' 22–23
Geneva Convention of 1864 10, 37–38, 68, 126
  Article 4 10
Geneva Convention III of 1949 (Prisoners of War Convention) 93, 102
  Article 4 102, 107
Geneva Convention IV of 1949 22–23, 29, 30
  Part III 76
Geneva Convention Relative to the Treatment of Prisoners of War of 1929 68
Geneva Conventions of 1929 13–14
Geneva Conventions of 1949 8, 13–14, 18, 24, 29, 60, 68, 70, 74, 76, 84–85, 92–95, 97, 99, 101–2, 105, 114, 173, 180
  Common Article 2 103
  Common Article 3 70, 103–5, 173
Geneva law 24, 27, 67–68, 85, 129, 156
Gentili, Alberico
  De jure belli libri tres (*Three Books on the Law of War*, 1598) 9
Gong, Gerrit 62
Goodman, Ryan 132–34
Goodrich, Peter
  Legal Discourse 33
Google Books Corpus 47
Great Depression 70
Greenwood, Christopher 104
Greimas, Algirdas Julien 33
Grotius, Hugo 76
  De jure belli ac pacis 9–10
Guantanamo Bay 1, 104, 105
Gutteridge, Miss (UK) 93

Habermas, Jürgen 111
Hague Conferences 69, 95, 102
Hague Convention II of 1899 11, 69, 84
  Article 1 11
  preamble 74
Hague Convention III of 1907
  Article 1 11
Hague Convention IV of 1907 11, 22, 69, 75
  Article 54 75
  preamble 75
Hague Conventions of 1899 11, 64, 68–70, 84–85, 86, 88
Hague Conventions of 1907 11, 68–70, 85, 86, 88–92, 97, 101
  preamble 90
Hague law 24, 27, 68, 85, 88, 89, 129, 156
Hague Regulations of 1899 11
Hague Regulations of 1907 11, 24, 71
  Article 1 11
Halliday, MAK 37, 41, 49
Hamdan, Salim Ahmed 105
Hamdan v Rumsfeld 105
Hampson, Françoise J. 24, 28
Hansen, Michelle 136
Heinsch, Robert 71
Himmler, Heinrich 120, 153
Holocaust 120
homophobia 117, 119, 125, 137, 155
Hostage Case 77
'hostilities' 13, 107, 183
Human Rights Watch 25
'humanitarian' 14, 24, 27, 28, 60, 67
'humanitarian Conventions' 14
'humanitarian law' 15–16
'humanitarian pause' 2
'humanitarian principles' 14, 27
'humanitarian rules' 27
humanity, principle of 41, 73–75, 118, 122, 133, 138
humanization 130–31, 134–35, 137, 146

ICC 36, 49
ICC Statute. *See* Rome Statute of the International Criminal Court
ICJ 24, 71, 78, 161, 174
ICRC. *See* International Committee of the Red Cross
ICTY 163
Inspector-General of the Australian Defence Force Afghanistan Inquiry Report (Brereton Report) 81
Instructions for the Government of Armies of the United States in the Field. *See* Lieber Code
International Commission of Jurists 25
International Committee of the Red Cross (ICRC) 8, 12–13, 15–16, 24, 25, 30, 36, 42, 68, 72–73, 98, 102, 109, 132–34, 163
  Commentaries to the Conventions 13–15
  Commentary to the Additional Protocols 107
  Conference of Government Experts 16–17, 25
  International Humanitarian Law treaties database 36, 42–43
  Interpretive Guidance on the Notion of Direct Participation in Hostilities under International Humanitarian Law 109–10, 132
International Conference of the Red Cross
  17th 92
  21st 15
International Convention for the Protection of All Persons from Enforced Disappearance 39
International Court of Justice (ICJ) 24, 71, 78, 161, 174
International Criminal Court (ICC) 36, 49
  Statute of. *See* Rome Statute of the International Criminal Court
International Criminal Tribunal for the Former Yugoslavia (ICTY) 163
'international humanitarian law' 2, 7–8, 14–30, 33, 115, 128–30
'international instruments' 20, 26–27, 28, 30
'international law' 20, 28, 30
Israel–Lebanon war 29
Israel–Middle East conflict 8, 19
Israel–Palestine conflict 8, 19, 26–31
Israeli Defense Force 153
Israeli Supreme Court 105, 110

James, Henry 119
  The Bostonians 145
Japan–China conflict 12
Jarvis, Michelle 78–79

Jennings, Robert 162
Jochnick, Chris 34
Johnson, James Turner 70, 84, 85, 88
Journal of International Humanitarian Legal Studies 2

Keegan, John 67
Keene, Edward 63
Killingsworth, Matt 3–4
Kimmel, Michael 116, 117
Kinsella, Helen 114
Kolb, Robert 69–70
Korean War 1
Koskenniemi, Martii 63, 67*n*30
Kosovo intervention 79
Kriegsraison 76–77, 119–22
Künzli, Arnold 89

Lauterpacht, Hersch 128
'law(s) of armed conflict' 2, 7, 17–22, 23–24, 27–30, 33, 115. *See also* 'armed conflict'
'law(s) of war' 2, 7, 9, 10, 16, 18, 20, 23–24, 28, 29–30, 33, 37–38, 115, 122–23, 129. *See also* 'war'
Legality of the Threat or Use of Nuclear Weapons (Advisory Opinion) 78, 174
Lenin, Vladimir 96
lex specialis derogat generalis 135–36
Libyan Arab Jamahiriya v United Kingdom (*Lockerbie* case) 161
Lieber, Francis 119
Lieber Code 10, 36–39, 63–64, 71, 75
  Article 11 10
  Article 14 48
Linklater, Andrew 62
LiVecche, Marc 153
Lockerbie case (*Libyan Arab Jamahiriya v United Kingdom*) 161
Lorimer, James 61
Lukin, Annabelle 2–3, 46
Luttrell, Marcus 80–81

MacBride, Seán 25
Macquarie Laws of War Corpus (MQLWC) 42, 43, 45, 47, 57
Macquarie University 42
Malešević, Siniša 35, 39, 43–44
Manstein, Erich von 140
Mao Tse-Tung (Mao Zedong) 96–98
Marshall, John 76
Martens, Friedrich 88–90
Martens Clause 63–64, 74–75, 90
Marxism 95–96, 111
masculinities 4–5, 34, 113–57
Matthiessen, Christian MIM 37
Maurice, John Frederick 12*n*20
Mazower, Mark 64
Mégret, Frédéric 4–5, 28, 34, 53, 56, 64, 79
Melzer, Nils 109
Merleau-Ponty, Maurice 95–96
Meron, Theodor 131
Middle East conflict 8–9
military advantage 55. *See also* military necessity, principle of
'military necessity' 24, 41, 46–48, 55, 119
military necessity, principle of 18, 24, 26, 41, 46–48, 55, 60, 64, 68–69, 71, 74, 75–79, 81–82, 88, 129, 133, 138, 146
Ministry of Defence (UK)
  Manual on the Law of Armed Conflict 71
MINUSCA 169–70
MINUSMA 161, 168, 169*n*45, 175, 179
misogyny 117, 125, 134–37, 155
'mode' 38, 39, 42
Morris, Tamer 5
Moltke, Helmuth von 119, 144
MONUSCO 165, 177–78
Mowbray, Jacqueline 2–3
MQLWC 42, 43, 45, 47, 57
Murphy, Sean 103

NATO 79
Neocleous, Mark 91
neutrality, principle of 11, 41, 68, 100, 117
Neutrality Act (US) 12
News on the Web 45, 47
Nietzsche, Friedrich 91
Nightingale, Florence 126
noblesse oblige 121–22, 123, 157
Normand, Roger 34
Nuclear Weapons (Advisory Opinion) 78, 174

O'Hagan, Jacinta 65
obfuscation 1–2, 102, 140
Otto, Dianne 145
Oxford Manual 69, 128

pacifism 123, 143–45, 151, 156, 157
Paris Declaration Respecting Maritime Law 36, 37–39, 43
PCATI 105–7
peacekeeping 5, 134, 158–85
Pert, Alison 41
Pictet, Jean
  'The Principles of International Humanitarian Law' 15
'police action' 1
principles of international law 71–82
  distinction 41, 60, 71–72, 73, 76, 98, 114–15, 182
  humanity 41, 73–75, 118, 122, 133, 138
  military necessity 18, 24, 26, 41, 46–48, 55, 60, 64, 68, 69, 71, 74, 75–79, 81–82, 88, 129, 133, 138, 146
  neutrality 11, 41, 68, 100, 117
  prohibition on causing unnecessary suffering and superfluous injury 41, 50–54, 133
  proportionality 41, 60, 68, 71, 72–73, 76, 107, 133, 182
'prisoners of war' 14
Prisoners of War Convention. *See* Geneva Convention III of 1949
prohibition on causing unnecessary suffering and superfluous injury, principle of 41, 50–54, 133
proportionality, principle of 41, 60, 68, 71, 72–73, 76, 107, 133, 182
protection of civilians mandate 5, 158–85
Protocol Additional to the Geneva Conventions of 1949
  Annex II 43
Public Committee Against Torture in Israel (PCATI) v Israel (Targeted Killings Case) 105–10, 112
Public Committee Against Torture in Israel (PCATI) 105–7
Putin, Vladimir 1

queer theory 115, 154–56

Rahusen, Mr (Netherlands) 90
raison d'état 4, 60, 69, 70, 77–82
'recourse to force' 13
Red Cross movement 127. *See also* International Committee of the Red Cross (ICRC)
Reed, Mr (US) 101
'register' 3, 35–36, 37–42, 57
Regulations Respecting the Laws and Customs of War on Land. *See* Hague Regulations
responsibility to protect (R2P) doctrine 168–71, 172, 179, 183–85
Rivlin, Eliezer 107
Roberts, Adam 37, 39
Rochelle, Pierre Drieu de la 137
Rome Statute of the International Criminal Court 36, 43, 48, 49–57, 74
  Article (2)(e) 56
  Article 8 49, 54, 55, 56
  Article 8(2)(a) 55
  Article 8(2)(b) 55
  Article 8(2)(b)(iv) 50, 52
  Article 8(2)(b)(xx) 50, 51
  Article 8(2)(c) 55
  Article 8(2)(e) 55, 56
  Article 30 54
Roosevelt, Theodore 142
Rousseau, Jean-Jacques 86, 95, 153
Rues-Smit, Christian 69, 70
Russia–Ukraine conflict 1
Rwanda conflict 26, 30, 161*n*4, 166

Saul, Ben 81
Saussure, Ferdinand de 115
Schmitt, Carl 104
Schmitt, Michael 75, 77
Schutzstaffel (SS) 120, 153
Second World War 12, 13, 65, 68, 70, 93, 120, 123, 128, 142, 152
September 11 terrorist attacks 144, 153. *See also* War on Terror
sissyphobia 125
Six Day War 19
Slavin, General (USSR) 93
Snyder, Timothy 125
Solis, Gary 74, 77
Spanish Civil War 105
Special Court of Sierra Leone 166
'special military operation' 1
SS (Schutzstaffel) 120, 153
St Petersburg Declaration 10–11, 63, 68–69, 70
'standard of civilisation' 3–4, 59–82
'States Parties' 39–40
Steinberg, Major (Israel) 93

Supreme Court (Israel) 105, 110
Supreme Court (US) 76
Sydney Corpus Lab 42–43

Targeted Killings Case 105–10, 112
'tenor' 38, 42, 49
terminology 2–3, 7–31
  changes in 3, 7–8, 39
  future analyses of 27–29
  history of 9–18
  meaning of 2–3
  State practice regarding 2–3, 7–31
terms
  'armed conflict' 1, 7, 9, 13–14, 18, 36, 174. *See also* 'law(s) of armed conflict'
  'armed conflict between States' 13
  'ceasefire' 2
  'collateral damage' 2
  'Contracting Parties' 39–40
  'Contracting Powers' 39–40
  'General Armistice Agreement' 21
  'Geneva Convention' 22–23
  'hostilities' 13, 107, 183
  'humanitarian' 14, 24, 27, 28, 60, 67
  'humanitarian Conventions' 14
  'humanitarian law' 15–16
  'humanitarian pause' 2
  'humanitarian principles' 14, 27
  'humanitarian rules' 27
  'international humanitarian law' 2, 7–8, 14–30, 33, 115, 128–30
  'international instruments' 20, 26–27, 28, 30
  'international law' 20, 28, 30
  'law(s) of armed conflict' 2, 7, 17–22, 23–24, 27–30, 33, 115. *See also* 'armed conflict'
  'law(s) of war' 2, 7, 9, 10, 16, 18, 20, 23–24, 28, 29–30, 33, 37–38, 115, 122–23, 129. *See also* 'war'
  'military necessity' 24, 41, 46–48, 55, 119
  'police action' 1
  'prisoners of war' 14
  'recourse to force' 13
  'special military operation' 1
  'standard of civilisation' 3–4, 59–82
  'States Parties' 39–40
  'war' 1, 8, 9, 10, 13–14, 151
Thirty Years War 76
Tigray conflict 182
Treitschke, Heinrich von 144
Trump, Donald 125, 139

Ukraine–Russia conflict 1
UN. *See* United Nations
UNAMIR 161*n*4
UNAMSIL 158–59, 172
Union Army (US) 10
United Nations (UN) 5, 24, 49, 70, 137, 159, 160, 162, 166–67, 169, 175, 176, 178, 183
  Draft Operational Concept on Protection of Civilians 165
United Nations Assistance Mission for Rwanda (UNAMIR) 161*n*4
United Nations Charter 159, 161–62, 166, 176
  Article 2 167
  Article 2(1) 166
  Article 2(7) 166–67
  Article 24 161–62, 176, 177
  Article 25 161–62
  Chapter VII 158, 161, 167
United Nations Conference on Human Rights of 1968 15
United Nations Department of Peace Operations (DPO) 168, 171
  Protection of Civilians Handbook 165–66
United Nations General Assembly 24, 31, 183
  Resolution A/RES/3237 (XXIX) 20
  resolutions of 3, 8–9, 18–23, 26–27, 28, 30–31
United Nations General Debate Corpus 27
United Nations Human Rights Committee 183
United Nations Mission in Mali (MINUSMA) 161, 168, 169*n*45, 175, 179
United Nations Mission in Sierra Leone (UNAMSIL) 158–59, 172
United Nations Mission in South Sudan (UNMISS) 161, 164, 168, 170, 180
United Nations Mission in the Central African Republic (MINUSCA) 169–70
United Nations Mission in the Democratic Republic of the Congo (MONUSCO) 165, 177–78
United Nations resolutions. *See* United Nations General Assembly, resolutions of; United Nations Security Council, resolutions of

United Nations Secretariat 171
United Nations Security Council 24, 27, 31, 158–85
  Resolution 2118 161
  resolutions of 3, 8–9, 18–23, 27, 28, 29, 30–31, 159–85
United States v List (*The Hostage Case*) 77
UNMISS 161, 164, 168, 170, 180

van Dijk, Boyd 114
Vattel, Emer de 121
  Le droit des gens, ou Principes de la loi naturelle, appliqués à la conduite et aux affaires des nations et des souverains 9
Vietnam War 139
Vitoria, Francisco de
  De Indis et de jure belli 9

'war' 1, 8, 9, 10, 13–14, 151
War on Terror 4, 60, 79–82. *See also* 9/11 terrorist attacks
Weber, Max 39, 87–88, 91, 111
  Economy and Society 91
  Politics as a Vocation 87
Willacy, Mark
  Rogue Forces 81
Wilson, Page 24–25, 27, 28, 29
Wolff, Christian
  Jus naturae methodo scientifica pertractatum 9
World War I 69, 70, 127, 142, 144, 152
World War II 12, 13, 65, 68, 70, 93, 120, 123, 128, 142, 152

Yom Kippur War 19

www.ingramcontent.com/pod-product-compliance
Lightning Source LLC
Chambersburg PA
CBHW031347230926
51848CB00002B/422
* 9 7 8 9 0 0 4 7 1 2 4 6 1 *